KING'S COLLEGE LONDON

MEDIEVAL STUDIES

I

KING'S COLLEGE LONDON MEDIEVAL STUDIES

CAMBRIDGE PEMBROKE COLLEGE MS. 25:

A Carolingian sermonary used by Anglo-Saxon preachers

James E. Cross

KING'S COLLEGE LONDON
1987

ISSN 0953-217X
ISBN 0 9513085 0 5

Printed By
Short Run Press Ltd.
Exeter
December 1987.

CONTENTS

PREFACE

In 1982 I was asked to help to initiate a group activity which would consider the sources of Old English literature. For the lecture (at the Kalamazoo Medieval Conference in May 1983) I thought to speak about the use of unpublished mediaeval Latin manuscripts whose value had already become clear to me in a study of saints' legends as sources for the notices in The Old English Martyrology. Looking for new illustrations, I first consulted Helmut Gneuss's list of Anglo-Latin manuscripts from the Anglo-Saxon period (Anglo-Saxon England 9 (1981), pp.1-66) on the simple assumption that an English writer was more likely to read a manuscript in his native land than one from the Continent. There I noted a rarity, the unpublished MS 25 of Pembroke College, Cambridge, which was the only large collection of homilies/sermons in the list not designated as a version of Paul the Deacon's influential homiliary. M. R. James's catalogue of Pembroke manuscripts had indicated the sources for about a quarter of the items (although the identifications should be credited to H. Schenkl). Those identified were from the same Latin writers whose works were already known to have been used in the Old English vernacular, but, presumably, the unidentified items did not have contact with these works or with the other major sources of the period, such as the homiliary of Paul the Deacon, the Roman homiliary of Alanus of Farfa, the ninth-century homiliaries of Smaragdus, Hrabanus Maurus or Haymo of Auxerre, otherwise the well-read cataloguer would have noted these. The collection, I suspected, could contain much new and perhaps relevant material and I argued (now in Studies in Medieval Culture 20 (Kalamazoo, 1986), pp.77-101 at pp.84-85) that it should be read.

The microfilm, which I saw later in 1983, proved my suspicion well-founded, but, for those interested in the ironies of life as humane antiquarians often are, I record that I had used one section of the manuscript for the edition of the sermon Legimus in ecclesiasticis historiis (Traditio 33, 1977), but, at that time, did not ask to see more.

Results below illustrate the relevance of this collection to students of Old English vernacular sermons, their words, ideas and methods of composition. But our new group project to catalogue known sources of literature in the Anglo-Saxon period, and, if possible, to discover new sources, embraces both vernacular and Anglo-Latin works. Most of the original work in this monograph is thus on the Latin collection itself, notably on the Pembroke 25 copy made at Bury in the eleventh century, possibly as a companion volume to the copies there of parts of Paul the Deacon's homiliary (Pembroke MSS. 23 and 24 of the same date and place of origin). It is a valid object of study within the terms of our general project. As a result, however, the monograph is a hybrid, mainly about a Latin collection by one primarily interested in the Old English vernacular. The presentation of the Latin illustrations below is not a considered edition for Latinists, but a reading edition for Anglo-Saxonists, presenting a base text, Pembroke 25, with as many variants as possible. This, I have argued elsewhere, is the most helpful kind of presentation for vernacular source-analysts, since it is unlikely that the actual Latin manuscript of the source used by Old English writers will be discovered, and, often, no single manuscript will offer all the readings which have been used. The Old English texts below are taken from the most up-to-date editions for convenience since it has not been my intention to re-edit these.

A monograph about anonymous works, such as this, will have no wide sale. We have thus tried to produce it as cheaply as possible so that individual scholars may own copies if they wish. This has led to some problems for printing because our excellent typists, first Joan Welford, then Catherine Rees and Tina Benson, have had to work out what they could do with the word-processor as I was presenting material to them in sections. One decision at an early stage was to discard footnotes in the descriptive essays, and to refer to earlier discussions in brief, within parentheses, in the text. This practice already obtains in essays on linguistics and mediaeval history, and should present no problem to our intelligent readers who may refer to the bibliography, presented early in the volume, for full descriptions. Secondary material which is not listed in the bibliography is given adequate reference within the relevant discussion. Another decision was to print twenty lines of the Latin text per page, even though the textual variants sometimes do not fill the remaining space but sometimes would have over-run the space and have had to be presented in a different way. The material, we think, is accessible and readable, if not always pleasing to the pedantic eye. With more elaborate machinery and, no doubt, with more expertise in printing, we might have done better.

My own major difficulty (and one eventually for the typists) has been the nature of the study since source-analysis is a progressive activity, and a newly-found source necessitates insertion and correction. It may be that correction is not made in all places that it should be, also that the so-named 'art work', in our case insertion of umlauts etc., may not always have been made. I trust that any such oversights will be few and will not mislead.

In a study such as this which has to ignore the boundaries of separate disciplines, single or multiple questions are formulated and asked of different kinds of specialists, here of librarians, palaeographers, historians, experts on Latin and Celtic writings who have become friends, and fellow Anglo-Saxonists who already are friends. All my enquiries have been speedily and generously answered. Their names are already known for their varied contributions to scholarship of that unified Middle Ages which we seek to recall and explicate. They include: Bernhard Bischoff, Raymond Étaix, Francois Dolbeau, Raymond Page, Michael Lapidge, David Dumville, Simon Keynes, Malcolm Godden, Thomas Hill, J. D. Pheifer, Donald Scragg, Paul Szarmach, Charles Wright, Denis Brearley, Teresa Paroli, Jean Rittmueller, Joseph Kelly, Michael Herren, Michael Winterbottom, Richard Sharpe, R. L. Thomson, D. H. Turner and Penelope Bullock. My own colleagues in Liverpool have allowed me to test my speculations against their knowledge, Joyce Bazire, David Mills, Andrew Hamer and now Clare Lees; and our student Jane Moores has considered aspects of this study.

My reading of unpublished manuscripts has been eased by the courtesy and efficiency of the directors of major libraries in Europe and in Britain: Rome (Vatican Library), Paris (Bibliothèque Nationale), the municipal libraries at Orléans, Grenoble and Lyons, Munich (Staatsbibliothek), Vienna (Nationalbibliothek), London (The British

Library), Oxford (The Bodleian Library) and the cathedral libraries at Canterbury, Hereford and Worcester.

For permission to publish items from the Latin collection I primarily and gratefully thank the Master and Fellows of Pembroke College, Cambridge, but also the Master and Fellows of St. John's College, Cambridge, of Balliol College, Oxford, and the Librarians of the municipal libraries at Chartres and Grenoble.

The British Academy funded my visit to see the fragments of Chartres MS. 25 (44), and my own university has always been generous in purchasing microfilms from its limited resources during hard times, particularly for the humanities, in British provincial universities. I trust that this monograph will be some repayment for their help.

J. E. Cross
Liverpool
February 1986

BIBLIOGRAPHY

I   The Latin Collection

A   Manuscripts

i.   Chartres, Bibliothèque Municipale MS. 25 (olim 44) fols. 119-162; (saec. X-XI, Saint-Père, Chartres). The manuscript was burned in 1944 and is extant only as a succession of fragments, now boxed, interleaved and numbered.

ii. Cambridge, Pembroke College MS. 25, fols. 3r-180v; (saec. XI, Bury).

iii. Oxford, Balliol College MS. 240, fols. 56r-136r; (saec. XIV).

iv. Cambridge, St. John's College MS. 42 (B. 20), fols. 13r-62v, 70v-71v; (saec. XII, Worcester?).

v.   Canterbury Cathedral MS. Addit. 127/12, fragment; (saec. XI in.). Sermons for Purification of Mary and part of Septuagesima, as Pembroke 25 nos. 15, 16.

vi. London, British Library MS. Royal 5 E XIX, fols. 21r-36v (probably 1089-1125, Salisbury). Twelve sermons in order varied from Pembroke, as Pembroke 25 nos. 76, 1, 2, 77, end of 27 (folio missing), 29, 34, 36 (beginning only), 39, 37, 52, 53.

vii. Paris, Bibliothèque Nationale MS. lat. 3794, fols. 18r-31r; (saec XII, Germany?). Seven sermons included within another homiliary, Purification of Mary to the second sermon for Dom. i in Quadragesima entitled in Pembroke: In die initii, as Pembroke 25 nos. 15-21 inclusive.

viii. Grenoble, Bibliothèque Municipale MS. 278 (470); (saec. XII, Grande-Chartreuse). Sermons (or part-sermons) as in the Pembroke-type homiliary, interspersed in the Grenoble collection, as Pembroke nos. 20 (fols. 6r-8r), 38 with adaptation and omission (fols. 34v-35v), 36 (fols. 37r-39v), 40 incomplete (fols. 72v-74v), 24 (fols. 77r-79v), 93 incomplete (fols. 79v-81v), 16 (fols. 86r-89r), 15 (fols. 89r-92r), 29 (fols. 92r-94r), 92 incomplete (fols. 94r-94v).

B. Studies and manuscript catalogues

H. Barré, Les Homéliaires Carolingiens de l'école d'Auxerre, Studi e Testi 225 (Città del Vaticano, 1962), pp.17-25. (Discusses and catalogues the Latin collection).

Catalogue Général des Manuscrits des Bibliothèques Publiques de France: Départements: Tome VII: Grenoble (Paris, 1889), pp.112-13 (Grenoble MS.); Tome XI: Chartres (Paris, 1890), pp.11-12 (Chartres MS.).

R. Étaix, 'Le Sermonnaire Carolingien de Beaune', Revue des Études Augustiniennes XXV (1979), pp.106-149 (Paris MS.).

M. R. James, 'On the Abbey of S. Edmund at Bury', Cambridge Antiquarian Society, Octavo Publications, XXVIII (1895), no.168 (Pembroke MS.).

M. R. James, A descriptive catalogue of the manuscripts in the library of Pembroke College, Cambridge (Cambridge, 1905), pp.25-29 (Pembroke MS.).

M. R. James, A descriptive catalogue of the manuscripts in the library of St. John's College, Cambridge (Cambridge, 1913), pp.57-64 (St. John's MS.).

N. R. Ker, 'Salisbury Cathedral manuscripts and Patrick Young's catalogue', The Wiltshire (Archaeological) Magazine LIII (1949), pp.158-83 (Royal MS.).

N. R. Ker, 'The beginnings of Salisbury Cathedral Library', Medieval Learning and Literature; Essays presented to Richard William Hunt ed. J. J. G. Alexander and M. T. Gibson (Oxford, 1976), pp.23-49 (Royal MS.).

N. R. Ker, Medieval Manuscripts in British Libraries II, Abbotsford-Keele (Oxford, 1977), pp.316-17 (Canterbury MS.).

G. Morin, Études, Textes, Découvertes (Maredsous, 1913), p.60. (Notes the Latin collection).

R. A. B. Mynors, Catalogue of the manuscripts of Balliol College, Oxford (Oxford, 1963), pp.260-63 (Balliol MS.).

H. Schenkl, Bibliotheca Patrum Latinorum Britannica 3 vols. in parts (Vienna, 1891-1908), III.2 pp.17-19 (Pembroke MS.); III.2 pp.49-51 (St. John's MS.).

C.   Sources and Analogues of the Latin items

i.   Reference-works and/or commonly-cited series

Bibliotheca Hagiographica Latina Antiquae et Mediae Aetatis (BHL) ed. Socii Bollandiani, 2 vols. (Brussels, 1898-99, 1900-01).

Clavis Patrum Latinorum (CPL), A. Gaar and E. Dekkers, Sacris Erudiri III (editio altera, as separate volume, Steenbrugge, 1961).

Codices Latini Antiquiores (CLA), E. A. Lowe, 11 vols. (Oxford, 1934-66), Supp. (1971), vol. II (2nd edn., 1972).

Corpus Scriptorum Ecclesiasticorum Latinorum (CSEL) (Vienna, 1866 seq.).

Corpus Christianorum, Series Latina (CCSL) (Turnhout, 1953 seq.).

J. F. Kenney, The sources for the early history of Ireland: ecclesiastical. (New York, 1929, repr. 1966).

Patrologia Graeca (PG), J. P. Migne (Paris, 1857-68).

Patrologia Latina (PL), J. P. Migne (Paris, 1844-55), but individual volumes were sometimes re-issued with different pagination and publication-dates. Readers should use references other than column numbers if these differ from those in the volumes of their own libraries.

Patrologiae Latinae Supplementum, (PL Supp.), A. Hamman, 5 vols. (Paris, 1958-1974).

F. Stegmüller ed., Repertorium Biblicum Medii Aevi, 11vols. (Madrid, 1940-80).

ii.   Printed texts

Pseudo-Abdias in Acta Apostolorum Apocrypha, sive Historia Certaminis Apostolici, adscripta Abdiae in Codex Apocryphus Novi Testamenti ed. J. A. Fabricius (Hamburg, 1703).

Acta Apostolorum Apocrypha ed. R. A. Lipsius and M. Bonnet, 2 vols. in 3 parts, (Leipzig, 1891, 1898, 1903, repr. Hildesheim, New York, 1972).

Adomnán, <u>Adamnan's De Locis Sanctis</u> ed. Denis Meehan, <u>Scriptores Latini Hiberniae</u> vol. III (Dublin, 1958). Also in <u>Itineraria et Alia Geographica</u>, as no. VI ed. L. Bieler, CCSL CLXXV (Turnhout, 1965), also in PL 88 and CSEL XXXIX.

Alanus of Farfa, see Grégoire; presented as two sections, <u>pars hiemalis</u>, <u>aestivalis</u>, cited as I, II.

Alcuin, <u>De Virtutibus et Vitiis liber ad Widonem Comitem</u>, PL 101, cited by chapter.

Alcuin, <u>Opusculum primum scriptum de Vita S. Martini Turonensis</u>, PL 101.

Alcuin, <u>Sermo de Transitu Sancti Martini</u>, PL 101.

Pseudo-Alcuin, <u>De Divinis Officiis Liber</u>, PL 101.

Pseudo-Alcuin, <u>De Septem Sigillis</u>, PL 101, but noted as in the edition of E. Ann Matter, 'The Pseudo-Alcuinian "De Septem Sigillis": an early Latin Apocalypse exegesis', <u>Traditio</u> 36 (1980), pp.113-116.

Amalarius, <u>De Ecclesiasticis Officiis Libri Quatuor ad Ludovicum pium Imperatorem</u>, PL 105, also in <u>Amalarii Episcopi opera liturgica omnia</u> ed. J. M. Hanssens, 3 vols., vol. 2 as <u>Liber Officialis</u>, <u>Studi e Testi</u> 139 (Città del Vaticano, 1948-1950). Cited by book and chapter.

Ambrose, <u>Sancti Ambrosii Mediolanensis Opera</u> pars IV: Expositio Evangelii Secundum Lucam, ed. M. Adriaen, CCSL XIV (Turnhout, 1957), also in PL 15 and CSEL XXXII. iv.

Andrew, <u>Passio</u>, see <u>Acta Apostolorum Apocrypha</u>.

Angelom of Luxueil, <u>Commentarius in Genesin</u>, PL 115.

Augustine, <u>S. Augustini in Iohannis Evangelium Tractatus CXXIV</u> ed. R. Willems, CCSL XXXVI (Turnhout, 1954), also in PL 35.

Pseudo-Augustine, <u>Appendicis, Classis II, Sermones de Tempore</u>, <u>Sermo</u> CXV seq., PL 39, 1973 seq.

Pseudo-Augustine, Novae Patrum Bibliothecae, tomus primus ed. A. Mai(us) (Rome, 1852).

Pseudo-Augustine, Sermones ad Fratres in Eremo commorantes, et quosdam alios, PL 40.

Pseudo-Basil, Admonitio ad Filium Spiritualem, PL 103.

Bede, Bedae Venerabilis, Expositio Actuum Apostolorum et Retractio ed. M. L. W. Laistner, Mediaeval Academy of America (Cambridge, Massachusetts, 1939), also in Bedae Venerabilis Opera pars II, Opera Exegetica CCSL CXXI (Turnhout, 1983), also in PL 92.

Bede, Chronica Minora, in Chronica Minora saec. IV. V. VI. VII. vol. III ed. T. Mommsen, Monumenta Germaniae Historica, Auctorum Antiquissimorum XIII (Berlin, 1898), also in PL 90.

Pseudo-Bede, Excerptiones Patrum, Collectanea, Flores ex Diversis, Quaestiones et Parabolae, PL 94.

Pseudo-Bede, Homiliae, liber tertius, Homiliae Subdititiae, PL 94.

Pseudo-Bede, In Pentateuchum Commentarii, Expositio in primum librum Mosis, PL 91.

Pseudo-Bede, Quaestionum super Genesim ex Dictis Patrum, Dialogus, PL 93.

Caesarius of Arles, Sancti Caesarii Arelatensis Sermones ed. G. Morin, 2 vols., CCSL CIII, CIV (Turnhout, 1953), cited by sermon and paragraph.

Pseudo-Caesarius, Sermones, PL 67.

Cassiodorus, Magni Aurelii Cassiodori . . . Opera Pars II, 2: Expositio Psalmorum LXXI-CL, ed. M. Adriaen, CCSL XCVIII (Turnhout, 1958).

Catechesis Celtica in A. Wilmart, 'Reg. Lat. 49: Catéchèses celtiques' Analecta Reginensia, Studi e Testi LIX (Città del Vaticano, 1933). Also noted in a typescript edition of the manuscript by R. E. McNally.

Collectio Canonum Hibernensis in Die Irische Kanonensammlung ed. H. Wasserschleben (2nd edn., Leipzig, 1885), cited by book and chapter.

Corpus Antiphonalium Officii, vol. III Invitatoria et Antiphonae, vol. IV Responsoria, Versus, Hymni et Varia, ed. R-J. Hesbert, Rerum Ecclesiasticarum Documenta, Series Maior, Fontes IX, X (Rome, 1968, 1970).

Cross, J. E., 'Legimus in ecclesiasticis historiis': A sermon for All Saints, and its use in Old English prose', Traditio 33 (1977), pp.101-35. An abbreviated text of this sermon is in PL 94, 452-55.

Cross, J. E., 'Portents and events at Christ's birth: comments on Vercelli V and VI and the Old English Martyrology', Anglo-Saxon England 2 (1973), pp.209-20.

Cyprian, De Mortalitate in Opera Omnia ed. G. Hartel, CSEL III Pars I (Vienna, 1868).

Pseudo-Cyprian, De Duodecim Abusivis Saeculi ed. S. Hellmann, Texte und Untersuchungen zur Geschihte der Altchristlichen Literatur, Reihe 3, Band 4, Heft 1, (Leipzig, 1909). Also in PL 4 and PL 40.

Dynamus Grammaticus (al. Patricius), Ad discipulum suum ait; Novae Patrum Bibliothecae, tomus primus, pars secunda ed. A. Mai(us) (Rome, 1852).

Evangelia Apocrypha ed. Constantinus Tischendorf (Leipzig, 1853).

Pseudo-Fulgentius (of Ruspe), Sermones, PL 65. The sermon noted, no. 2 (PL 65, 859) for Pembroke 25 item 8, is regarded as Pseudo-Fulgentius in CPL no. 844.

Gildas, Liber querulus de excidio et conquestu Britanniae in Chronica Minora saec. IV.V.VI.VII, vol. III ed. T. Mommsen, Monumenta Germaniae Historica, Auctorum Antiquissimorum XIII (Berlin, 1898).

Gildas, The Ruin of Britain and other works ed. and trans. Michael Winterbottom, History from the sources (London and Chichester, Totowa, New Jersey, 1978), also in PL 69.

Grégoire, Réginald, Les Homéliaires du Moyen Âge, Rerum Ecclesiasticarum Documenta, Series Maior, Fontes VI (Rome, 1966). Grégoire includes the fullest description of the homiliaries of Alanus of Farfa and Paul the Deacon. This book is the one cited below under Grégoire. Grégoire has now reprinted his material with revision in Homéliaires Liturgiques Médiévaux: Analyse de Manuscrits (Spoleto, 1980).

Gregory, Regulae Pastoralis Liber ad Joannem episcopum civitatis Ravennae, PL 76.

Gregory, XL Homiliarum in Evangelia, libri duo, PL 76.

Pseudo-Gregory, Liber Responsalis sive Antiphonarius, PL 78.

Pseudo-Hildefonsus, Sermones Dubii, PL 96.

Hieronymus (see Jerome).

Hrabanus Maurus, De Clericorum Institutione ad Heistulphum Archiepiscopum, libri tres, PL 107. Cited by book and chapter.

Hrabanus Maurus, Homiliae: I. Homiliae de Festis Praecipuis, item de Virtutibus, PL 110.

Isidore, De Ortu et Obitu Patrum, PL 83, col. 129 seq. (There is also Pseudo-Isidore, De Ortu etc. in PL 83, 1275 seq.).

Isidore, Isidori Hispalensis Episcopi Etymologiarum sive Originum libri XX ed. W. M. Lindsay, 2 vols. (Oxford, 1911), also in PL 82. Cited by book and chapter.

Isidore, Sententiarum libri tres, PL 83.

Isidore, Synonyma de Lamentatione Animae Peccatricis, PL 83.

Pseudo-Isidore, Liber de Numeris (see McNally, R. E.).

James, Montague R., ed., Latin Infancy Gospels (Cambridge, 1927).

Jerome, S. Hieronymi Presbyteri Opera, Pars I, Opera Exegetica 7, Commentariorum in Matheum libri IV CCSL LXXVII (Turnhout, 1959), also in PL 26.

Pseudo-Jerome, Expositio Quatuor Evangeliorum, PL 30.

Kelly, Joseph F., ed., Scriptores Hiberniae Minores, CCSL CVIII C (Turnhout, 1974).

Köberlin, K., ed., Eine Würzburger Evangelienhandschrift (Mp. th. f. 61, s. VIII.), (Augsburg, 1891).

Liber de Numeris (see McNally, R. E.).

Liber Responsalis sive Antiphonarius (see Pseudo-Gregory, Liber Responsalis).

Maximus (of Turin) and Pseudo-Maximus, Sancti Maximi Episcopi Taurinensis Homiliae in Quatuor Classes Distributae PL 57, 221 seq.; Sermones in tres classes distributi PL 57, 529 seq.; identified by homily or sermon number and PL volume and column number. Only one of the items noted as sources is included in Maximi Episcopi Sermones ed. A. Mutzenbecher, CCSL XXIII (Turnhout, 1962), (for item 37).

Pseudo-Matthei Evangelium (Liber de Ortu Beatae Mariae et infantia Salvatoris), see Evangelia Apocrypha.

Pseudo-Miletus (Mellitus), Liber de Actibus Joannis Apostoli a Leucio conscriptis, PG 5.

McNally, Robert E., Der irische Liber de numeris; Eine Quellenanalyse des pseudo-isidorischen Liber de numeris (Diss., Munich, 1957). Within the dissertation McNally, often but not always, prints a text for a section at the head of his discussion; if so, the page reference is given. The text is also partially printed for nos. I, II and the beginning of III in PL 83, 1293-1302. Otherwise citations are from a typescript edition prepared by R. E. McNally before his death, and generously made available to me by his literary executors at Fordham University, New York.

Old English Martyrology (OEM); Das altenglische Martyrologium ed. Günter Kotzor, Bayerische Akad. der Wissenschaften, Phil.-Hist. Klasse, Abhandlungen,

Neue Folge, Heft 88, 1, 2 (Munich, 1981), also in The Old English Martyrology ed. G. Herzfeld, EETS, OS 116 (London, 1900).

Orosius, Pauli Orosii Historiarum adversum paganos libri VII, ed. Carolus Zangemeister, CSEL V (Vienna, 1882). The edition by Zangemeister (Leipzig, 1889), has different pagination. Cited by book, chapter and paragraph.

Pascasius Radbertus, Pascasii Radberti Expositio in Matheo libri XII, ed. Bedae Paulus, CC Continuatio Mediaevalis LVI, A, B, (Turnhout, 1984).

Paul the Deacon (Paulus Diaconus), see Grégoire; presented as two sections, pars hiemalis, aestivalis, cited as I, II.

Paulinus (of Aquileia), Liber Exhortationis, vulgo De Salutaribus Documentis, ad Henricum Comitem seu Ducem Forojuliensem, PL 99.

Protevangelium Jacobi. A Latin version is not extant. For the Greek text see Evangelia Apocrypha.

Rufinus, Historia Ecclesiastica, in Eusebius Werke, zweiter Band, Die Kirchengeschichte ed. E. Schwartz; Die lateinische Übersetzung des Rufinus ed. Theodore Mommsen, Die Griechischen Christlichen Schriftsteller (Leipzig, 1903, 1908).

Sulpicius Severus, Vita Sancti Martini in Sulpicii Severi Libri qui supersunt ed. Carolus Halm, CSEL I (Vienna, 1866).

Theodulf (of Orléans), Capitula ad presbyteros parochiae suae, PL 105; the editors of Monumenta Germaniae Historica are preparing a collated edition of which I have seen a page-proof.

Tischendorf, see Evangelia Apocrypha.

Transitus Mariae, the Transitus C, in A. Wilmart, 'Reg. Lat. 119 (fol. 132-135v); L'ancien récit latin de l'Assomption', Analecta Reginensia, Studi e Testi LIX (Città del Vaticano, 1933).

<u>Visio S. Pauli</u>. Redactions of this popular apocryphal text have been variously edited. For the fullest presentation under one cover see Theodore Silverstein, ed., <u>Visio Sancti Pauli: The History of the Apocalypse in Latin together with Nine Texts, Studies and Documents</u> 4 (London, 1935).

iii   Manuscripts

Cracow, Cathedral Chapter 140 (olim 43). This collection of sermons is described by Pierre David, 'Un recueil de conférences monastiques Irlandaises du VIIIe siècle', <u>Revue Bénédictine</u> 49 (1937), pp.62-89, where selected passages are printed. Bernhard Bischoff (in McNamara p.159 note 124) notes: 'Although Irish elements can be traced in it . . . the language is, to a considerable degree, romanised. In my opinion it is Italian, after 800, not French'. For fuller references to Bischoff and McNamara see below sub Paris, Bibliothèque Nationale lat. 11561.

Munich, Bayerische Staatsbibliothek Clm. 6233. The manuscript includes a commentary on Matthew's Gospel (fols. 1r-110v) and homilies (fols. 110v-172v). Lowe, CLA IX (1959) no. 1252 notes: 'Written in Southern Bavaria, presumably in a scriptorium in the Freising diocese, under the supervision of Dominicus', and dates the manuscript saec. VIII^{ex}. He adds that Dominicus 'often started the page' (fols 1, 3^v, 6^v etc.) for his pupils to pick up where he left off, and 'a contemporary Anglo-Saxon hand makes corrections throughout'. Bernhard Bischoff, (in McNamara 23, pp.126-27) regards the commentary as a Hiberno-Latin composition, dates it saec. VIII^2, but thinks that it probably did not originate in Ireland. In my view there are 'Irish symptoms' in some of the homilies.

Paris, Bibliothèque Nationale lat. 11561. This is one manuscript of a commentary on selected passages or verses from the whole of Scripture, now designated as a Hiberno-Latin composition by Bernhard Bischoff, 'Wendepunkte

in der Geschichte der lateinische Exegese im Frühmittelalter', Sacris Erudiri 6
(1954), p.223, and there dated saec. IX med-^{2}, and named 'Bibelwerk' (p.211).
Bischoff revised the essay in his Mittelalterliche Studien Band I (Stuttgart, 1966),
and this has been translated in Biblical Studies: The Medieval Irish contribution,
ed. Martin McNamara, Proceedings of the Irish Biblical Association 1 (Dublin,
1976). The German 'Bibelwerk' has been translated 'Reference Bible'. Other
manuscripts of this commentary are noted by Bischoff (in McNamara 1A, p.97):
Vatican Regin. lat. 76 (saec. VIII-IX, only Genesis, incomplete); Munich,
Bayerische Staatsbibliothek Clm. 14276 (Old Testament) and Clm. 14277 (New
Testament) (saec. IX in.), and some fragments. Bischoff (in McNamara 1B and
1C, pp.97-98) also indicates that Paris, Bibliothèque Nationale lat. 614 A (saec.
IX^{2}or IX/X) contains excerpts, and that Lyons, Bibliothèque Municipale 447 (376)
(saec. IX) reworked excerpts of the material in dialogue form.

Paris, Bibliothèque Nationale lat. 10457 and lat. 10616 (saec. VIII-IX). This is
one manuscript bound as two volumes under the numbers noted. It contains a
commentary on Genesis 1,1-9,6 (lat. 10457 fols. 2r-159r), 'perhaps of continental
origin . . . certainly formed under Irish influence' (Bischoff in McNamara 3,
pp.103-4), Isidore, Liber de Natura Rerum (lat. 10457 and 10616) (CLA V no.
601), and a dialogue between a Discipulus and Magister (lat. 10616 fols. 94r-131r)
'Written doubtless at Verona by an expert scribe of the time of Egino, Bishop of
Verona between 796 and 799, who died at Reichenau in 802' (CLA V no. 601).

Paris, Bibliothèque Nationale lat. 12021. This manuscript contains comments on
selected statements from the Gospels, under chapter headings, on fols. 1r-27v,
followed by a recension of the Collectio Canonum Hibernensis. On the
commentary see Stegmüller, Repertorium VII no. 10457, pp.101-02; on the
Collectio see Wasserschleben p.LXVII. Stegmüller records the manuscript as
saec. IX. Wasserschleben notes that it was 'formerly at St. Germain's, previously
at Corbie, originally in Brittany'. Bernhard Bischoff has confirmed that it is
'saec. IX, Breton' by private communication.

Orléans, Bibliothèque Municipale 65 (62). This manuscript (saec. IX med.) contains a commentary on Matthew, which has contacts with other anonymous commentaries and one named commentary. For further information see Bischoff in McNamara 16 I, pp.113-14, where the manuscript is erroneously designated Orléans 65(2), and J. F. Kelly, 'Frigulus: an Hiberno-Latin commentator on Matthew', Revue Bénédictine 91 (1981), pp.363-73. The commentary once survived in four other manuscripts, two of which, in fragment, are now destroyed. These are: Paris, Bibliothèque Nationale lat. 2384, fols. 1r-54v, 61r-62v, saec. IX med. (breaks off at Matthew cap. 23); Paris BN Lat. 12292 fols. A-D, saec. VIII-IX, Irish script (see CLA V no. 642); Turin, Biblioteca Nazionale F VI.2 no. 4, saec. IX, the fragment burned in 1904; Dresden, Sächsische Landesbibliothek R 52um, saec. VIII-IX, German Anglo-Saxon script (see CLA VIII no. 1181), the fragment destroyed in 1945. Orléans BM 65 (62) is the only complete manuscript. Kelly (p.371) also notes similarities between this commentary and a fragment in Hereford, Cathedral Library P II 10 (saec. VIII) written in Northumbrian uncials (see CLA II no. 158) and demonstrates that our commentary is similar in content and word to a, then 'lost' but now found, commentary on Matthew by a certain Frigulus, (Figulus), which had been postulated by previous scholars from abstractions used by Smaragdus of Saint-Mihiel in his Collectanea in Epistolas et Evangelia, (PL 102). In May 1980 Bernhard Bischoff indicated to me by letter that the 'lost' commentary by Frigulus was in Halle. Now Jutta Fliege, Die Handschriften der ehemaligen Stifts-und Gymnasialbibliothek Quedlinburg in Halle, Universitäts- und Landesbibliothek Sachsen-Anhalt in Halle a. d. Salle, Band 25 (Halle-Saale, 1982), pp.218-20, has demonstrated that Quedlingburg Codex 127 (Upper Italy, saec. IX med.-3/4) contains the lost commentary fols. 1r-69v, under the title Fribolus (Frigulus?): Commentarius in Evangelium secundum Mattheum. Unfortunately, a microfilm of this unpublished manuscript is inaccessible at present.

Vatican Library, Reginensis lat. 542. A Poncelet, Catalogus Codicus Hagiographicorum Latinorum Bibliothecae Vaticanae (Brussels, 1910), lists the contents of the manuscript, pp.368-70, and dates it, p.368, as saec. XII.

Vatican Library, Reginensis lat. 703 B. A Poncelet, ibid, pp.397-98, notes the one hagiographical item, and dates the manuscript, p.397, as saec. XII. Marjorie Chibnall, ed., The Ecclesiastical History of Orderic Vitalis vol. 1 (Oxford, 1980), p.121, indicates that manuscript contains a text of the history, dates the manuscript as saec. XII and notes that it is from St. Stephen's, Caen.

Vienna, Österreichische Nationalbibliothek MS. lat. 940; saec. VIII-IX, Salzburg. Bernhard Bischoff in Die südostdeutschen Schreibschulen und Bibliotheken in Karolingerzeit: Teil II; Die vorwiegend osterreichischen Diözesen (Wiesbaden, 1980), p.111 calls this an 'Irish commentary on the Gospel of Matthew'. In McNamara no. 17 I p.115 he notes that it occupies fols. 13r-141v.

II   **Vernacular texts**

A.   Editions

Die Vercelli-Homilien I-VIII Homilie, ed. Max Förster, Bibliothek der angelsächsischen Prosa: XII Band (Hamburg, 1932; reprint Darmstadt, 1964).

Vercelli Homilies IX-XXIII ed. Paul E. Szarmach, Toronto Old English Series (TOES) 5 (Toronto, 1981).

The Vercelli Homilies, typescript edition (including Vercelli homilies XIX, XX, XXI), in preparation for The Early English Text Society by Donald G. Scragg. These texts are used in the discussion below.

Eleven Old English Rogationtide Homilies, ed. Joyce Bazire and James E. Cross, TOES 7 (Toronto, 1982). Includes variant texts of Vercelli XIX and XX.

Angelsächsischen Homilien und Heiligenleben ed. Bruno Assmann, Bibliothek der angelsächsischen Prosa: III Band (Kassel, 1889; reprint Darmstadt, 1964).

Twelfth-century Homilies in MS. Bodley 343 ed. A.O. Belfour, EETS, OS 137 (1909, repr. 1962).

R. Brotanek, Texte und Untersuchungen zur altenglischen Literatur und Kirchengeschichte (Halle, 1913).

A. M. Luiselli Fadda, Nuove omelie Anglosassoni della Rinascenza Benedettina (Firenze, 1977).

Hildegard L. C. Tristram, Vier altenglische Predigten aus der heterodoxen Tradition, mit Kommentar, Übersetzung und Glossar sowie drei weiteren Texten im Anhang (Diss., Freiberg im Breslau, 1970).

Robert Atkinson, The Passions and the Homilies from Leabhar Breac: Text, Translation and Glossary, Royal Irish Academy, Todd Lecture Series II (Dublin, 1887).

B. **Selected studies and Reference-work**

Bazire-Cross, Rogationtide, pp.6-15, 25-30. Discussion of the content of Vercelli XIX and XX.

Max Förster, 'Der Vercelli-Codex, CXVII nebst einiger altenglischer Homilien der Handschrift', Festschrift für Lorenz Morsbach ed. F. Holthausen und H. Spies, Studien zur Englischen Philologie (Halle, 1913), pp.20-179.

T. D. Hill, 'The Seven Joys of Heaven in Christ III and Old English Homiletic texts', Notes and Queries 214, NS 16 (1969), pp.165-66; see also Bazire-Cross pp.11-12.

Karl Jost, 'Einige Wulfstantexte und ihre Quellen', Anglia 56 (1932), pp.306-12. Considers the sources of Assmann XI and XII.

Karl Jost, Wulfstanstudien; Schweizer Anglistische Arbeiten, Swiss Studies in English, Band 23 (Bern, 1950).

N. R. Ker, Catalogue of Manuscripts containing Anglo-Saxon (Oxford, 1957).

Donald G. Scragg, 'The compilation of the Vercelli Book', Anglo-Saxon England 2 (1973), pp.189-207.

Donald G. Scragg, 'Napier's "Wulfstan" homily XXX: its sources, its relationship to the Vercelli Book and its style', Anglo-Saxon England 6 (1977), pp.197-211.

Celia Sisam (ed.), The Vercelli Book (Vercelli Biblioteca Capitolare CXVII), Early English Manuscripts in Facsimile XIX (Copenhagen, 1976), Introduction.

Helen L. Spencer, 'Vernacular and Latin versions of a sermon for Lent: "A lost penitential homily found"', Mediaeval Studies 44 (1982), pp.271-305. Edits Pembroke 25 item 22 and demonstrates that a text of this Latin item is the source of Vercelli III.

Paul E. Szarmach, 'Caesarius of Arles and the Vercelli Homilies', Traditio 26 (1970), pp.315-23.

Paul E. Szarmach, 'The Vercelli Homilies: Style and Structure', in The Old English Homily and its Backgrounds ed. Paul E. Szarmach and Bernard F. Huppé (Albany, New York, 1978), pp. 241-67.

Joan Turville-Petre, 'Sources of the Vernacular Homily in England, Norway and Iceland', Arkiv för Nordisk Filologi 75 (1960), pp.168-82.

Joan Turville-Petre, 'Translations of a lost penitential homily', Traditio 19 (1963), pp.51-78. Constructs the Latin homily (which Spencer later finds) from its vernacular derivatives.

THE LATIN COLLECTION

Sources

A number of scholars have considered sources for individual items of this collection, although such identification was not the main purpose of their separate studies. I have gratefully accepted their accurate identifications but have silently corrected their oversights. In addition to definable sources I have noted 'popular' themes and ideas which may help our understanding of what was available to 'insular' writers. Abbreviated references to authors and titles, below and following, should be easily identified within the preceding bibliography. The numbering of items below is as in Barré's analysis of the Pembroke 25 manuscript (Homéliaires pp.18-24) since the Pembroke numbering goes awry in places. Items which are not edited here are analysed with reference to folio and line numbers of the Pembroke manuscript.

Heinrich Schenkl (Bibl. Pat. Brit. III.2, pp.17-19) identified whole sources where a single patristic sermon was used (items 6, 38, 39, 64, 66, 76, 77) and partial sources otherwise (items 20, 21, 37, 46, 65), and M. R. James (Pembroke MSS. pp.25-29) accepted all the suggestions without question. These identifications helped to alert me to the possibilities of the Pembroke-type collection.

Henri Barré added a few more sources among his general comments on the composer's reading (Homéliaires pp.24-25) and within his list of initia (pp.239-343). These identifications included whole sources (items 17, 74, 75) and partial sources (items 15, 26). He also used helpful BHL numbers for apocryphal stories and legends (items 9-10 and 51), generally recorded the use of antiphons but without specific exemplification, and corrected Schenkl by noting the use of the long version of the sermon 'Legimus in ecclesiasticis historiis' (items 56-63), in the reference to the edition of Combéfis (p.17 note 60), as opposed to that in Migne. Most importantly, he referred to Amalarius, De Eccles. Off. (items 16, 31) a text which plays its part in the dating of the composition of the collection. Raymond Étaix (Revue Aug. 25 pp.109-10) has identified in close detail the six items (15-21 inclusive) which were abstracted from the Pembroke-type collection for the homiliary of Beaune (Paris MS.).

But studies of vernacular sermons, which are now known to be based on the Pembroke-type collection, have obviously contributed valid identifications for the appropriate Latin items. Joan Turville-Petre's brilliant reconstruction of the Latin source for Vercelli Homily III (Traditio 19) by using vernacular derivatives, identified the multiple sources for item 22, and I have merely deleted some alternatives, rightly noted by her, out of my present knowledge of the Latin composer's habits of reading. Karl Jost, on Assmann Homilies XI and XII, and Paul Szarmach, on Caesarius in Vercelli Homilies XIX and XXI, have ascertained sources for items 20, 21 and 23 (Jost) and for items 34 and 38 (Szarmach) where the Old English and Latin correspond. Years ago, so far as I can trace, Max Förster, discussing Vercelli Homily XX in the Morsbach Festschrift, first noted the use of Alcuin's De Virt. and thus provided the main source for item 93.

For my continuing analysis (following) I have had generous help from Abbé Raymond Étaix, in an invigorating correspondence, in which he has confirmed some of my findings and added a number of his own, particularly for minor echoes which are most difficult to clarify. He would, I realise, wish to have only these general thanks. I should finally record gratitude to my friends J. D. Pheifer of Trinity College, Dublin, who quickly spotted the source for item 54 from his close acquaintance with Isidore, and Thomas D. Hill of Cornell University, who wrote about the persistent theme of the Seven Joys of Heaven.

My own most pleasing discoveries have been the recording of the link between our collection and those collections of sermons and commentaries on Scripture which reveal 'insular' influences, i.e. with the unpublished series of homilies in Munich Clm. 6233 (items 11, 12, 13, 14, 43, 44, 45, 46, 50), with those in Rome, Vatican Reg. lat. 49 (Catechesis Celtica) (items 26, 27, 29), with (some unpublished) commentaries on Scripture (items 11, 12, 15, 30), and also the note of the use of Dynamius Grammaticus (item 89), a man, apparently, of limited literary production. Most of the remaining identifications were made by following the principles of source-analysis.

1. Incipit omelia in quarta Dominica ante natale Domini: Primum omnium oportet nos memorari, fr. k., et recitare de Deo ueraciter et loqui caeli ac terrae conditore...

    P 3r; B 57r; Royal 23v.

    P 3r ll.4-10. Phrases from a Creed, but ll.5-6, 9-10 as Caesarius 3 (Morin, I 20, 21), the Athanasian Creed. The words in ll.5-6, 9-10, are repeated within a longer passage from Caesarius 3 at P 48r ll.12-23.

    P 3v ll.6-12. Ps.-Caesarius 17 (PL 67, 1079 CD). See the use of this sermon in item 30, 67v l.8-68r l.7, and comment there.

    P 3v ll.17-19. Statement on Adam's expulsion from Paradise, also at P 45r ll.4-6 (Hieronimus ait) and at P 67r ll.11-12. At P 45r the source is Coll. Can. Hib. 12, 2 (ed. p.33), but cf. Alcuin, De Virt. cap. 16 (PL 101, 625) for P 3v and 67r.

    P 3v ll.23-27. Ps.-Caesarius 17 (PL 67, 1079D).

    P 4r ll.4-20. Testimonies of Christ's Advent from Isaiah 7, 14; 11, 1-3 (seven gifts of Holy Spirit); John I, 32 and 34.

    P 4r l.20-4v l.26. Theme of seven gifts of Holy Spirit in the patriarchs: sapientia in Adam, intellectus in Noah, consilium in Abraham, fortitudo in Isaac, scientia in Jacob, pietas in Moses, timor domini in David, all in Christ. The theme is found in printed texts and in unpublished manuscripts, some of which have 'insular' connections (scribal hand, Irish foundation, or defined Hiberno-Latin material in the manuscript). Printed texts are Ps.-Bede, Collectanea, De Septem Donis Spiritus Sancti (PL 94, 553) and Ps.-Alcuin, De Septem Sigillis (ed. Matter, pp.115-116). For unpublished manuscripts see McNally, Der irische Liber de Numeris, pp.108-109. Allocation of gift to patriarch is constant, but reasons, supported by Scriptural testimonies, vary.

    There are many quotations from Scripture in this sermon.

2. Omelia in iii Dominica ante natale Domini: Factum est autem cum impleta essent omnia quę de aduentu Domini in carne temporibus praedicta per prophetas fuerant ...

    P 5v; B 58r; Royal 26r.

    Mainly a narrative from Scripture, an introduction on John the Baptist as precursor of Christ (P 5v l.16-6r l.5), followed by the story of Gabriel's visitation to Mary as in Luke 1, 26-48. Non-scriptural sources are:

P 5v l.28-6r l.4 eulogy of John cf. Caesarius 216.3 (Morin, II 860) (as Ps.-Aug. 197.3, PL 39, 2114) chosen as Alanus of Farfa II.39.

P 7r l.16-7v l.7 Based on Caesarius 188.6 (Morin, II 769-70) (as Ps.-Aug. 116.6, PL 39, 1976-77), but with insertion of phrases from Caesarius 187.3 (Morin, II 764) (as Ps.-Aug. 115.3, PL 39, 1974). See also P items 3 and 4 below.

3. In ii^a Dominica ante natale Domini: Illud scire et in corde frequenter meditari, et animo uoluntarie recordari debemus, fr. k., quod iam prope est dies aduentus Domini ...

P 7v; B 59r; J 13r.

Caesarius 187 (Morin, II 763-766) (as Ps.-Aug. 115, PL 39, 1973-1975) chosen as Alanus of Farfa II. 84, with omissions, adaptations and variant readings from the printed texts.

4. Omelia in prima ante natale Domini: Sanctam et gloriosam solemnitatem natiuitatis Domini nostri I. C., saluatoris cosmi, fideli deuotione, fr. k., caelebraturi, totis uiribus nos debemus cum Dei adiutorio preparare...

P 9r; B 60r; J 13v.

Caesarius 188 (Morin, II 767-70) (as Ps.-Aug. 116, PL 39, 1975-1977) chosen as Alanus of Farfa II.85, with omissions, adaptations and variant readings from the printed texts.

5. Omelia in natale Domini nostri Iesu Christi: Oportet nos, fr. k., gaudere hodie et exultare et in unum conuenire, ad laudandum et benedicendum et praedicandum nomen Domini, saluatoris mundi...

P 10v; B 60v; J 15r.

P 10v l.28-11r l.26. Portents and events at Christ's nativity (with significations) as follows: (i) circulus aureus circa solem; (ii) fons olei ... in Roma; (iii) omnia debita regis laxata sunt; (iv) sol obscuratus est; (v) terraemotus ... magnus; (vi) bella ab orbe terrarum cessauerunt; (vii) animalia fari humana locutione non dubitatur: bos ... in Roma ... agnus in Egypto. Some items are found in Orosius, Hist. adv. Paganos lib. VI.xx.5-8 (ed. pp. 419-20), some in Cat. Celt. (ed. Wilmart pp.99-100), some in Ps.-Alcuin De Divin. Off.

cap. 1 (PL 101, 1174). For some discussion of these portents and events in OE. texts see Cross, Anglo-Saxon England 2 (1973), pp.209-20. Item (i), circulus aureus appears to be an adaptation in insular texts; item (vii), bos in Roma, agnus in Egypto, appears in the Old English Martyrology (ed. Kotzor, II p.2).

P 11v 11.10-14. Three 'O' apostrophes: O felices panni ... O felices uagitus ... O presepe splendidum ...; cf. Ps.-Aug. 119.5 (PL 39, 1984).

P 11v 11.18-22. Sequence of five hodie's as antiphons and responses in Hesbert, Corpus IV no. 6859, III no. 3093. P omits a sixth hodie in other MSS as Hesbert, Corpus III no. 3093. Three of the items are as Ps.-Aug. 121.3 (PL 39, 1988).

6. Item alia: In illo tempore, exiit edictum a Cesare agusto, ut discriberetur uniuersus orbis... (Luke 2, 1). Quia largiente Domino missarum solemnitatem hodie caelebraturi sumus ...

    P 11v; B 61r.

    Gregory, Hom. 8 in Evang. (PL 76, 1103-1105) chosen as Paul the Deacon I.24, on Luke 2, 1-14, with some variant readings from the printed text.

7. Item alia: Venerandus est hic dies, fr. k., ab omnibus fidelibus, in quo natiuitas Domini nostri I. C. totum mundum noua ac preclara aduentus sui luce resplenduit ...

    P 13v; B 62r; J 15v.

    Based on Ps.-Aug. 123 (PL 39, 1990-91) (as Ps.-Fulgentius 36, PL 65, 898-900) chosen as Alanus of Farfa I.7.
    There are many insertions:-

    P 13v 11.13-17. Response, Hesbert, Corpus IV no. 6858.

    P 14r 11.3-21. Section on Mary; the first lines (P 14r 11.3-11) from Ps.-Aug.193.2 (PL 39, 2104), chosen as Alanus of Farfa I.8.

    P 14r 11.27-28. Two facta est phrases from Ps.-Aug. 195.1 (PL 39, 2107), chosen as Alanus of Farfa I.5.

    P 14v 11.24-15r 1.6. Echo and adaptation of antiphons and responses as Hesbert, Corpus IV no. 7068, III no.4091, IV no. 7569, and cf. III no. 3093.

8. Omelia in natale Sancti Stephani: Oportet nos disputare, fr. k., de sancto
    Stephano primo apostolorum diacono. Septem enim ab ipsis ad diaconatus
    officium electi sunt ...

    P 15r; B 62v; J 16r.

    P 15r ll.14-18. Ps.-Aug. 210.3 (PL 39, 2138). Ps.-Aug. 210 is chosen as
    Alanus of Farfa I.19. Ps.-Aug. 210.2-6 is now Caesarius 219 (Morin, II
    867-70).

    P 15r l.23-15v l.23. Ps.-Aug. 215.1-3 (PL 39, 2145-46) (as Ps.-Fulgentius 2,
    PL 65, 859-60). Verbal echoes but phrases re-ordered with insertions.

    P 15v l.27-16v l.16 (end). Ps.-Aug. 210.4-6 (PL 39, 2138-40) with
    omissions.

9. Omelia in natale Sancti Iohannis euangelistae: Sanctum Iohannem
    adoptiuum Domini filium uenerari oportet, fr. k., cui supra pectus eiusdem
    Domini recubanti reuelata sunt secreta cęlestia ...

    P 16v; B 63v; J 16v.

    P 16v ll.18 (beginning)-21. Introduction including an antiphon, Hesbert,
    Corpus III no. 3425.

    P 16v l.21-18r l.12 (end). Ps.-Miletus (Mellitus), Liber de Actibus Joannis
    Apostoli (PG 5, 1241-43; BHL 4320) with variant readings from the
    printed text and a little omission.

10. Item alia: Factum est, fr. k., cum implesset Iohannes haec et multa his
    similia, et cum annorum esset nonaginta .vii., apparuit ei Dominus I.C. cum
    discipulis...

    P 18r; B 64r; J 17v.

    P 18r ll.14-26. Ps.-Miletus (see no. 9 above) (PG 5, 1249).

    P 18r l.26-19v l.2 (end). Acta Apostolorum Apocrypha sive Historia
    Certaminis Apostolici, adscripta Abdiae ... Babyloniae episcopo in
    Codex Apocryphus Novi Testamenti ed. J. A. Fabricius (Hamburg,
    1703), lib. II pp.582-589, with omissions and adaptation. This is BHL
    4316.

11. Omelia in Natale Innocentum: Glorificare oportet et honorare hanc
    solemnitatem beatorum ac felicium infantium, fr. k., quorum hodie
    triumphalem passionis gloriam caelebramus...

P 19v; B 65r; J 18r.

P 19v l.11-20r l.2. The flight into Egypt, quoting Matthew 2, 13-15, Isaiah 19, 1 and 18, with extending explication. Cf. Commentary on Matthew in Vienna Nb lat. 940 fol. 28v (noted under Bibliography I C iii). See illustration below on 'Insular connections' within discussion of 'The Collection and its background'.

P 20r ll.2-28 Cf. Commentary on Matthew in Orléans BM. lat. 65 (62) pp.38-39 (noted under Bibliography I C iii). See illustration below on 'Insular connections'. Two ideas as in Pseudo-Matthaei Evangelium in Evangelia Apocrypha ed. Tischendorff, that is, idols destroyed in Egypt in cap. 23 (ed. p.86); Christ stayed four years in Egypt in cap. 24 (ed. p.88). Note however the place in Ps.-Matt. is named Hermopolis cap. 22 (ed. p.85) as Orléans 65 (62) p.38, not Hieropolis, Ieropolis as in Pembroke 25, fol. 20r l.3. See also discussion on the number of Innocents under 'Insular connections' below.

P 20v l.1-21r l.10 (end). Selections from an unpublished sermon found in Munich Clm. 6233 fols. 122v-125r, with additions and variant readings. See J. E. Cross, 'The insular connections of a sermon for Holy Innocents' in Medieval Literature and Antiquities: Studies in honour of Basil Cottle ed. M. Stokes and T. Burton (Boydell and Brewer, Cambridge, 1987), for a presentation of this sermon with commentary on its sources.

12. Omelia in Circumcisione Domini: Intelligendum est, fr. k., et exponendum omnibus noui Testamenti fidelibus, quod post consummationem octo dierum ...

P 21r; B 65v; J 18v.

P 21r l.13 (beginning)-21v l.9. Cf. phraseology and ideas in Comm. in Lucam (Vienna Nb. lat. 997) ed. Kelly (CCSL CVIII C) pp.16-17. See illustration below on 'Insular connections' within discussion of 'The Collection and its background'.

P 21v l.9-23r l.8. Based on selections from a sermon found in Munich Clm. 6233 fols. 125r-127v, chosen as Alanus of Farfa I. 31, and printed in part from Vatican manuscripts in PL Supp. 2, 1213-18. Our selections are as PL Supp. 2.1-4 (1213-16) but where readings vary those in P are nearer to those in Munich Clm. 6233.

13. Omelia in die Theophaniae: Predicanda sunt et recolenda miracula, fr. k., et uirtutes, quę huius solemnitate dies peracta sunt ...

P 23r; B 66v; J 19v.

P 23r l.14 (beginning)-23v l.17. Eulogy of the festival; echo of response at P 23r ll.20-21 (Hesbert, Corpus IV no. 6821); testimony, cf. Numbers 24, 17, at P 23v ll.5-10.

P 23v l.17-24r l.10. Scripture verses from Matthew 2, 1-11, (Coming of Magi) with commentary.

P 24r l.10-24v l.1. Various significations of the Magi's gifts. See discussion below on 'Insular connections' within the section on 'The Collection and its background'.

P 24v ll.10-24 (end). Caesarius 194.4-5 (Morin, II 788), with omissions and adaptation.

14. Item alia: Haec sunt mirabilia, fr. k., quę in die solemnitatis sui baptismatis Dominus noster I.C. ostendere dignatus est...

P 24v; B 67v; J 20r.

P 25r ll.1-16. The miracle of five loaves and two fishes, basically John 6, 3-14, with additions.

P 25r l.16-25v l.4. The wedding at Cana, John 2, 1-11; with adaptation, and addition as Munich clm. 6233 fols. 131v-132r. N.B.: et fecit uinum de aqua, id est, .cl. modios et mutauit speciem aque conuertens in colorem et saporem uini. (P 25r ll.24-26, Munich 131v).

P 25v l.4-26r l.8. Baptism of Christ. Sentences and phrases interwoven from Munich 6233 fol. 132v and 133v and Ps.-Aug. 136.1-2 (PL 39, 2013-14).

P 26r l.9-26r l.28. Eulogy of John and the feast. Echoes of antiphons most conveniently presented in Ps.-Gregory, Liber Responsalis (PL 78, 743-44); as Hesbert, Corpus III, nos. 1552, 1553, 5062, 1554, 3678, 1768, 1788.

P 26r l.28-26v l.8. Ps.-Aug. 136.5 (PL 39, 2015).

P 26v l.8-27r l.2 (end). Selections from Munich 6233 fols 133v-135(bis)v, with adaptation.

15. Omelia in Purificatione Sancte Marie: Conueniendum est in unum nobis, fr. k., ad huius diei sollempnitatem, quia hodie Christus cum substantia nostre carnis in templo est dignatus presentari...

> P 27r; B 68v; J 21r; Paris 18r; Grenoble 89r; Canterbury (whole sermon, but two folios cut and material excised).

> P 27r l.15-27v l.11. Ps.-Hildefonsus 4 (PL 96, 258) with additions, omissions and differences.

> P 27v ll.12-17. Antiphons as in Ps.-Gregory Liber Responsalis (PL 78, 799 and 746); and Hesbert, Corpus III no. 3078, IV no. 6759, III no.2925.

> P 27v l.26-28r l.11. Based on Ambrose, Expositio secundum Lucam lib.II cap.58 (CCSL XIV, 56).

> P 28r l.16-28v l.13. Cf. phraseology in Comm. in Lucam (Vienna Nb. lat. 997) ed. Kelly (CCSL CVIII C) pp.17 and 19. See illustration below on 'Insular connections' within discussion of 'The Collection and its background'.

> P 28v ll.18-27 (end). Concluding exhortation.

16. Omelia in Septuagesima: Inquirendum est, fr. k., et subtiliter discutiendo inuestigandum quid mysterii continetur in officiis, quae scripta sunt in antiphonario et missali libello...

> P 28v; B 69v; J 21v; Paris 19v; Grenoble 86r; Canterbury (part sermon).

> P 29r l.1-31v l.3. Apart from brief introduction (P 29r ll.1-9) and a few lines at the end (from P 31r l.27), Amalarius, De Eccles. Off. 1, 1 (PL 105, 993-97).

17. Omelia in Sexagesima: Primum in predicatione christianus debet populus silentium tenere; deinde, qui habet aures audiendi audiat, id est, qui intellectum mentis continet, humiliter audiat sermones quos annuntiat sacerdos. Sacerdotis est enim in pace populum ammonere quod debeat agere; populi est cum humilitate et silentio audire que monet sacerdos...

> P 31v; B 70v; J 22v; Paris 21v.

> P 31v l.4(beginning)-22. Introduction with Scriptural quotation.

> P 31v l.26-32r l.21. Pericope, Luke 8, 5-15.

> P 32r l.21-33v l.17. Gregory (Gregorius dicit) Hom.15 in Evang.1-4 (PL 76, 1131-33), chosen as Paul the Deacon I.71.

18. Omelia in Quinquagesima: Hoc denuntiare uobis oportet, fr. k., et uos diligentius considerare debetis, ut per terrenorum medicorum exempla peruenire studeatis ad caelestia...

P 33v; B 71v; J 23v; Paris 23v.

P 33v l.26-34r l.15.   Caesarius 57.1-2 (Morin, I 251-52) (as Ps.-Aug. 249.1-2, PL 39, 2206), with omission and adaptation.

P 34r l.15-35r l.10. Caesarius 197.1-4 (Morin, II 794-97), with omission and adaptation.

P 35r l.10-35v l.26. Seven ways of forgiveness for sins. Theodulf, Capit. cap.36 (PL 105, 203).

P 36r l.1-36r l.16(end). Caesarius 197.4-5 (Morin, II 798).

19. Omelia in caput ieiunii: Precauendum est omnibus bona opera exercentibus, fr. k., quod Dominus dicit in aeuangelio: Adtendite, ne iustitiam uestram faciatis coram hominibus.....

P 36r; B 73r; J 24r; Paris 25v.

P 36r ll.19-28. Matthew 6, 1-4 (haec lectio).

P 36r l.28-38r l.14(end). Caesarius 146.1-3 (Morin, II 599-602) (as Ps.-Aug. 63.1-3, PL 39, 1864-66).

20. Omelia in Quadragesima, Dominica I: Audite, filioli mei, et intelligite, quomodo sacra scriptura uos ammonet, et ad regna caelorum inuitat, et uiam ostendit...

P 38r; B 74r; J 25r; Paris 27r; Grenoble 6r.

Sources presented with text printed below, from: Sermo 64 ad Fratres in Eremo (PL 40, 1347); Caesarius 183.1 (Morin, II 744) (this paragraph as Ps.-Aug 287.1, PL 39, 2287-88); Theodulf, Capit. caps.28, 34, 37-39, 41, 44 (PL 105, 200-05); Alcuin, De Virt. cap. 3 (PL 101, 615).

21. Item alia in die initii: Rogo et ammoneo uos, fr. k., ut in isto legitimo ac sacratissimo tempore quod de suo sancto ieiunio Dominus consecrauit...

P 40r; B 74v; J 25v; Paris 29r;

Sources presented with text printed below, from: Caesarius 199.1-3 and 8 (Morin, II 803-05 and 807) (as Ps.-Aug. 142.1-3, 8, PL 39, 2022-25), chosen as Alanus of Farfa I. 52; Caesarius 188.3, 4, 6 (Morin, II 768-70); Theodulf, Capit. cap.23 (PL 105, 198).

22. Omelia in Dominica ii in Quadragesima: Primum omnium tria quaedam unicuique homini pernecessaria sunt: fides, spes, caritas...

P 42v; B 76r; J 26v.

This sermon is now printed by Spencer, Mediaeval Studies 44 (1982), 283-91, and analysed by Turville-Petre, Traditio 19 (1963), 56-60, in relation to its direct derivative Vercelli Codex homily III. Sources as from Turville-Petre, but now modified, are: Alcuin, De Virt. caps. 4, 10, 12, 13, 16, 17 (PL 101, 616-626); Hrabanus, De Cler. Inst. 2, 9 (PL 107, 328-29); Coll. Can. Hib. 12.2-4, 12.8-9, 13.1-2, 14.2-3, (ed. pp.33-41); Theodulf, Capit. cap.31 (PL 105, 201). There are variations from the printed texts.

23. Omelia in Dominica iii in Quadragesima: Oportet nos, fr. k., omni die dominico ad ǥcclesias Dei cum humilitate et silentio et sobrietate conuenire...

P 46r; B 77r; J 27v.

Sources presented with text printed below, from: Caesarius 13.3 (Morin, I 66); Theodulf, Capit. caps. 24-27 (PL 105, 198-200); Alcuin, De Virt. caps. 21 and 26 (PL 101, 629 and 632). There are variations from the printed texts.

24. Omelia in Dominica iiii in Quadragesima: Quicumque uult saluus esse, ante omnia opus est ut teneat catholicam fidem...

P 48r; B 78r; J 28r; Grenoble 77r.

P 48r l.12(beginning)-l.23. Caesarius 3 (Morin, I 20-21) on the Creed, cf. P 3r, under Item 1 above.

P 48v l.14-49r l.1. Phrases from Caesarius 57.4 (Morin, I 252-53), Christ accuses the sinner.

P 49r l.1-50v l.2. Theme (unidentified). Sinners reply we did not know, no-one told us; prophets, patriarchs, Peter, Paul, evangelists, martyrs. Then, from a group of saints, replies from Noah, Abraham, Moses, David, Isaiah and Christ himself (including ubi sunt passage). Sinners say: Have mercy. Christ replies: Discedite a me maledicti.

25. Omelia in Dominica vᵃ in Quadragesima: Spiritus sanctus per Isaiam prophetam hortatur nos et ammonet dicens: Querite Dominum dum inueniri potest...

P 50v; B 79v; J 29r.

P 50v l.22. Isidoro dicente (unidentified).

P 51r ll.1-6. Soul as domina; body as ancilla. cf. Coll. Can. Hib. 60.2 ed. p.226).

P 51r ll.6-13. Alimenta spiritalia cf. Galatians 5, 22-23.

P 51r ll.20-22. Augustinus ait, on peace, cf. Caesarius, 188.6 (Morin, II 770) 224.4 (Morin, II 887), but common in Caesarius.

P 51r ll.22-26. Alcuin, De Virt. cap. 6 (PL 101, 617), on peace.

P 51v ll.5-8. Isidorus dicit, on four ways of perverting judgement. Probably Coll. Can. Hib. 21, 13 (ed. p.66), citing Isidore, but cf. Alcuin, De Virt, cap. 21 (PL 101, 629).

P 51v ll.8-11. In libris Clementis scriptum est. Coll. Can. Hib. 22,2 (ed. p.74).

P 51v l.13. Sicut scriptum est: O principes uindicate super latrones... (unidentified).

P 51v l.17. Sicut scriptum est: Ideo enim redundat omne peccatum... (unidentified).

P 52r ll.1-9. Against Kalendas Ianuarias and pagan customs (unidentified).

P 52r ll.10-26. A list of virtues opposing vices (unidentified), but such lists are common.

P 52v ll.18-20. Seven Joys of Heaven theme; see T. D. Hill in bibliography.

26. Omelia in Dominica die Palmarum: Dominus per prophetam predicatoribus loquitur dicens: Aperi os tuum, et ego adimplebo illud ...

P 52v; B 80r; J 30r.

P 53r l.1-54v l.8. As Omelia in dominica die palmarum, no. XIII in R. E. McNally's typescript edition of Catechesis Celtica, Vat. Reg. lat. 49, fols. 13r-14r, with minimal difference of word. Pembroke 25 (and Vat. Reg. lat. 49) draws on Gregory Hom. 2 in Evang. 1 and 7 (PL 76, 1082 and 1084) at P 53r l.24-53v l.1 and P 54r l.17-54v l.4 respectively, and has verbal echoes of Jerome in Matt. (CCSL pp.180, 181) at P 53v l.3-54r l.16.

P 54v l.8-55v l.25. Scriptural citations from within Matthew 21, 1-13, (Christ's entry into Jerusalem and the clearing of the temple), with adaptation from the other gospels, and with explication. The great majority of the explications are verbally close to those in <u>Cat.</u> <u>Celt.</u> No. XV (McNally edition), Vat. Reg. lat. 49 fols. 15r-15v. There are some insertions for which an antiphonal base may be suspected at P 55v ll.10-13, 16-17.

P 55v l.25-56r l.26 (end). As <u>Cat.</u> <u>Celt.</u> No. XV (McNally edition), Vat. Reg. lat. 49 fols 15v-16r (end of item).

N.B. P 56r ll.8-10: <u>dicit quidam tractator principibus et doctoribus ecclesiarum</u>: Cauete ne dimittatis in aecclesiis dei crescere illa que dominus cum indignatione eiecit de templo suo . . . (unidentified). The passage enclosing this quotation (P 55v l.27-P 56r l.21, in illo tempore . . . in regnum, as Vat. Reg. lat. 49) is verbally close to Cracow Cathedral MS. 140 (olim 43)p.121. See discussion in the section on 'Insular connections' below.

27. Item alia: Factum est autem postquam emundasset Iesus templum suum ab omnibus scandalis, accesserunt ad eum caeci et claudi...

P 56r; B 81v; J 31r; Royal 29r (ending only).

P 56r ll.27-28. Brief introduction, echo of Matthew 21, 12.

P 56v ll.1-6. Matthew 21, 14-16 but with slight additions as in citation in <u>Catechesis Celtica</u> no XIV (McNally edition), Vat. Reg. lat. 49 fol. 14r.

P 56v ll.6-10. Explication as <u>Cat. Celt.</u> no. XVI (McNally edition), Vat. Reg. lat. 49 fol. 16r.

P 56v ll.10-12. Matthew 21, 16 adapted.

P 56v ll.13-21. Cf. <u>Cat. Celt.</u> no. XIV (McNally edition), Vat. Reg. lat. 49 fol. 15r for ideas, and some verbal echoes.

P 56v l.21-57v l.12. As <u>Cat. Celt.</u> no XIV (McNally edition), Vat. Reg. lat. 49 fol. 14v, based on Jerome <u>in Matt.</u> (CCSL, p.189) and Scripture.

P 57v ll.12-24. Matthew 21, 17, with explication as <u>Cat. Celt.</u> no. XVI (McNally edition), Vat. Reg. lat. 49 fol. 16r, with brief echo of Jerome <u>in Matt.</u> (CCSL p.190).

P 57v l.25-58r l.3. Continuation of Matthew 21, 17 with explication as <u>Cat. Celt.</u> no. XIV (McNally edition), Vat. Reg. lat. 49 fol. 15r.

P 58r ll.3-12 (end). As <u>Cat. Celt.</u> no. XVI (McNally edition), Vat. Reg. lat. 49 fols 16r-16v.

28. Alia omelia in die Palmarum: Dominus ad prophetam Iezechiel, cum
    mitteret eum ad predicandum filiis Israel, dicit: Mitto ego te ad filios populi
    mei...

    P 58r only; omitted also from list of contents in Balliol 240.

    P 58r l.16-61r l.18. Exhortation to preachers with many scriptural
        quotations including opera carnis cf. Galatians 5, 19-21.

    P 61r l.18-62r l.23. Explication of Matthew 20, 30 and scriptural verses
        within Matthew 21, 7-13.

    P 62r l.23-63r l.27 (end). Exhortation on destruction of earthly cities and
        on praise of heavenly city.

29. Omelia in Caena Domini: Oportet hoc scire et intelligere, fr. k., quod hęc
    dies, id est quinta feria, in qua caena Domini ab apostolis, pridie quam
    pateretur, secundum consuetudinem legis preparata est....

    P 63r; B 82v; J 31v; Royal 29r; Grenoble 92r.

    P 63v l.1 (beginning)-65v l.2 (end). As Omelia in Cena Domini in
        Catechesis Celtica no. XVII (McNally edition), Vat. Reg. lat. 49 fols.
        16v-17r with slight variation of individual words. The item is, first, an
        explication of John 13, 5-14 (P 63v l.1-64v l.20) using some ideas of
        Augustine, Tract. in Ioh. 55, 7; 56, 1; 56, 3; 58, 5 (CCSL pp.466, 467,
        468, 474-5), then an extract, with a little adaptation, from Caesarius
        202.1 (Morin, II 814-5, De Cena Domini) (P 64v l.20-65r l.18), and
        finally an exhortation (P 65r l.19-65v l.2 (end)).

30. Omelia in Parasceuen de Passione Domini: Hoc primum omnium inquirendum
    est humano generi, qualiter mundus a principio creatus et formatus est...

    P 65v; B 83v; J 32r.

    P 65v l.4 (beginning)-67v l.8. Story of Creation, Adam and Eve, and the
        expulsion from Paradise with quotation of Scriptural verses from
        Genesis caps 1-3 and insertions of explanation.

    P 65v ll.8-16. cf. Ps.-Bede, Expositio in primum librum Mosis (PL 91, 191).

    P 66r ll.4-5. cf. Ps.-Bede, Expos. in primum lib. Mosis (PL 91, 201).

P 66r ll.17-20 cf. Paris B.N. lat. 10616 fol. 114r, and see illustrations from this manuscript, noted here and immediately below, in the discussion on 'Insular connections', within the section on 'The Collection and its background'.

P. 66v ll.18-23. Hieronimus dicit (on Genesis 3, 7) cf. Paris B.N. lat. 10616 fols. 116r-116v.

P 67r ll.11-12. See above under item 1, fol. 3v.

P 67r ll.16-26. Hieronimus ait (on Genesis 2, 17), theme, four kinds of death, cf. Paris B.N. lat. 10616 fols. 115r-115v and Paris B.N. lat. 12021 fol. 5v.

P 67r l.26-67v l.8. cf. Paris B.N. lat. 10616, in order, fols. 117r-117v, 114v, 115v-116r.

P 67v l.8-68r l.7. Ps.-Caesarius 17 (PL 67, 1079 CD). Compare the use of this sermon in item 1, 3v ll.6-12, 23-27. The passages in items 1 and 30 are very close in phrase, notably in extensions on the printed text in PL. The Latin sermon is found in a number of manuscripts, but the text varies so greatly that a critical edition is complicated (R. Étaix).

P 68r l.15-72r l.25. Scriptural story from Matthew caps 24, 26, 27 with insertions, some from Jerome, in Matt; Jerome sometimes named.

P 72r l.26-73r l.6. Agustinus ait; Augustine 80.1-3 Sermo de Passione Domini; Mai, Novae Patrum Bibliothecae. I, 156-158, selections.

31. Item alia: Parasceven, id est sexta dies sabbati, que preparatio interpretatur, eo quod omnia que in sabbato necessaria sunt, in illa preparantur...

P 73r; B 87r; J 35r.

The sermon uses two main sources, Hrabanus, De Cler. Inst. 2, 37 (PL 107, 347-49) and Amalarius, De Eccles. Off. 1, 14 (PL 105, 1028-1032); but insertions from: Amalarius, De Eccles. Off. 1, 13 occur at P 73r ll.18-20; and Adomnán, De Locis Sanctis III, 3.11 (ed. Meehan p.110) at P 74v ll.1-4, and III, 3.12-14 (ed. p.110) at P 74v ll.16-25.

32. Omelia in Sabbato Sancto: Sabbati paschalis ueneratio ideo caelebratur et colitur, quia in eadem die Dominus in sepulchro quieuit. Vnde et bene in Ebreo sermone sabbatum requies interpretatur.

P 75r; B 88r; J 35v.

P 75r 1.6 (beginning)-75v l.l. Hrabanus, De Cler. Inst. 2, 38 (PL 107, 349-50), with omissions.

32a. (Barré omits as separate item). Item alia in Sabbato.

Iudẹi ergo quoniam Parasceue erat ut non remanerent in cruce corpora Sabbato; erat enim magnus dies ille Sabbati...

P 75v; B 88r; J 35v.

Extracts from Alanus of Farfa I.93, being selections from Augustine, Tract. in Ioh. 120.1-5 (CCSL pp.661-63), with interpolated passages printed by Grégoire, Homéliaires, pp.46-47.

33. Omelia in die Sancto Paschae: Spiritus sanctus per prophetam populo christiano diem solemnem constituere hortatur et ammonet dicens: Constituite diem solemnem in condensis, id est, in multitudinibus...

P 77r; B 89r; J 36r.

P 77v l.10. Hieronimus ait : Qui cotidie eucharistiam accipiunt... (unidentified).

P 77v ll.14-16. Cassiodorus ... dicens, Cassiodorus, Expos. in Psalm. CXVII (CCSL, p.1057).

P 78r l.10-78v l.6. Extracts from Jerome, in Matt. (CCSL, pp.279-80).

P 78v l.9-79r l.24. Agustinus ait, Ps.-Aug. 167 (PL 39, 2069-70), selections with insertions.

34. Item alia de Resurrectione Domini: Uidete, fr. k., et considerate quam carissimos nos Dominus habere dignatus est, et quomodo nos amare disposuit...

P 79v; B 90r; J 37r; Royal 30v.

Sources presented with text printed below from: Ps.-Caesarius 17 (PL 67, 1080 A), Caesarius 57.3 (Morin, I 252) and Ps.-Aug. 136.6 (PL 39, 2015).

35. Omelia Octavas Paschẹ: Paulisper de ministratoribus persecutionis Christi, quid actum sit uideamus, fr. k., primus itaque Herodes, sub quo passi sunt infantes, nunc finem habuit...

P 81r; B 91r; J 37v.

P 81r 1.18(beginning)-82r 1.4. Death of Herod and his son and Pilate; siege of Jerusalem etc. cf. Rufinus, Hist. Eccles. I.8, II.10, II.7, II.6, III.6, III.7, III.8 (ed. pp.65-71, 129-31, 123, 121, 209, 211, 217-18).

P 82r 1.10-83r 1.26. Ps.-Aug. 160 (PL 39, 2059-61) chosen as Alanus of Farfa II.2, with omissions and variant readings from the printed text.

36. Omelia in Rogatione: feria ii: Scitis, fr. k., quod istos quattuor dies cum summa diligentia custodire debetis, in grandi humilitate, in patientia, in caritate, in castitate, in puritate, in uigiliis, in ieiuniis, in orationibus...

P 83v; B 92r; J 38v; Royal 31v (incomplete); Grenoble 37r.

Text printed below. No sources identified.

37. Alia in iii feria, Sermo beati Maximi episcopi: Legimus in prophetis cum Niniue ciuitati subuersio immineret...

P 85v; B 93r; J 39r; Royal 33r.

P 85 1.12(beginning)-P 87r 1.22. Maximus of Turin 90 (PL 57, 459-62) chosen as Alanus of Farfa II.17 and Paul the Deacon II.17, with omissions and variant readings from the printed text. Also in CCSL XXIII, 332-34.

P 87r 1.27-P 87v 1.20. Coll. Can. Hib. 12,3; 13,2 (ed. pp.34, 38-39), cf. use of this material under item 22 above.

38. Alia in iiii feria in Letania Maiore: Ecce, fr. k., dies sancti ac spiritales et animę nostrę medicinales adsunt, et ideo quicumque uult sanare peccatorum suorum uulnera...

P 87v; B 94r; J 40r; Grenoble 34v (with adaptation and omission).

Caesarius 207 (Morin, II 828-31) (as Ps.-Aug. 173, PL 39, 2076-78) with additions and variant readings from the printed text.

39. P. no title; J, item alia, B, Alia: Scire et intelligere debemus, fr. k., quod dies conpunctionis et poenitentię modo cęlebramus, et ideo oportet nos precauere...

P 90r; B 95r; J 40v; Royal 32r.

Caesarius 208 (Morin, II 832-34) (as Ps.-Aug. 174, PL 39, 2078-79) chosen as Alanus of Farfa II.18, with additions and variant readings from the printed text.

40. Item alia: Oportet nos, fr. dil., annuntiare uobis, quod modo dies sanctificati ac uenerabiles sunt, in quibus a uitiis et peccatis possumus nos mundare...

P 91r; B 95v; J 41r; Grenoble 72v-74v (incomplete).

Text printed below. No sources identified.

41. Omelia in Ascensione Domini: Uocem iocunditatis ac dulcedinis de resurrectione Domini ac uictoria Christi annuntiate, fr. k., in medio catholici [populi], et usque ad extremum terrę dicite...

P 93v; B 97r; J 42r.

Sources presented with text printed below, from: Gregory, Hom. 29 in Evang. 1-4 (PL 76, 1214-16) chosen as Paul the Deacon II.28, Bede, Expositio Actuum Apostolorum (ed. Laistner p.8), antiphon in Hesbert, Corpus III no. 4079, and extracts from an unpublished sermon in Munich Clm. 6233 fols. 158v-159v.

42. Item alia in eodem die: Gloriari nos oportet semper, fr. k., et gaudere, quia Dominus ac Redemptor noster post redemptionem humani generis et diaboli triumphum, hodie cum magna uictoria ad cęlos ascendisse legimus...

P 95v; B 98r; J 43r.

Themes presented with text printed below, from: Ps.-Aug. 136.6 (PL 39, 2015), Visio. S. Pauli (tortures of sinners) in various redactions, ed. Silverstein, and Seven Joys of Heaven theme; see T.D. Hill in bibliography.

43. Omelia in die Sancto Pentecosten: Factum est, fr. k., cum impleta essent omnia quę de aduentu Domini in carne predixerant prophete...

P 97r; B 99r; J 43v.

P97r ll.17(beginning)-28. Introduction on Pentecost including Scriptural quotations.

P97v l.4-99v l.20. Selections from an unpublished sermon in Munich Clm. 6233 fols. 161v-166r, with insertions of Scriptural quotations and two sections: P97v ll.22-24 cf. Hrabanus, De Cler. Inst. 2, 41 (PL 107, 354); P 99v ll.1-7, Gregory Hom. 30 in Evang.7 (PL76, 1224-25), chosen as Paul the Deacon II.33.

44. Omelia in natale Sancti Iohannis Baptistae: Ad inluminandum humanum genus, quod per inuidiam diaboli perierat, scire et intelligere debemus...

P 99v; B 100r; J 44v.

P 100r l.1. Phrase from Munich Clm. 6233 fol. 167r (see below on Item 50).

P 100r ll.2-3. John born 5198 years and 6 months from creation of world. This figure relates to Christ's nativity at 5199, a number found in Orosius, Hist adv. Paganos preface (ed. p.6), Bede, Chron. Min. cap. 22 (PL 90, 290; ed. Mommsen p.281) and The Old English Martyrology (ed. Kotzor II p.1).

P 100r l.13-100v l.25. Scripture, Luke 1,9-80, selections.

P 100v l.26-102r l.15. Caesarius 216 (Morin II, 858-61) (as Ps.-Aug. 197, PL 39, 2113-15) chosen as Alanus of Farfa II.39; selections with insertions.

45. Omelia in natale Sancti Petri Apostoli: De sancto Petro apostolo, primo et principe apostolorum, hodie nos oportet loqui...

P 102r; B 101v; J 45v.

P 102r l.18 (beginning)-105r l.14. Selections from an unpublished sermon in Munich Clm. 6233 fols. 135v (bis)-142v, with insertions and adaptation.

P 105r l.21-105v l.12. Echoes of phrases from Passio (BHL 6657) as in text or variants printed in Acta Apostolorum Apocrypha I.i; ed. Lipsius pp.171 and 173.

46. Omelia in natale Sancti Pauli Apostoli: Audite me, filioli mei, et liberate uos; currite pro uobis in bonis operibus et nobis beneficium prestate et uobis...

P 105v; B 103r; J 47r (incomplete).

P 105v l.17(beginning)-107r l.3. Ps.-Aug. 204, (PL 39, 2124-25) chosen as Alanus of Farfa II.48, with omissions, and insertions of Scriptural texts and phrases from Munich Clm. 6233 fols. 143v-144r.

P 107r l.3-108v l.13. Selections from Munich Clm. 6233 fols. 144r-150r with insertions, sometimes of Scriptural texts.

47. Omelia in Natale Martyres in Kalendas Agusti: Uenerari nos oportet, fr. k., hanc solemnitatem Machabeorum, quę hodie celebratur et colitur. Machabei enim ex Iudaeis erant...

P 108v; B 104v; J 48r col.2 l.9 (as P 110v l.13), incomplete at beginning.

P 108v l.27-110r l.19. A narrative, from II Maccabees caps. 6 and 7, of the mother and her seven sons, but these chapters are a common basis for narratives for 1 August within legendaries as indicated by BHL 5106-5111. The story includes non-scriptural features, as P 109r ll.4-7: <u>Haec sunt autem nomina illorum, Eleazarus et Felicitas et septem filii eius, Dardanus, Dardianus, Antiochus, Mentonius, Anchius, Anchialius, Heubresius.</u> Eleazar as the father and Felicitas as the mother are noted elsewhere in the text. Obviously some confusion with Felicitas and her seven sons (BHL 2853-2855) but note Ps.-Isidore (Irish) <u>Liber de Numeris</u> VII, 36: <u>Septem fratres, filii Felicitatis, de quorum triumphys et cruciatibus in Machabeis scriptum est.</u>

P 110v l.16-111v l.5. <u>doctrina sancti Agustini.</u> Caesarius 13.1-4 (Morin, I 65-67) (as Ps.-Aug. 265.1-4, PL 39, 2238-39), with omissions, additions and variant wording.

48.   Item alia de Sapientia: Primum omnium inquirendum est omni homini Deum scire uolenti, fr. k., quę sit uera scientia ueraque sapientia, quia sapientia huius seculi stultitia est apud Deum...

P 111v; B 106r (incomplete); J 48v.

P 111v l.21 (beginning)-112r l.3. Alcuin, <u>De Virt.</u> cap. 1 (PL 101, 614-15).

P 112r ll.3-11. Hrabanus, <u>De. Cler. Inst.</u> 3, 37 (PL 107, 414).

P 112r l.12-P 113v l.5. Scriptural quotations but including the story of Solomon's judgement on the disputed child, 3 Kings, 3, at P 112r l.24-113r l.15.

49.   In Assumptione Sanctę Mariae: Sciendum est, fr. k., et omnibus exponendum fidelibus, quod post ascensionem Domini nostri I. C. saluatoris mundi, cum magna gloria ab alto caelorum descendit angelus Domini ad sanctam Mariam, cum esset in templo Dei...

P 113v; B, J omit, but in the index of B.

P 113v l.14 (beginning)-P 117v l.5. Selections with adaptation from a text of <u>Transitus Beatae Mariae</u>, the designated <u>Transitus C</u>; see the edition by Wilmart, 'L'ancien récit latin de l'Assomption', pp.325-56. A variant text of parts of our sermon has been printed by G. Marocco, <u>Marianum</u> 12, (1950), pp.449-51.

P 117v ll.5-10 (end). Based on antiphons or responses as in Ps.-Gregory <u>Liber Responsalis</u> (PL 78, 798-99) and in Hesbert, <u>Corpus</u> III nos. 1566, 2762, 3105; IV nos. 6165, 6851, 6867.

50. Omelia in Passione Sancti Iohannis Baptisțe: Ualde honorandus est nobis, fr. k., sanctus Iohannes Baptista, cuius hodie solemnitatem agimus, qui statim ut ualuit, heremum concupiuit in aetate puerili ...

P 117v; B 107r(lacks opening); J 49r.

The sermon is based on selections from an unpublished sermon found in Munich Clm. 6233 fols. 167r-171r, but with insertions notably from: Adomnán, De Locis Sanctis II, 23.2,3 (ed. Meehan p.92) at P 118v ll.15-22, and from Scripture, Mark 6, 17-29, on the death of John at P 119r l.13-119v l.8.

51. Omelia in Natiuitate Sancte Mariae: Inquirendum est, fr. k., et explanandum per ordinem de origine generis Mariae, et natiuitatis eius solemnitate. Quidam uir nob[il]is fuit in tribu Iuda, Ioachim nomine, ex genere Dauid, honorabilis ualde in xii tribus Israel...

P 119v; B 107v; J 50r.

P 119v l.19-121v l.18. Extracts, with verbal echoes but adaptation, from a Latin version of the Greek Protevangelium Jacobi 1-8.

P 121v l.21-122r l.9. Based on responses for the festivals of Mary as in Ps.-Gregory, Liber Responsalis (PL 78, 798 and 802), and in Hesbert, Corpus IV nos. 7455, 7199, 6854, cf. III no. 3852.

A variant text of our sermon has been printed by F. Vattioni, 'Frammento latino del Vangelo di Giacomo', Augustinianum 17 (1977), pp.507-08.

52. Omelia in iiii^or Tempora: Ecce dies confessionis et humillimae supplicationis adsunt, fr. k., et ideo ammoneo uos, filii in Christo dilectissimi, ut gaudeat unusquisque uestrum, quia pro salute uestra...

P 122r; B 109r; J 51r; Royal 34v.

No sources identified. Many Scriptural quotations.

53. Item alia: Oportet nos, fr. k., ad primum sancțe religionis fundamentum catholicam fidem tenere, in qua salus animarum corporumque redditur...

P 123v; B 109v; J 51v; Royal 36r.

No sources identified. Many Scriptural quotations.

54. Omelia in festiuitate Sancti Michaelis Archangeli: Angeli grece vocantur, aebraice malaoth, latine uero nuntii interpretantur, ab eo quod Domini uoluntatem populis nuntiant. Angelorum autem officii nomen est...

P 125r; B 110r; J 52r.

P 125r l.2(beginning)-127r l.23(end). Isidore, Etym. lib. VII cap. V (PL 82, 272-74).

55.   Item alia: Memorari et recitare decet memoriam Sancti Michaelis, fr. k., cunctis gentibus, toto orbe terrarum dispersis, qui constitutus est a Deo dux et princeps super omnes animas hominum suscipiendas...

P 127r; B 111r; J 53r.

P 127r l.27-127v l.6. Based on antiphons and responses for the festival as in Ps.-Gregory, Liber Responsalis, (PL 78, 805-06) and Hesbert, Corpus III nos. 1474, 3757, IV nos. 6826, 7834.

P 127v l.11-128r l.24. A story of Michael fighting a dragon in Asia as in Vat. Reg. lat. 703B (noted as BHL 5956b), Vat. Reg. lat. 542 (noted as BHL 5951b), both in BHL Supp., and The Passions and the homilies from Leabhar Breac ed.   Atkinson, text pp.213-19; translation pp.451-57. N.B. Insertion of antiphons at P128r ll.1-5, as in Liber Responsalis, (PL78, 805-06) and Hesbert, Corpus IV nos. 6535, 6715, 7151.

P 128r l.28-128v l.26. Extracts from Isidore, Etym. lib. VII cap. V (PL 82, 272-74) as in previous sermon (no. 54).

P 128v l.26-129r l.19. Based (with verbal echoes of phrases) on the sermon Legimus in ecclesiasticis historiis, ed. Cross, Traditio 33 (1977), pp.108-10, as in succeeding sermon (nos. 56-63).

For a detailed discussion of this sermon (no. 55) see J.E. Cross, 'An unpublished story of Michael the Archangel and its connections', in Magister Regis: Studies in honor of Robert Earl Kaske, ed. A. Groos et al. (Fordham U.P. New York, 1986), pp.23-35.

56-63. Omelia in solemnitate omnium sanctorum in Kalendis Nouembris: Legimus in aecclęsiasticis historiis, fr. k., quod Sanctus Bonifatius, qui quartus a beato Gregorio Romanę urbis episcopatum tenebat...

P 129r; B 112r; J omits.

The basic source for this sermon is an anonymous sermon Legimus in ecclesiasticis historiis, which is found in augmented versions of Paul the Deacon's homiliary.   For collations of this text, and some sources for it (Gregory, Hom. 19, 27, 28, 34 in Evang., PL 76) see Cross, Traditio 33 (1977), pp.101-35.   As noted (Cross, pp.122-23) the Pembroke item inserts two sections, P 131v ll.7-12 and P 132v 1.14-133r 1.8. The second, larger, section echoes phrases, but with adaptation, from Cyprian, De Mortalitate cap. 26 (CSEL III i, pp.313-14) (information from Malcolm Godden).

64. Item alia de ordinibus omnivm sanctorvm: Hodie, dilectissimi, omnium sanctorum sub una solemnitatis lҽtitia caelebramus festiuitatem...

P 133r; B 114r; J omits.

P 133r 1.12(beginning)-133v 1.23. Ps.-Bede, Homiliae Subdititiae 70 (PL 94, 450-52) (which appears in augmented versions of Paul the Deacon's homiliary), with sizeable omissions and one addition (P 133v ll.23-25).

65. Omelia in natale Sancti Martini Episcopi: Postquam Dominus noster I. C. triumphator ad alta caelorum ascendit et in maiestate paterna consedit...

P 133v; B 114r; J 53v.

Based on Alcuin, De Vita S. Martini caps. 1-10 (PL 101, 657-62; BHL 5625), but with additional information presented in interwoven phrases from Sulpicius Severus, Vita Sancti Martini caps. 2-8, 19 (ed. pp.111-18, 128; BHL 5610).

66. Item alia: Oportet nos omnes unanimiter gaudere, fr. k., et prҽclarum diem obitus Sancti Martini fideliter uenerari. Sed precipuҽ qui in occidentalibus mundi partibus sunt fideles Christi...

P 136v; B 115v; J 55r.

Alcuin, Sermo de transitu S. Martini (PL 101, 662-64; BHL 5626) with variant readings from the printed text.

67. Omelia in natale Sancti Andreae Apostoli: Ecce adest dies honorabilis Sancti Andreҽ apostoli; uiriliter agite, fr. k., sectando precepta saluatoris....

P 138v; B 116v; J 55v.

P 138v ll.8(beginning)-15. Based on Scripture, Matthew 4, 18-20; the calling of Peter and Andrew.

P 138v ll.15-20. The mission-fields of the apostles, Andrew in Scithia et in Achia (sic); these two areas are named in Isidore, De ortu et obitu Patrum cap. 70 (PL 83, 151).

P 138v 1.20-140v 1.24(end). Passio Sancti Andreae apostoli ed. M. Bonnet, Acta Apostolorum Apocrypha II.i, pp.3-37, (BHL 428); extracts with verbal echoes and one addition of a Scriptural quotation.

68-72. Natale omnium apostolorum: Benedictus Deus et Pater Domini nostri I. C., cui quidem soli ab hominibus reddenda est benedictio...

P 140v; B 117v; J 56v.

No sources identified. Moral injunctions with many Scriptural quotations. Each numbered item ends with a benediction.

73.   In natale plurimorum martyrum: Qvotiescumque, fr. k., sanctorum martyrum solemnia uoluntarie caelebramus...

P 145v; B 120r; J 58r.

P 145v l.11(beginning)-147v l.13. Caesarius 223 (Morin, II 882-85) (as Ps.-Aug. 225, PL 39, 2160-62) chosen as Alanus of Farfa II.94, with small omissions, additions, and variant readings from the printed text.

P 147v l.13-148v l.8. Ps.-Maximus of Turin 88 (PL 57, 707-10) chosen as Alanus of Farfa II.95, with omissions and adaptation.

74.   Omelia in natale plurimorum confessorum: Scriptum est, fr. k., in evangelica lectione quod homo quidam peregre proficiscens uocauit seruos suos... Homo iste paterfamilias Dominus Christus est, qui ad patrem post resurrectionem uictor ascendens...

P 148v; B 121v; J 59v.

Ps.-Maximus of Turin 24 (PL 57, 893-96) chosen as Alanus of Farfa II.102, with additions, omissions and variant readings from the printed text.

75.   Omelia in natale unius confessoris: Ad sancti ac beatissimi istius patris nostri cubb̗, cuius hodie festa celebramus, fr. k., laudes addidisse aliquid boni decerpsisse est atque deducere. Uirtutum enim eius gratia....

P 151r; B 122v; J 60r.

Ps.-Maximus of Turin 78 (PL 57, 417-22) chosen as Alanus of Farfa II.103 and Paul the Deacon II.106, with additions, omissions and variant readings from the printed text.

76.   Omelia in natale uirginum: Saepe uos ammoneo, fr. k., praua opera fugere huius mundi...

P 152v; B 123v; J 61r; Royal 21r.

Gregory, Hom. 12 in Evang. (PL 76, 1118-23) chosen as Paul the Deacon II.122, with small additions within the body of this sermon, with variant readings from the printed text, and an addition at the end (P 157r ll.1-5).

77. Omelia in natale ecclesiae: Qvotiescumque, fr. k., altaris uel templi festiuitatem colimus, si fideliter...

P 157r; B 125v; Royal 27r; J omits.

Caesarius 227 (Morin II, 897-900) (as Ps.-Aug. 229, PL 39, 2166-68, and Ps.-Maximus of Turin 18, PL 57, 879-82) chosen as Alanus of Farfa II.106 and Paul the Deacon II.127, with omissions, additions and variant readings from the printed text.

NB Barré, p.18, regarded the items recorded below as additions to the original homiliary. See discussion under 'The "original" collection' below.

78-88. De officio misae et misterio atque orationibus canonicorum horarum; Sermo Rabani Mauri: Officium quidem missę magna ex parte ad solum pertinet sacerdotem...

P 159r; B 126v.

P 159r l.23(beginning)-160r l.24. Hrabanus, De Cler. Inst, 2,1 (PL 107, 325-26) but with a large insertion at P 159r l.25-159v l.12 on the necessities for a priest at communion.

P 160r l.26-162v l.17. Sections with captions as Hrabanus, De Cler. Inst. 2, 2-10 (PL 107, 326-29) with adaptations.

P 162v l.20-165r l.28. Abstracts from Hrabanus, De Cler. Inst. 3, 37 (PL 107, 413-14) and also from Gregory, Regulae Pastoralis Liber, Tertia Pars, Prologus and caps. 1-5 (PL 76, 49-56). Gregory's work was used by Hrabanus, but P contains phrases which are found in each author alone. Other extensions are from Scripture and from Coll. Can. Hib. 24, 1, 2 (P 165r ll.8-11; 13-14; 24-25) and 24, 4 (P 165r ll.16-19) (ed. pp.75-76).

P 165v ll.1-21. Unidentified, including a citation from Agustinus (P162v l.4 seq.).

89. Predicatio commvnis omnibus popvlis: Iuxta qualitatem audientium formari debet sermo doctorum ut ad sua singulis congruat, hoc est, ut iuxta uniuscuiusque actus conueniat....

P 166r; B 129v, incomplete at beginning; J 70v.

P 166v ll.2-3. Seven Joys of Heaven theme; see T.D. Hill in bibliography.

P 166v l.8-167r l.7. Tractator sapiens dixit. Dynamius Grammaticus (al. Dynamius Patricius), A. Mai, Novae Patrum Bibliothecae I.ii, 182, with insertions.

P 167r ll.9-17. Theme, three reasons why the Lord conceals the day of death for a man, unidentified.

P 167r ll.20-24. Ubi sunt sequence similar to Isidore, Synonyma II.91 (PL 83, 865).

P 167v l.23-168r l.2. Dynamius Grammaticus ibid.

90. Predicatio de principibus et populis: Doctorum est omnes cum modestia ammonere quęcumque debeant agere. Illorum est humiliter audire ortamenta doctrinę quę illorum procedat ex ore sacerdotum est quę non licet fieri prohibere populorum est non facere.

P 168r; B 130v.

Sources presented with text printed below, from: Gildas, De excidio Britonum cap. 62, 2-4; Coll. Can. Hib. 25,15; 25,3; 25,4; 24,2; 24,4; 24,2 (ed. pp.75-81); Ps.-Cyprian, De duodecim abusivis saeculi, chapter-headings as list, as in e.g. Ps.-Bede, Collectanea (PL 94, 545); Ps.-Basil, Admonitio ad Filium Spiritualem cap. II (PL 103, 686).

91. Predicatio bona omnibus Christianis: Quicumque uoluerit placere Deo primum requirat quo possit modo diligere eum, quia primum et maximum mandatum est ...

P 170r; B 131v.

Sources presented with text printed below, from: Alcuin, De Virt. caps. 3, 4 (PL 101, 615-16) but closer in word to item 22 above, P 43r ll.1-11; Coll. Can. Hib. 21,7 (ed. p.64). Themes - Sex sunt quę odit dominus et septimum detestatur (Proverbs 6, 16-19) cf. lists in Ps.-Bede, Collectanea (PL 94, 545) and Ps.-Isidore (Irish) Liber de Numeris VII.16 (without supporting Scriptural texts as in our sermon); Vias domini, unidentified; Seven Joys of Heaven; see T. D. Hill in bibliography.

92. Sermo S. Agustini ad predicandum cotidianis diebus: Oportet nos, fr. k., ut tota mentis intentione inquirere et intelligere studeamus quare Christiani sumus...

P 171v; B 132r; Grenoble 94r (beginning only).

Apart from small addition at end (P173r ll.5-6), Caesarius 16 (Morin I, 76-78), omitting first eight lines of Caesarius.

93. Predicatio bona de VIII vitiis idemque virtvtibus: Precauere nos oportet semper, fr. k., octo ultla principalia quę assidue animas hominum iugulant...

P 173r; B 133r; Grenoble 79v (incomplete).

Sources presented with text printed below. Apart from a brief introduction, abstractions with adaptation from Alcuin, De Virt. caps. 27-35 (PL 101, 633-38) inclusive, on the eight vices and the four cardinal virtues.

94. Predicatio de preceptis Dei: Sciendum est, fr. k., quod primum credulitatis fundamentum est fides....

P 175r; B 134r.

Apart from the introduction (P 175v ll.1-3), abstractions, with adaptation and addition from Alcuin, De Virt. caps. 2-4, 6-10, 12-17, (PL 101, 615-26) sometimes out of Alcuin's order.

95. Item alia: Oportet nos, fr. k., in sanctitate et iustitia semper seruire et placere Deo...

P 177v; B 135v.

Apart from the introduction (P 177v ll.25-28) and ending (P 180r ll. 6-10), abstractions, with adaptation and addition from Alcuin, De Virt. caps. 18-22, 24-26 (PL 101, 626-632).

96. De eo quod a cantoribus placide ac suaue canendum sit: Studendum summopere cantoribus est, ne donum sibi diuinitus conlatum uitiis foedent, sed potius illud humilitate, castitate, et sobrietate et caeteris sanctarum uirtutum ornamentis exornent....

P 180r; B 136v.

No sources identified.

The 'original' collection.

Henri Barré (Homéliaires p.18) suggested that the original collection was limited to the pieces for the 'cycle liturgique', that is, up to Pembroke 25 item 77, Omelia in natale ecclesiae, and he regarded the remaining items as 'apparemment étrangères'. In my view however, the evidence of the extant manuscripts and of the composer's methods indicate that Pembroke 25 most nearly represented the original compilation.

1.   **The evidence of the manuscripts**

(a)   Chartres 25(44).

Presumably the earliest extant manuscript was Chartres 25(44) which was already damaged when described in Cat. Gén. pp.11, 12. Then it was a manuscript containing identifiable works by named authors, notably (for its date of composition) some by Hrabanus Maurus, and also our collection at the end of the manuscript (fols. 119-162), but, even then, with both beginning and ending already lost or mutilated. The first complete item of the Chartres collection was numbered: XXXII, Omelia in die sancto Pascels (sic): Spiritus Sanctus per prophetam populo Christi, corresponding to Pembroke no. 33; and the concluding folios (157-162) were damaged. It was a pity that it was not described in greater detail, since the manuscript was burned in 1944 and now exists only as a succession of fragments, boxed, interleaved and numbered. Abbé Raymond Étaix examined the fragments, and left a letter, dated 21st January 1957, at Chartres BM identifying many of these, particularly of the items corresponding to phrases from the works by named authors in the manuscript. He also made suggestions for six fragments of the sermon collection. Abbé Étaix now agrees that one of these identifications is in error, and I have added ten more, as now reported to the Librarian. The fifteen identified fragments correspond to phrases within isolated folios from Pembroke fols. 81v-108v. Eight of these fragments have legible words or part-words on both recto and verso which offer some evidence towards a speculation about the original extent of the Chartres 25(44) collection, at least before the manuscript was burned in 1944. Four of these eight may serve as examples in discussion. The words in these fragments are placed as on original lines but not vertically in relationship to each other since the leaves are warped.

1. Fragment 7 recto.

   impleta qui ex

   e filioque proced

   conseruandu nos

   descendit et com

   Pembroke 99r.

   26. de c̨elo uenientis consummata sunt atque impleta qui ex

   27. patre filioque procedens ad conseruandum nos descendit

   28. et commonet...

   Fragment 7 verso.

   OI L

   NATALE SCI

   NIS BABTISTI

   as deinde

   rophetas inter

   ime scs iohann

   Pembroke 99v.

   22. XLIIII. OMELIA IN NATALE SANCTI IOHANNIS BAPTISTAE

   26. mundo, primum patriarchas, deinde prophetas inter quos

   27. maxime sanctus iohannes...

2. Fragment 52 recto.

   magnu reme

   animabus suis nos

   Pembroke 91r.

   6. ... non subducunt se magnum remedium

   7. animabus suis noscuntur...

Fragment 52 verso.

non biberent

ando uidit deus tant

affliccione et tant

Pembroke 91v.

6. ...gustarent quicquam nec pascerentur et aquam ne bi -

7. -berent et quando uidit deus tantam afflictionem et tantam...

3. Fragment 54 recto.

facere (?)

rones deus

micidium nullus

Pembroke 93r.

5. ...Furtum nullus presumat facere quia fures et latro-

6. -nes deus non amat. Homicidium nullus homo presumat facere...

Fragment 54 verso.

faciat iusti

plific castitas

Pembroke 93v.

3. spem certam fideliter sperare faciat iustitiam amplificet castita-

4. -tem mentis...

4. Fragment 55 recto.

rogo et

mone uos fideles

ut in istis die

unium et oratione

et elimosina cu b

Pembroke 92r.

24. .....Et ideo rogo et ammoneo uos fideles Christi ut in

10   25.   istis die<u>bus</u> ieiuni<u>um</u> et oratione<u>m</u> et aelymosina<u>m</u> cu<u>m</u> bona...

Fragment 55 verso.

homo rog

dimittat ill

commissa caueat

Pembroke 92v.

24.   quis<u>que</u> homo rogare d<u>eu</u>m ut dimittat illi peccata com<u>m</u>issa.

25.   Caueat autem...

A comparison of words and lines in the fragments with corresponding folio- and line-numbers of Pembroke 25 indicates that the Chartres folios were originally written in double columns since the script is about the same size as that in Pembroke, and yet, for three (Fragments 52, 54, 55) out of the four illustrations Chartres had approximately the same number of words to a page as Pembroke, since the line-numbers on succeeding pages of the relevant Pembroke parallels are exactly or approximately the same. The four other identified fragments (with recto and verso readings), which are not presented here, confirm this suggestion. The first complete sermon in Chartres 25(44), noted above, was as Pembroke no. 33 on fol. 77r and the collection occupied fols. 119-162, or 44 folios of the Chartres manuscript. Unless items were omitted from the Chartres succession of sermons, this sequence would be as from Pembroke item 32 (i.e. a part-sermon preceding the first complete sermon in Chartres) approximately to Pembroke item 51 (ending at Pembroke fol. 122r) and thus far short of a series for the liturgical year.

The comparison of the Chartres fragments with the Pembroke text also indicates that Chartres was not the exemplar. On Fragment 52 verso we note <u>non biberent</u> (as B and J) for Pembroke <u>ne biberent</u>, on Fragment 54 verso we read <u>castitas</u> for Pembroke (as B and J) <u>castitatem</u>, and for Fragment 7 verso the Chartres words correspond to the Pembroke title but appear to omit a considerable part of the opening of the Pembroke sermon which reads (fol. 99v):

Ad inluminandum humanum genus, quod per inuidiam diaboli
perierat, scire et intelligere debemus, dilectissimi fratres, quia
dominus et saluator noster multas lucernas accendere dignatus
est in (B omits) mundo, primum patriarchas, deinde prophetas
inter quos (B: quas) maxime sanctus Iohannes sicut sol inter
omnia sidera clarior lucessit (B, J: lucescit) in caelo.

Some suspicion also attaches to the dating of Chartres 25(44) in <u>Cat. Gén.</u> (p.12)
as 'saec. X-XI except folios 31-36 (saec. XII)', since the fragments of the
sermon-collection are clearly in a different hand from that in other fragments
(identified by Abbé Étaix) in other sections of the manuscript. One date (saec. X-XI)
is not satisfactory, I suspect, for both hands, but a palaeographer can confirm or deny
this suspicion.

(b)   The remaining manuscripts.

When Henri Barré (<u>Homéliaires</u> p.18) made his comment about the 'original'
collection, he had available St. John's 42, Royal 5 E XIX and Paris lat. 3794. N. R.
Ker (<u>Med. MSS.</u> pp.316-17) has added the Canterbury fragment (Add. 127/12) and
Raymond Étaix informed me of Grenoble 278 (470) and Balliol 240. All the
manuscripts attest the existence of a Pembroke-type collection, and three of these
offer evidence for Barré's opinion about the 'original' extent. Ker noted the number
XV on fol. 1 of the Canterbury fragment against a caption <u>Omelia in Purificatione</u>
<u>Sanctae Mariae</u>, matching the Pembroke enumeration, and that the succeeding
Canterbury sermon is as no. 16 in the Pembroke manuscript. The fragment, obviously,
is from a larger collection of the Pembroke type. The sermons in Royal 5 E XIX are
items for the liturgical year in a different order from those in Pembroke 25, but one
number, XXVIII, against the title <u>Omelia in Cena Domini</u> (fol. 29r), indicates that the
items were selected from a larger collection like that of Pembroke 25. As Étaix
indicated (<u>Rev. Aug.</u> 25) in his analysis of the Sermonary of Beaune, the composer of
Paris lat. 3794 clearly chose a sequence of items from a Pembroke-type collection for
insertion into the Beaune collection. All the items contained in these manuscripts,
however, are for the liturgical festivals.

A comparison of the items in Pembroke 25, St. John's 42 and Balliol 240, together with the list of contents in Balliol 240, hints at a larger extent of the 'original' collection. Barré (p.18) noted that St. John's 42 omitted certain items extant in Pembroke 25 (and Balliol 240), nos 1-2, 56-63 (the 'Legimus' sermon on All-Saints) but included no. 89 of the general sermons. Other items were also omitted, nos. 6, 28, 49, 64 and 77, and folios were probably missing from the exemplar, since item 46 ends incompletely at fol. 48r col. 2 (as Pembroke 25 fol. 108r 1.14) but, without break in the script, St. John's continues item 47 with a loss of material at the beginning (as Pembroke 25 fol. 110v 1.13). St. John's also has an extra item for the Nativity of Christ between items 4 and 5 of Pembroke and Balliol with incipit at fol. 14r:-

> Apparuit benignitas et humanitas saluatoris nostri dei non ex operibus iustitie̜ que fecimus nos sed secundum suam misericordiam saluos nos fecit (cf. Titus 3, 4-5). Adquiserat sibi, fratres karissimi, genus humanum astucia diabolice̜ fraudis...

This sermon is a variant text of one printed under the name of Hildebert, bishop of Mans, archbishop of Tours (PL 171, 390-94). The collection in PL 171 is now regarded, however, as a mélange of sermons from different authors, and our sermon 'Apparuit benignitas' has now been firmly attributed to Geoffrey Babion, a preacher of the twelfth century, in a detailed study by Jean-Paul Bonnes (Revue Bénédictine 56 (1947), pp.174-215). The sermon is listed among Geoffrey's authentic works at p.200. If the attribution is correct the sermon was not in the original Pembroke-type collection, which is extant in manuscripts earlier than the twelfth century.

St. John's 42 ends its group of items for the liturgical feast-days as Pembroke item 76, omits item 77 as noted, and then presents a text of the Gesta Salvatoris, before continuing to an extensive collection of sermons on general topics, the first of which is a variant text of Pembroke 25 no. 89 Predicatio communis omnibus populis, the first of the Pembroke general sermons. This may suggest that the St. John's scribe saw a Pembroke-type collection which included the general sermons (nos. 89-96), substituted the Gesta for Pembroke nos. 78-88 (a series of extracts mainly from Hrabanus Maurus, De Clericorum Institutione), accepted no. 89, but then chose different general sermons. Even St. John's 42 may hint at an original collection larger than Barré surmised.

Balliol 240 lacks sermons corresponding with Pembroke items 28 and 49, but material is clearly missing from the Balliol manuscript to explain the omission of no. 49 In Assumptione Sancte Mariae. The script in Balliol 240 at fol. 106v col. 1 ends before the bottom of a ruled column at: Ego domine et mulier (as Pembroke 25 no. 48, fol. 112v l.21); fol. 106v col. 2 although ruled, is blank, and fol. 107r col. 1 begins: appropinquabit enim regnum celorum (as Pembroke 25, no. 50, fol. 117v l.28), but the index of Balliol 240 fol. 56r col. 2 reads in sequence: De Sapientia (no. 48); In assumptione Sancte Marie (no. 49); In decollatione Sancti Iohannis baptiste (no. 50). The index itself omits certain items but the sermons under such omitted titles are in the Balliol text.

The composer of the collection in Grenoble 278 (470) also drew on an earlier collection which included general sermons, since the manuscript includes items 92 and 93, from the group which Barré rejected, as well as sermons for the liturgical festivals.

The evidence of Balliol 240, Grenoble 278 (470) and possibly St. John's 42 suggests that Pembroke 25 is the fullest representative of the original collection, with the possible exception of Pembroke item 28 Alia omelia in die Palmarum which is in Pembroke 25 only, and is omitted from the index of Balliol 240. Pembroke 25 contains three items for Palm Sunday, nos. 26-28. Item 28 is an exhortation to preachers based largely on Scriptural quotations, so it is possible that the other copyists felt that enough material had been presented for this festival and that such exhortation had no special relevance for the day. But such sermons, drawing largely on Scripture, are found elsewhere within the Pembroke-type collection, notably two items for Quattuor Tempora (nos. 52, 53) and one In natale omnium apostolorum (nos. 68-72). Item 28 may be left as part of the original collection.

2.   Methods of composition and sources.

Firm evidence from the content of the sermons indicates that one author composed the pieces presented in Pembroke 25.

The identifications already made in the list of sources noted above indicate that our composer normally used and adapted material from his predecessors and rarely abstracted a whole sermon or homily from an earlier author without some change. His practice is not rigid, but only one item (no. 6) in the whole collection, the second of three items In natale Domini, appears to be solely a sermon of a patristic author (Gregory, Hom. 8 in Evang.), and one other (item 29, In Caena Domini) is a variant text of a sermon in Catechesis Celtica. Even where single sources appear to be the basis for individual items, as nos. 3, 4, 39, 92 (Caesarius of Arles), 17, 76 (Gregory, in Evang.), 74, 75 (Ps.- Maximus or Maximus of Turin), 93, 94, 95 (Alcuin, De Virt.), 66 (Alcuin, Sermo S.   Martini), 56-63 (the sermon 'Legimus') and 64 (Ps.-Bede, Hom. Subdit. 70), introductions and/or conclusions are sometimes added, selections are often made or material added within the text. All the remaining items (of those whose sources are identified) clearly use more than one source, sometimes multiple sources.

The use of homilies by one writer over the whole collection is not conclusive, since individual homilies are commonly selected from a patristic author's collection for separate use in homiliaries. But persistent quotation from individual books or established and firm collections offers some evidence of common authorship. We may thus ignore the fact that sermons now attributed to Caesarius of Arles were used commonly in the first part and once in the second part (no. 92), but consider repeated citations from, and use of, Alcuin, De Virt, Hrabanus Maurus, De Cler. Inst. and the Collectio Canonum Hibernensis.

Alcuin, De Virt is quoted in no. 20 (cap. 3), 22 (caps. 4, 10, 12, 13, 16, 17), 23 (caps. 21, 26), 25 (cap. 6), 48 (cap. 1), and, among the general sermons, no. 91 (caps. 3, 4), 93 (caps. 27-35 inclusive), 94 (caps. 2-4, 6-10, 12-17), 95 (caps. 18-22, 24-26). Hrabanus, De Cler. Inst. is used in no. 22 (2, 9), 31 (2, 37), 32 (2, 38), 48 (3, 37) and may have been used for an idea in no. 43 (2, 41). As the earlier scholars noted, nos. 78-88, which Barré regarded as the beginning of the addition to the collection, are based on Hrabanus 2, 1-10 inclusive and 3, 37. Wasserschleben's edition of the Collectio Canonum Hibernensis is, unfortunately, an insufficient text for a detailed comparison with the words of the Pembroke-type collection. As his footnotes indicate, passages are omitted from the edition which are extant in certain of his manuscripts. I have confirmed some of these by reading Oxford, Bodley, Hatton MS. 42 (4117), written in Brittany, saec IX[2], and thereafter at Christ Church, Canterbury and Worcester (Gneuss, Anglo-Saxon England 9, (1981), no. 629, p.39), and Paris BN lat. 12021, saec. IX, Brittany (Wasserschleben p. LXVII). Publication of the omitted passages, at least, would be helpful. But the printed edition itself indicates that Coll. Can. Hib. was largely used for item 22 (12, 2-4; 12, 8 and 9; 13, 1 and 2; 14, 2 and 3); and also in the general sermon no. 90 (25, 15; 25, 3 and 4; 24, 2; 24, 4). The sections 12, 3 and 13, 2 were also used as a final addition in no. 37, and probably 12, 2 was echoed in item 1, and 21, 13 in item 25. More contacts may be distinguished when Coll. Can. Hib. is fully collated and edited.

Quotation from favoured books is some indication of common authorship, but one persistent habit of composition by our author, repetition of favoured passages, is conclusive. The best illustration is where the author appears to recall his own words, after a brief quotation from Alcuin De Virt. cap. 4.

Item 22, Omelia in Dominica ii in Quadragesima (fol. 43r) begins:

> Primum omnium tria quaedam (J: quidem) unicuique homini pernecessaria (J: necessaria) sunt, fides, spes, caritas; fides, ut credat in deum patrem omnipotentem et filium et spiritum sanctum, tres personas (B: persone) et unam (B, J: unum) substantiam (B, J: substantia); spes, ut certe speret eterna premia; caritas, ut sit plenus in (B, J: omit) dilectione dei et proximi quia omnes in baptismo filii dei sanctificamur ut fratres simus spiritaliter in caritate perfecta (J: omits) secundum deum. Manere ergo debemus in dilectione dei et proximi ut ipse semper in nobis perseueret quia (J: omits) sicut Iohannes ait: Deus caritas est, et qui manet in caritate, in deo manet, et deus in illo (J: eo) (I John 4, 16).

Item 91, Predicatio bona omnibus Christianis (fol. 170v) reads:

> Tria ergo haec pernecessaria sunt unicuique homini, fides, ut credat in deum (B adds: patrem) omnipotentem, trinum persona

> et unum substantia; spes, ut certe speret aeterna premia;
> caritas, ut sit plenus dilectione dei et proximi quia omnes in
> baptismo filii dei sanctificamur ut fratres simus spiritaliter in
> caritate perfecta secundum deum. Maneamus ergo in dilectione
> dei et proximi sicut predictum est ut ipse in nos semper
> perseueret, sicut Iohannes ait: Karissimi (B: omits), deus
> caritas est, et qui manet in caritate, in deo manet, et deus in eo
> (B: illo) (I John 4, 16).

Differences between the two passages even in the base text, Pembroke 25, are minimal and only in word. In a considered edition these dissimilarities would be fewer. The only point to note in the second passage is the addition of 'sicut predictum est', because the idea of 'love of God and neighbour' has been presented earlier in the sermon. But a notable point of similarity is that a considered edition would read 'deus in illo', within the Scriptural quotation at the end of both passages, because it is not the Vulgate reading 'deus in eo'.

The habit of using favoured passages more than once is confirmed by other examples, although these are among the items for the liturgical year. As indicated within the list of sources, words taken from Caesarius Sermo 3 on the Creed in item 1 are again used in item 24 for Lent; item 3 draws solely on Caesarius Sermo 187, item 4 on Sermo 188, but phrases from these two sermons are used to fill out item 2; and in item 37 an extract from Coll. Can. Hib. 12, 3 and 13, 2 extends a sermon closely based on one by Maximus of Turin, but the passages had already been used in item 22 for Lent, which is the source for Vercelli Homily III; the second item for Michael the archangel, no. 55, is a composite sermon as indicated, using extracts from Isidore Etym. lib. VII cap. V, a chapter which was wholly used for item 54, and also using phrases from the anonymous sermon 'Legimus in ecclesiasticis historiis', which was the source for items 56-63.

The evidence already presented has offered a positive argument for single authorship of the whole collection as in Pembroke 25. We may now consider why Henri Barré may have rejected items 78-96. The crucial items probably were nos. 78-88, the extracts mainly from Hrabanus Maurus De Cler. Inst., which appear in Balliol 240 but for which St. John's 42 (the only other large collection known to Barré) alternatively has a text of the Gesta Salvatoris. The caption in Pembroke fol. 159r reads: De Officio misae et misterio atque orationibus canonicorum horarum: sermo Rabani Mauri; and succeeding sections are entitled as in Hrabanus as for the canonical hours. Hrabanus (and the Pembroke-type collection), however, is not describing ritual for the hours but giving reasons for the different prayers at the appropriate hours; in other words, the emphasis is on spiritual exhortation, not on mechanical establishment of ritual. The emphasis could well fit the addition in the caption 'et misterio' and the piece could certainly be entitled Sermo Rabani Mauri. But the whole sermo is extended by our author even within the first section (which is based on Hrabanus 2, 1) with a presentation of the qualities of a priest (running to sixteen lines of manuscript), and the final section, drawing on Hrabanus 3, 37 and Gregory's Regulae Pastoralis Liber (with additions) discusses the different kinds of preaching to dissimilar kinds of audience. The whole item ends (fol. 165v) with a benediction as with a normal sermon: Largiente domino nostro Iesu Christo qui cum patre et spiritu sancto uiuit et regnat in secula seculorum. Amen. In presentation this appears to be a sermon very like the sermon on All-Saints, item 56-63, the sections of which are sometimes numbered separately and sometimes entitled, as e.g. LVIII De angelis atque archangelis (fol. 130r). This sermon is even more clearly sectionalized than item 78-88 since each section of the 'Legimus' sermon ends with a benediction, unlike other manuscripts of the text presented in Traditio 33 (1977), pp. 105-121.

Henri Barré (Homéliaires p.25) rightly commented on the similarity of our collection to that prepared by Hrabanus Maurus for Archbishop Haistulph (PL 110, 9-134), and there entitled, Homiliae de festis praecipuis, item de uirtutibus. In this collection, after forty items for liturgical festivals, Hrabanus apparently added others on diverse topics beginning: XLI In dominicis diebus, and including discourses on virtues and vices and on aspects of Christian behaviour. As I have argued above, the composer of the Pembroke-type collection had the same intention and fulfilled it, as best witnessed now in the Cambridge, Pembroke College MS. 25.

The collection, its purpose and its background.

Milton McG. Gatch, speaking of Carolingian homiletic collections in his
Preaching and Theology in Anglo-Saxon England (Toronto, 1977), says (p.30) that 'one
of the most difficult tasks ... is to ascertain which collections lay behind them and for
what purpose they were compiled'. Fortunately Henri Barré (Homéliaires p.24) has
given a lead on the second of these problems in his brief but accurate remarks on our
collection: 'Dans un cadre liturgique assez reduit, cet Homéliaire entend fournir aux
prêtres des modèles et des suggestions pour leur allocutions au peuple chrétien; de là,
enseignements doctrinaux, exhortations morales, explications d'ordre liturgique et
récits édifiants sur la vie des Saints'.

Preachers were the immediate audience for the collection as illustrated within a
number of items by choice of source-material and/or by direct statement. Theodulf of
Orléans's Capitula, which was addressed to 'fratribus et compresbyteris nostris
Aurelianensis parochiae sacerdotibus', is used largely for two sermons for Lent (nos. 20
and 23). In no. 20 (Dom. i in Quad.) the Theodulfian extracts emphasise the need for
teaching, and, for this day, the special observations of Lent. These statements are
interwoven with admonitions from Sermo 64 ad fratres in eremo entitled (in PL 40,
1347): 'De exhortatione ad sacerdotes, ut doceant quid populum Christianum scire et
observare oporteat', and from Caesarius of Arles, Sermo 183 entitled (in Morin II, 744):
'Omelia sancti Augustini de periculo sacerdotis . . .'. The main topic of no. 23 (Dom.
iii in Quad.) is the celebration of Sunday, but its Theodulfian extracts direct the reader
to preach on the need for giving hospitality and of avoiding perjury and false
testimony, while its short introduction is taken from Caesarius of Arles Sermo 13,
entitled (in Morin I, 64): 'Sermo in parochiis necessarius'.

Caesarius, himself, whose value in the extension of preaching and teaching was
recognised by use in the Anglo-Saxon vernacular as well as by his successors in Latin,
provides many sources, some directed towards preachers. The item for Quinquagesima
(no. 18) is based on his Sermo 57 (Morin I, 251) and Sermo 197 (Morin

II, 794). The extract in our collection from Sermo 57 admonishes priests to prescribe harsh remedies, using the obvious analogy of physical doctors, an analogy more fully developed in Sermo 197.

There are even practical hints on the manner of preaching, in one case (no. 88) drawing on the well-known manuals. This item is entitled (P 162v): 'De discretione dogmatum iuxta qualitatem audientium' and advises preachers how to teach different kinds of listeners by abstracting both from Gregory, Regulae Pastoralis Liber and from Hrabanus Maurus, De Clericorum Institutione, which itself uses Gregory's work. Item 89 entitled: 'Predicatio communis omnibus populis' begins 'Iuxta qualitatem audientium formari debet sermo doctorum ad sua singulis congruat ...'. Item 90, which is printed below, includes such phrases as: 'Primum igitur pre omnibus ammonendi sunt principes'. Sometimes direct comment to preachers serves as a brief introduction, as in no. 26 (Palm Sunday), where the words are taken directly from another similar sermon in the so-named Catechesis Celtica, and as in no. 17 (Sexagesima), where the introduction may be the author's own composition, since the body of this sermon is the Gospel lection for the day and Gregory's exegesis of this in his Homilia 15 in Evangelia. Obviously the teaching is on dogma and morals but often the expressions indicate that preachers are to teach it, rather than that a Christian congregation simply receive it; as in the first words of the first item in the collection (Dom. iv ante natale domini): 'Primum omnium oportet nos memorari, fratres karissimi, et recitare de deo ueraciter et loqui caeli et terrae conditore et omnium quę in eis sunt ...', and a little later: 'decet nos igitur narrare primum deo et loqui quia ipse fecit nos, cum non essemus, ad imaginem et similitudinem suam'. Also, quite clearly and extensively in no. 28 (Palm Sunday) the author addresses his fellows, particularly adapting God's instruction to the prophet Ezekiel, and in item 78 (P 159r)our writer inserts a long passage on the qualities of a priest.

The most striking point about this whole collection for these preachers is the amount of narrative presented, where, in other collections, one could have expected exegesis of pericopes or eulogistic sermons. The narrative is taken from apocryphal story, from hagiography, from history and itinerary, and from Scripture itself, whether ultimately or directly. Apocryphal story is used for John the evangelist (nos. 9 and 10), for the death of Peter (no. 45), for the Assumption and Nativity of Mary (nos. 49 and 51) and for Andrew (no. 67). Hagiographical accounts are abstracted, partially for the archangel Michael (no. 55) and wholly for Martin (nos. 65 and 66). The account of Herod's death in item 35 appears to be based on Rufinus's history, and Adomnán's De Locis Sanctis is quoted twice (nos. 31 and 50). Scriptural narrative is the base for the nativity and passion of John the Baptist (nos. 44 and 50) and also for the conversion and missionary journeys of Paul (no. 46). Scripture is the ultimate source for the narrative of the Maccabees (no. 47) although there is extension and misrepresentation. Such Scriptural narrative is notably a basis for the two items on Epiphany (nos. 13 and 14), which record the four manifestations of Christ, the coming of the Magi, the miracle of the five loaves and two fishes, the wedding at Cana and the baptism of Christ. Narrative is the mode for In Parasceuen (no. 30) and In Caena Domini (no. 29); and 'facts' are inserted in other less dominantly narrative items, e.g. on the Innocents (no. 11). This is not to say that explication, particularly moral explication, is omitted, but that information from memorable story is regarded as helpful reading for the preachers on certain days.

Apart from the narrative items, even where it appears that an exegetical homily is wholly or almost wholly used, as in no. 6 (in natale Domini), no. 17 (Sexagesima) and no. 76 (the Common for virgins), all based on Gregory, Homiliae in Evangelia and chosen by Paul the Deacon for the respective festivals, we see that Gregory's homilies are not dominated by the sequence of Scriptural verses within the lections. For no. 6, Gregory hom. 8 notes that he will speak only briefly on the lection; and for no. 17, Gregory hom. 15 envelopes the parable, of the seed falling on stony ground, in a moral discourse on human virtue and acts. Only in Gregory hom. 12 (for no. 76) on the wise and foolish virgins, does the explication follow the succession of Scriptural verses, but lengthy moralizations are offered by Gregory.

Precepts for morals, advice on Christian behaviour, and presentation, rather than explanation, of the tenets of the faith, form the majority of sentiments in the whole collection, but such comments are especially seen in those items using the sermons of Caesarius of Arles (and Pseudo-Augustine), or abstracting from the collections of sententiae such as Alcuin, De Virtutibus and the Collectio Canonum Hibernensis, and also in the items for the seasons of penance, Lent (nos. 20-25), Rogation Days before Ascension (nos. 36-40), In Quattuor Tempora (nos. 52 and 53), and among the general sermons at the end (nos. 89-95). Some of these, which were used by Old English homilists, are among those published below, and illustrate this emphasis.

Such precepts, and other statements, are sometimes presented in mnemonic form, as numbered lists or with summary titles. We note such themes: the seven gifts of the Holy Spirit exemplified in the patriarchs (no. 1), seven ways of forgiving sin (no. 18), three things necessary for faith (nos. 22 and 91, within passages discussed above), six things necessary for religion (no. 22), four ways of subverting justice (nos. 23 and 25), four kinds of death (no. 30), three reasons for Christ's Passion (no. 31), three things giving testimony (no. 34), four days of Rogations with parallel fours (no. 36), three kinds of wisdom (no. 48), three reasons why a man's day of death is concealed (no. 89), seven ways of admonishing princes (no. 90), twelve abuses of the world (no. 90), twelve virtues which adorn the just soul (no. 90), six things which the Lord hates (no. 91) and, of course, the eight vices and four virtues (no. 93). A few times lists have titles as e.g. alimenta spiritalia (no. 25), opera carnis (no. 28), ornamenta celorum (no. 43) and vias domini (no. 91). Some themes are presented in rhetorical form as e.g. the theme now known as The Seven Joys of Heaven (nos. 25, 89, 91). Some are merely lists as e.g. the portents and events at Christ's birth (no. 5), and the events which took place on Sunday (no. 33).

Throughout the collection the author helps his fellows to present the ideas that he has selected in a way which an audience can remember.

Gatch's first question on 'which collections lay behind' our collection is not exactly appropriate to our author, who, as Barré says (Homéliaires pp.24-25): 'D'ordinaire, il combine entre eux les textes qu'il emprunte ici et là, et il y insère volontiers des passages de l'Ecriture, des Antiennes liturgiques, des rappels doctrinaux ou des exhortations pratiques'. As noted above, only one homily from a patristic author was the sole source for one item (no. 6). Here, obviously, we should not limit ourselves to previous collections of homilies only. But many sources can be traced and give some indication of the cultural milieu of our composer.

Fairly certainly he would have access to the homiliary of his house, and I have listed among the sources above some which are homilies chosen either for the Roman homiliary of Alanus of Farfa or by Paul the Deacon. We can say initially that our author used fourteen sermons of Pseudo-Augustine chosen also by Alanus, eight of which are now assigned to Caesarius of Arles. Also, he used five of Gregory's Homiliae in Evangelia which were included within the homiliary of Paul the Deacon. But he drew on one other of Gregory's homilies which was not selected by Paul, and other Pseudo-Augustinian sermons which were in neither of the two earlier homiliaries. He thus seems to have known Gregory's homilies, and also sermons under the name of Augustine, other than in the influential homiliaries.

A prudent scholar would leave aside further speculation, since no text of the pieces within Alanus's homiliary is in print, and only early and uncollated editions of Paul the Deacon are available. At this time only those who have seen the manuscripts would know whether, say, a homily of Gregory's in either Alanus or Paul differs distinctively from that same homily within manuscripts of Gregory's Homiliae. But for one particular homily chosen in the Roman homiliary of Alanus of Farfa it appears that the Pembroke-type collection used Alanus. Grégoire has been conscious of the problem and has indicated major differences between the selections of Alanus and their apparent sources. One item for Holy Saturday (AF I.93) is seemingly based on passages from Augustine, Tractatus in Iohannis Evangelium. Grégoire does not print these passages so we cannot tell whether they are verbally different from those in Augustine, but he does publish certain interpolations within the Alanus version which expand the basic source. Item 32a (Item alia in Sabbato) within the Pembroke-type collection echoes those passages from Augustine designated as source for Alanus by

Grégoire and also those interpolated passages printed by him (pp.46-47). If no text of Augustine had those interpolations and if they are distinctive to the selection in Alanus, for this item our composer certainly used the recension of the Roman homiliary by Alanus. No such conclusion can be suggested for a relationship with Paul the Deacon's homiliary since the analysts suggest that Paul merely selected separate homilies from Gregory's Homiliae in Evangelia without distinctive adaptation.

Our author could also have seen other homilies as a group since he draws on eight sermons now extant as a series in Munich, Bayerische Staatsbibliothek Clm. 6233 (saec. VIII^2) and uses these largely for eight of his own items and slightly for two more. The manuscript contains a commentary on part of the Gospel of Matthew, followed at fol. 110v by a sequence of thirteen sermons and then, finally, a section of lessons for Vigils for the Dead. Only three of the thirteen Munich sermons are known in other homiliaries, as Abbé Étaix informed me, one for Circumcision, which is a text of Alanus of Farfa (I.31) for the festival and a variant text of its printing in PL Supp. 2, 1213-18, and two others, as yet unpublished, for Christ's Nativity and for the Holy Innocents. These last two are found in Cologne, Cathedral MS. CLXXI, which has the following inscription on its first folio: 'Codex sancti Petri sub pio patre Hildibaldo scriptus. omelia exerpta diuersorum patrum de diebus festis'. Henri Barré (Revue Bénédictine 17 (1961) p.79) has indicated that Hildebald, archbishop of Cologne (784-819), had this collection made towards the end of his life. A collation (from microfilm) of the two sermons in both Cologne and Munich indicates that the Cologne scribe did not use the Munich manuscript and that the Munich text was not the exemplar for these sermons. Nevertheless Hildebald's copyist for Cologne CLXXI regarded the anonymous Munich sermons as worthy to be placed among those of 'diverse fathers', such as Caesarius of Arles and Gregory the Great, some of whose sermons are among the items in the Cologne manuscript.

An interesting link exists between Munich 6233 and the homiliary of Alanus of Farfa, in that the earliest manuscript of Alanus's recension is Munich, Bayerische Staatsbibliothek Clm. 18092 (saec. VIII ex.) 'written in South Bavaria, presumably at

Tegernsee, by the scribe Dominicus: 'Ego Dominicus scripsi librum istum' (fol. 1),

perhaps identical with a priest of that name who in 769 wrote a charter concerning

Rottbach, near Freising' (CLA IX (1959), no. 1315), while Munich 6233 (saec. VIII[2]) was

'written in Southern Bavaria, presumably in a scriptorium in the Freising diocese,

under the supervision of Dominicus, scribe of Clm. 18092' (CLA IX (1959), no. 1252).

Apparently Dominicus 'often started the page by writing several lines obviously meant

to serve as a model for his pupils, who pick up where he left off (foll. 1, 3v, 6v, etc)'

(ibid.). It would seem that the Alanus recension was the main homiliary for the house

and copied by Dominicus, but that Munich 6233 was worth copying by the pupils. The

link, however, between 18092 and 6233, is relevant to us only if we can demonstrate

that our composer used distinctive readings of those two manuscripts and thus actually

saw them. Denis Brearley has been editing the Munich 6233 Gospel commentary; and

he will edit the Munich sermons together with the corresponding Pembroke-type

sermons in collaboration with me. We shall consider the problem but are not

optimistic about a firm result in view of the obvious loss of manuscripts and of the

adaptation of his source-material, on occasions, by our composer.

Yet one other collection may have been known as a group, the so-named

Catechesis Celtica, extant only in one manuscript, Vatican Library Reg. lat. 49 (saec.

IX or X, Brittany?). I had seen the manuscript, from which selections were published

by Wilmart (see bibliography), but now have had access to a typescript edition

prepared by the late R. E. McNally. As indicated in the list of sources, Pembroke nos.

26 and 27 (for Palm Sunday) use four items from Cat. Celt. as distinguished in

McNally's edition, and no. 29 (In Caena Domini) is a variant text of Cat. Celt. no. 18

for the same feast, but is not, in my view, using the text of Vat. Reg. lat. 49. At one

point Pembroke no. 29 (fol. 63v l.19) is explaining John 13, 4: 'et praecinxit se lintheo,

id est, induit se uestimentis nostrae mortalitatis' (all MSS), in opposition to Reg. lat.

49 (fol. 16v): 'uestimentis nostrae humilitatis'. The Pembroke-type reading is clearly

the original reading in its context and the Reg. lat. 49 scribe has miscopied another

text which the Pembroke-type scribes have recorded accurately. Nevertheless, the sermons of <u>Cat. Celt</u>. appear to be a distinctive series of compositions, copied as a group, which our composer could have seen as a volume.

Other named writers, apart from homilists, within the list of sources could have been used from volumes under their names, but, in view of the popularity of the Pembroke-type collection within Anglo-Saxon England, we should discuss what I name as 'insular connections', because familiarity with the material may have aided the popularity.

Insular connections

Writings of named Irish and Anglo-Saxon authors have been long known and some collections such as the <u>Collectio Canonum Hibernensis</u> and the <u>Catechesis Celtica</u> have been so named to indicate insular connections, but impetus for the general reading of anonymous commentaries on Scripture which had 'insular symptoms' came from Bernhard Bischoff's seminal paper 'Wendepunkte in der Geschichte der lateinischen Exegese in Frühmittelalter', <u>Sacris Erudiri</u> 6 (1954), pp.189-281. There Bischoff discussed features which he regarded as distinctive of Hiberno-Latin commentaries and named a number of these which were still unpublished. The list was revised in his collection of papers, <u>Mittelalterliche Studien</u> Band I (Stuttgart, 1966), pp.205-273, and this paper was translated in M. McNamara (ed.) <u>Biblical Studies: The Medieval Irish Contribution</u>; <u>Proc. of the Irish Biblical Association</u> no. 1 (Dublin, 1976), pp.74-160. Clare Stancliffe (<u>Studia Patristica</u> XII (1975), pp.361-370), attempted to modify Bischoff's assertions in various ways, but indicated (p.366) that 'we can allow the main picture to stand ... there is a hard core of commentaries which are definitely Irish, but outside this we have a gradual shading off ... through compilations in which an Irishman had a hand to ones in which some Irish influence is discernible'. She also warned against assigning certain works 'to an Irishman rather than a Continental or Anglo-Saxon exegete' (p.366).

But, with such reservations in mind a number of scholars now have been reading the works designated by Bischoff as, at least, unusual and distinctive. Certain notable ideas and formulas of presentation, even sequences of word, persist in such works, even if these may not have originated in Ireland (although some may). Limitation of reading by one's own lack of time, or loss of works originally extant in the Middle Ages, often makes it difficult to trace where an idea originates. But on the basis of reading in print, in manuscript, in microfilm, as well as in transcript and in typescript circulated through the good fellowship of generous medievalists, I shall attempt to demonstrate, not Irish influence, but insular influence, on this collection, since the comradeship and interconnection between Irish and Anglo-Saxons has been widely illustrated both in the homelands and in the Continental missionfields and centres of learning.

Four known insular writers were used, and one of them named. Alcuin's <u>De Virtutibus</u> was almost fully used over the whole collection as indicated in detail above; his <u>De Vita S. Martini</u> was abstracted and filled out from the account by Sulpicius Severus for item 65; item 66 closely follows Alcuin's <u>Sermo de transitu S. Martini</u>. Apparently there is some discussion about which works Alcuin wrote on the Continent and which in England, but, in terms of my argument, he is an Englishman wherever he wrote. Verbal echoes indicate that Adomnán, <u>De Locis Sanctis</u>, was abstracted in recognisable sections, on the shape and healing properties of the Cross (item 31), and on the locusts and wild honey of John the Baptist (item 50). Henri Barré (<u>Homéliaires</u> p.24 note 67) thought that item 15 (<u>in Purificatione Sancte Marie</u>) 'utilise ... peut-être le Vénérable Bède' but I see no verbal echoes of the relevant works of Bede for this item; yet in the first of two items for Ascension Day (no. 41) our writer abstracted a phrase from Bede's <u>Expositio Actuum Apostolorum</u>. The fourth insular writer, Gildas, is named (in no. 90) and his work <u>De Excidio Britonum</u> is given a title <u>Ormesta Britanniæ</u> (fol. 168v ll.5-6), known, at present, only elsewhere in the <u>Vita S. Pauli Leonensis</u> (information from M. Winterbottom). The meaning of the word <u>ormesta</u>, (used more often in the mediaeval title of Orosius's history as <u>Ormesta Mundi</u>) has been debated, particularly by Celtic scholars, and Patrick Sims-Williams (<u>History and Heroic tale</u> ed. T. Nyberg (Odense, 1985), p.116) has summed up earlier scholarship firmly: '<u>ormesta</u> is clearly a Latinization of <u>wormes</u> (> <u>gormes</u>) or of <u>armes</u>', Celtic words meaning 'oppressive conquest' (ibid. p.105). If the vernacular scholars are right the composer of the Pembroke-type collection used Gildas in a book whose title may have originally been 'insular'.

These are identifiable writers, two of whom, Bede and Alcuin, certainly were well-known on the Continent in many centres of learning. We now turn to anonymous and pseudonymous writings which are more likely to be limited to centres on the continent under insular influence and with insular connections, especially if, as Stancliffe notes (Studia Patristica XII p.367): 'the end of the eighth century is characterized by a 'recoil from Irishry' in both England and Gaul'.

The first is the Collectio Canonum Hibernensis, 'a reference book on the teaching of the Church with regard to practical matters of administration, discipline and the care of souls,' about which 'there has never been any reasonable doubt that the Hibernensis was of Irish origin' (Kenney, Sources p.248 and note 272). Our composer had access to a copy of this work, as detailed above within the list of sources.

The collection known as Catechesis Celtica is, however, one which Dr. Stancliffe regards as a 'compilation which reached its present form probably in Brittany, or possibly elsewhere in Gaul ... put together from diverse sources, both Irish and Carolingian ones' (Ireland in Early Mediaeval Europe ed. D. Whitelock et al. (Cambridge, 1982), p.25). Dr. Stancliffe is concerned about specific items which could be originally Irish, but if our composer had access to all the items as a collection, we may clearly say that he used a collection which revealed 'Irish/insular symptoms'. Our author used five items, at present in Cat. Celt., as in Vat. Reg. lat. 49, as detailed above. One of these was also demonstrably Irish, on the evidence which Dr. Stancliffe allows. Cat. Celt. no. 15 (McNally typescript edition), Vat. Reg. lat. 49 fols. 15r-16r, considers the pericope for Palm Sunday, Matthew cap. 21 (the entry into Jerusalem). Many of the explications are as Jerome In Matt., but one explanation within this item is, I think, unusual, where Mount Olivet is interpreted (fol. 15r): 'Ad montem Oliueti (Matthew 21, 1) id est, mons Oliueti interpretatur mons trium luminum, id est, refectio laboris, consulatio doloris, notitia ueri luminis, quod sine dubio est Christus', but has a parallel in Pseudo-Jerome Expositio quatuor evangeliorum PL 30, 574; PL 114, 884 (see

CPL no. 631) which reads: 'Mons Oliveti, id est, nomen trium luminum, id est, refectio

laboris, consolatio operis, notitia ueri luminis'. Pseudo-Jerome is regarded as Irish.

Obviously, more research would have to be undertaken to demonstrate the rarity of

the explication, except in texts which have 'Irish symptoms'. But a firmer link is

present. Cat. Celt. no. 15 (fols. 15v-16r) abstracts a long passage from a sermon

found, at present, only in Cracow Cathedral Chapter MS. 140 (olim 43) p.121. The

Cracow collection, termed 'un recueil de conférences monastiques Irlandaises du VIIIe

siècle' by Pierre David who described it (Revue Bénédictine 49 (1937) pp.62-89),

certainly has 'Irish symptoms' in some of its sermons. Cat. Celt. no. 15 either adapts

from the text in Cracow or abstracts from a variant text, but many verbal echoes and

echoes of idea indicate the connection between the two pieces. Within the abstracted

passage is a section which begins, in Cat. Celt., fol. 15v: 'Et ideo dicit quidam

tractator principibus et doctoribus aeclesiarum: Cauete ne dimittatis in aeclesiis Dei

crescere ... ' and in Cracow 140 (olim 43) p.121: 'Inde dicit unus tractator principibus

et doctoribus ecclesiarum: Nonne mittatis in ecclesia Dei crescere ... '. As Celtic

scholars, among them Dr. Stancliffe (Ireland in Early Mediaeval Europe, p.24), accept,

a feature of Celtic Latin usage was, as it were, translation-loans from their vernacular

into their Latin, among these princeps for abbas, 'so that we find ourselves reading

about "principes et doctores aeclesiae, qui principatum tene[n]t in aeclesia'" (ibid). On

this kind of evidence, if accepted, the tractator presumably was an Irishman, or the

Cracow composer, if he composed the description, was an Irish writer, or knew

distinctive Celtic Latin usages. Within this sermon in the Cracow manuscript are

other Celtic Latinisms distinguished by Celtic scholars. The passage, with the

description, was transmitted to the compiler/composer of the Catechesis Celtica

collection and so found its way to our composer who says (fol. 56r 1.8): 'Et ideo dicit

quidam tractator principibus et doctoribus ecclesiarum: Cauete ne dimittatis in

aecclesiis dei crescere ... ' Princeps for abbas in such a context may seem too slight

to speak of Celtic Latinisms but I shall return again to more distinctive usages of this kind in the Pembroke-type collection.

As noted above, the Pembroke-type collection also uses a number of sermons extant at present only in the Munich manuscript Clm. 6233, which manuscript exhibits the hand of a named scribe, Dominicus, active in an area in which there had been 'insular' missionary activity, and which manuscript apparently has been corrected by a 'contemporary Anglo-Saxon hand' (CLA IX (1959) no. 1252). The eyes related to that correcting 'hand' obviously read through this manuscript. Besides the sermons, Munich Clm. 6233 also contains a commentary on part of Matthew's Gospel which was regarded as Hiberno-Latin by Bernhard Bischoff (no. 23, in McNamara, p.126), who illustrated some of the 'Irish symptoms'. These comments, of course, merely indicate that some material in the manuscript was influenced by insular ideas, and, at present, and perhaps never, can we demonstrate a reading of the actual manuscript by our composer. The collection of homilies in Munich Clm. 6233 is, most probably, a compilation from disparate areas, since one item is found in the Roman homiliary of Alanus of Farfa (for Circumcision, I.31), and two more reveal insular features. Both of these, among others, were abstracted for Pembroke items. On fol. 122r, within a piece for Holy Innocents, these martyrs are numbered as 2,000: 'duo milia infantium qui pro Christo occisi sunt', and the number of the innocents was considered in commentaries which Bischoff identified among his 'Irish-influenced' texts. The debate is most clearly presented in Lyons BM 447 (376) (Bischoff IC in McNamara p.98) fol. 142v:

'Quanti infantes fuerunt occisi? RP: Alii dicunt cxliiii, ut in Apocalipsi dicitur, quod falsum est ut Primasius dicit; cxliiij hoc numero [e]lectos significare omnes finitus numerus pro infinito ponitur. Nullus estimet hunc numerum infantium esse; quis enim, imperitus et stultus, putat istum numerum de una tribu [n]ecasse (MS.: mecasse) quando omnium tribuum nomina hic secuntur item de tribu Ruben xij milia et cetera, et una tribu Iuda tantum occidit Herodes infantes. Ideo uerius [ii] milia fuerunt infantes quia sicut intrauit legio in duo milia porcorum innocentium secundum Marcum, ita seuit Herodes in dua (sic) milia puerorum innocentium'.

Lyons BM 447 (376) fol. 142v, has similar argument to that in the Irish Reference Bible (Bischoff IA in McNamara p.97) (as in two manuscripts, Munich Clm. 14277 fol. 230v and Paris BN lat. 11561 fol. 144r), while Vienna Nb 940 (Bischoff 17 I in McNamara p.115) fol. 29r-29v merely states: 'occidit omnes pueros ... id est, quasi duo milia paruulorum quasi chorus duorum legum martyrium ... '. Pembroke 25, however, takes its information from none of these commentaries when it says (fol. 20r l.13): 'Hii autem pueri a Bethleem et de omnibus finibus eius usque ad duo milia congregati in campis uiginti constituti sunt et in unoquoque campo centum propterea interfecti sunt'. The phraseology is closest, at present, to the commentary in Orléans BM 65 (62) (Bischoff 16 I in McNamara p.113) p.38: 'in omnibus in campis .xx., ut aiunt, .c. pueri in unoquoque campo', and to marginal annotations in the later text, the Gospel-book of Armagh of 1138 A.D., BL Harley 1802 fol. 11v: 'ii milia et cxl; xx enim campi sunt circa Betlem et occisi sunt .c. in unoquoque ex eis; .c. autem et xl in ipsa ciuitate' (cited by M. R. James, Latin Infancy Gospels (Cambridge, 1927), p.100) and also to the Irish vernacular text in the Leabhar Breac (in translation): 'Now Herod thereafter sends his soldiers ... to Bethlehem of Juda, and to the twenty plains that are around Bethlehem ... and by them were slain all the children inside ... so that two thousand two hundred were slain by them between the city and the plains ... One hundred and forty children, that is what were slain of them in Bethlehem' (cited from E. Hogan, The Irish Nennius ... and Homilies and Legends from L. Breac, Todd Lecture Series VI (Dublin, 1895), pp.80-81). The number, 2000 or thereabouts, appears to be a persistent Irish choice.

One other item in Munich Clm. 6233, in Theophaniam, shows Irish features, one noted from the wider reading of Bernhard Bischoff. As he noted (in McNamara, p.91): 'From "successors" the Magi became the "descendants" of Balaam'. Twice among the brief comments on the adoration of the Magi within its sermon (fols. 130r-130v), Munich Clm. 6233 (fol. 130r) notes that the wise men were 'de generatione Balaam' and (fol. 130v) speaks of 'Balaam cuius ex genere erunt'. One other minor hint, if Grosjean is right about Celtic Latin usage, is the phrase to describe the Creator (fol. 134r) 'qui facit celum et terram, stillas et omnia elimenta'. As Grosjean notes (Analecta Bollandiana 54 (1936), p.120) the words creator omnium elimentorum often are the name given to God in Irish: Dúlem Dúilem ... derives from dúil which corresponds to Latin elementum ... 'thing, creature, element'.

Apart from the use of named insular writers and of collections or of individual sermons which reveal insular influences, the Pembroke-type collection presents explications for a number of Scriptural statements within sequential narratives based on Scripture. For these explications we may suspect the use of commentaries if the explications are brief and pointed to the Scriptural verse, or perhaps, homiletic pieces of exegesis on a Gospel lection if the explications are more extended and if they elaborate on a given verse. The later the commentaries, however, the more derivative these become, and distinction between one and another is often not in idea but in phraseology and difference of choice of sources, leading to a distinctive compilation or composition. In such a situation it is obviously necessary to read all available commentaries, sometimes to trace a line of descent, but also to note distinctive differences. Patrick Sims-Williams has traced one explication, considered below, and modern editors of commentaries are expected to carry out similar extensive checking in earlier commentaries, as has been done, for example, for the commentaries of Bede on Mark and Luke, of Jerome and Pascasius Radbertus on Matthew in the CCSL editions of these works. For discussion here on varied Scriptural passages I would have wished to rely on such wide reading and checking of individual phrases and of works.

I can do that with confidence for one Hiberno-Latin commentary in print in a CCSL edition by Joseph Kelly (see in list of sources sub nom.) where he carefully distinguishes sources from what he calls 'literary parallels' from anonymous commentaries, some of these 'parallels' persisting in the 'insular' tradition.

The manuscript edited is Vienna Nationalbibliothek lat. 997 (saec. VIII-IX), containing commentaries on Luke and John, which use named patristic writers, but also (Kelly p.X) 'the Irish biblical commentary, the Expositio Quatuor Evangeliorum of Pseudo-Jerome'. Kelly's analysis of these commentaries confirms Bischoff's indication (nos. 30 and 31 in McNamara pp.134-37) that the commentaries reveal insular symptoms.

It is clear that passages within two items in the Pembroke-type collection have close verbal parallels with sections of the Vienna 997 Commentary on Luke. The sermon for Circumcision (no. 12), as noted within the list of sources, is based on selections from a sermon as in Munich 6233 fols. 125r-127v which is an item in the Roman homiliary of Alanus of Farfa, but also includes an introduction, not in the earlier sermon, referring to the circumcision of Christ, recalling the Scripture of Luke 2, 21, 22; 1, 28 and 31 (P fol. 21r l.13-21v l.9), and adding explications. One of these passages is clearly based on the words as in Vienna 997. P fol. 21r l.24-21v l.9 reads:

'Quicumque enim circumcisi cordibus fuerint regnum dei intrabunt. Et post octo dies a natiuitate illius uocatum est nomen eius Iesus (cf. Luke 2, 21). Hoc quidem significat quia nomen uniuscuiusque octo uitia capitalia (J: principalia) uincentis in libro uitae scribitur. Quod uocatum est ab angelo (Luke 2, 21). Angeli etenim hominibus reddunt testimonium ut, quoscumque dignos inuenerint, nomina eorum in libro uitę scribantur. Et nominibus scriptis postea salus sempiterna possideatur (B: possidetur) quod dicitur priusquam in utero conciperetur. Hoc etiam in (J omits: in) Isaac et Iacob et Iohanne (J: Iohannem) iam prefiguratum est qui ante natiuitatem suam propriis nominibus sunt uocati. Hoc quidam significat quod sicut nomina filiorum promissionis scribebantur (J: scribantur) ante natiuitatem suam. Ita procedunt (B: precedunt) merita sanctorum in caelis dum adhuc uiuunt super terram'.

Vienna 997 (ed. pp.16-17) reads:

' ... et in octauo die iudicii circumcisio cordibus regnum Dei introibunt ... Vocatum est nomen eius (Luke 2, 21): Id est, post octo uitia uincenda, nomen uniuscuiusque in libro uitae scribitur. Iesus (Luke 2, 21): Scriptis etenim nominibus in libro uitae, salus adest sempiterna. Quod uocatum est ab angelo (Luke 2, 21): Angeli etenim de hominibus reddunt testimonium ut, quoscumque dignos inuenerint, nomina eorum in libro uitae scriberentur. Priusquam in utero conciperetur: Quod in Isaac et Iacob et Iohanne figuratum est, qui ante natiuitate uocati sunt nomine. Praecedunt enim merita sanctorum in caelum antequam nascantur in uitam'.

The editor, Joseph Kelly, notes no source for this passage among the patristic authors consulted by him, so it appears that the composer of our item had access to this commentary, although not necessarily in the Vienna 997 manuscript.

The commentary is again used in the Pembroke item for the Purification of Mary (no. 15), narrated, of course, in Scripture immediately following the account of Christ's circumcision. As noted above, the sermon draws on various sources, but immediately after an abstraction from Ambrose's commentary on Luke our composer continues with Scripture, adapting Luke 2, 22, 23, but then he explains as follows (P fol. 28r l.16-28v l.1):

'Consuetudo itaque erat a circumcisionis die per xxxiii dies filium, (B, J, C add: filiam) autem per xlviii separari a templo. Non quia ipse (J omits: ipse) indiguit purgari in cuius conspectu caeli non sunt mundi sed ut (B omits: ut) suo exemplo instrueret mundum. Et (B omits: et) ut darent hostiam deo pro illo, secundum quod dictum est in lege domini, par turturum, aut duos pullos columbarum (cf. Luke 2, 24). Per turturem (C adds: igitur) castitas et (B, J, C: per columbam, for: et) (C adds: uero) innocentia designatur (B, J, C add the following: que a (B omits: a) nobis exigit Deus ut in nobis utraque (B, C add: semper) maneant, id est castitas et innocentia). Turtur enim post mortem sui (B: suam) coniugis alterum non sectatur coniugem (B, J, C: coniugium) usque ad mortem; et rubicundus colore maiestate (B, C: in estate) clamat et raro (J, C: nusquam; B: numquam) inuenitur nidus eius. Hoc quidem significat quia per castitatem spiritus sanctus in homine clamat, et uitam eius pre diabolo semper abscondit, quia iam conuersatio eius in caelis est'.

Vienna 997 (ed. p.17) reads:

'Completi sunt dies purificationis eius: Id est, L si filia, triginta autem si filius. Secundum legem Moysi (Luke 2, 22): Id est, non secundum necessitatem naturae, quia ipse non indiguit purgari in cuius conspectu etiam caeli non sunt mundi . . . Par turturum aut duos pullos columbarum (Luke 2, 24): Haec oblatio penuriam parentum significat, et ut castitas per turtures et gratia Spiritus sancti per columbas significaretur. Turtur namque, post mortem coniugis suae, coniugium non sectatur usque mortem. Et rubicundus est colore, et in aestate clamat, et nusquam inuenitur nidus eius. Per pudorem enim uirginitatis Spiritus sanctus in homine clamat, et uitam eius a diabolo abscondit. Vt Paulus ait: Vestra autem conuersatio in caelis est (cf. Philippians 3, 20)'.

The periods for purgation (which vary considerably among the commentators) have not been taken by our composer from this commentary, but the remaining phrases, for which again Kelly notes no source, are so close as to be a source for the item in Pembroke 25. Our writer continues with Scripture, sometimes with brief significations which are not in the Vienna commentary, but one more phrase is used from the commentary when, in reference to Luke 2, 34, et benedixit illis Symeon (P fol. 28v l.11), our author continues: 'more angeli Maria benedicentis: Benedicta tu inter mulieres et benedictus fructus uentris tui' (Luke 1, 42), cf. Vienna 997 (ed. p.19): 'Et benedixit illis Simeon: More angeli dicentis: Benedicta tu inter mulieres'.

At least four more anonymous commentaries with insular links could have been seen, but for this suggestion, the probability, at present, is less, since three are still in manuscript and the wide reading has not been undertaken which could demonstrate the distinctiveness of corresponding passages. One commentary is only in Vienna Nb lat. 940 (saec. VIII-IX, Salzburg), (Bischoff 17 I in McNamara p.115); another, as a complete text, is extant only in Orléans BM 65 (62) but has survived in part, fragment or record in four other manuscripts, one of these latter with Old Irish glosses, another in Irish script 'written probably in Ireland' (CLA V (1950), no. 642). On these variant texts see Bibliography I C iii on the Orléans manuscript. Both commentaries, as in Vienna 940, and as in Orléans 65 (62), are commentaries on the Gospel of Matthew, which alone tells the story of the Holy Innocents.

Pembroke 25 item 11, in Natale Innocentium, opens with a eulogy but takes up Scriptural narrative at fol. 19v l.13 with a near-citation of Matthew 2, 13-15 inclusive, on the command of the angel and the flight into Egypt, ending with the quotation of the prophecy: 'Ex Egypto uocaui filium meum'. The text continues, l.21:

'Hanc quidem fugam longe ante Isaias prophetauerat dicens: Ecce dominus ascendet super nubem leuem et ingredietur in (B omits: in) AEgyptum, et conterentur simulacra AEgypti ante conspectum eius (cf. Isaias 19,1). Haec nubs (B: nubes) leuis corpus sanctae Marie uirginis est quod, quia sine peccato semper fuit, leue reputatur super cuius (B: huius) igitur (J omits) humerum Christus deportatus est in AEgyptum; de qua dictum est: Erunt quinque ciuitates in terra AEgypti et una ex illis uocabitur ciuitas/20r/solis (cf. Isaias 19,18). Uere ciuitas solis est illa ciuitas in qua Iesus Christus inhabitauit qui est uerus sol iustitie (cf. Malachias 4,2)'.

Cf. Vienna 940, fol.28v:

'Et fuge in AEgyptum; nunc impletur quod legitur; Ascendens (corr. to: ascendit) super nubem leuem et ingreditur AEgyptum et conterentur simulacra AEgypti ante faciem eius (cf. Isaias 19,1). Nubem leuem dicit, id est, corpus sine peccato sanctae uirginis Mariae in cuius umero Christus erat deportatus in AEgyptum. Et illud impletur: Erunt quinque ciuitates in terra AEgypti et una uocabitur ciuitas solis (cf.Isaias 19,18) est uere ciuitas in qua uerus sol iustitiae (Malachias 4,2) Iesus Christus habitat'.

We note the similarity of the non-Vulgate conterentur within the quotation of Isaias 19,1, but a difference in Pembroke: ante conspectum, for Vienna: ante faciem, Vulgate: a facie. But such a passage as this in Vienna 940 was the base for the corresponding ideas and words in Pembroke 25.

Pembroke 25 fol. 20r l.2 continues:

'In illa igitur ciuitate, quae Hieropolis (B: Ieropolis) uocatur, in nocte aduentus domini in (J: ad) eam, comminuta (B, J: commutata) sunt omnia et ad nihilum redacta sunt idola. Haec autem fuga Iesu in AEgypto (J: Egyto) significat spiritaliter Christum ad gentes iturum (B adds: uenturum) esse ut crederent in eum. In qua etiam per quattuor expectauit annos iuxta preceptum patris loquentis ad eum: Esto in gentibus donec omnes credant (J: credent). Tunc autem Herodes cruentus cum cognouisset quod inlusus esset a magis, nolentibus Iesu (B, J: inuento ad se reuerti) iratus est ualde. Et mittens (B: mittensque) ministros suos occidit omnes pueros qui erant in Bethleem et in omnibus finibus eius, a bimatu et infra secundum tempus quod exquisierat a magis. Hii autem pueri a Bethleem et de omnibus finibus eius usque ad duo milia congregati in campis uiginti constituti sunt, et in unoquoque campo centum propterea interfecti sunt; et non solum duodecim dierum uel unius anni infantes sed a puero duorum annorum usque ad puerum unius noctis occisi sunt.

Quaerendum est autem quare sub hac temporis mensura rex crudelis occidit pueros, id est, ut Christus inter innocentes filios occideretur. Nonne rex iniquus nouerat quod regi et deo nascenti (B: nascendi) possibile erat utrum cresceret in breui tempore et oculis omnium quasi unius anni uel duorum puer appareret aut crescens in paruitate corporis se caelaret. Ideo autem sub hac conditione temporis omnes occidit pueros siue quia magi post annum a natiuitate domini ab Oriente aduenerant et per annum alterum quia diu expectauit eos ualde iratus istos occidit infantulos (J: infantes). Refulgent igitur isti in regno dei'.

Cf. Orléans 65 (62) p. 38:

'Sic et fuga Ioseph usque dum dicam quattuor annis ... In Egyptum: in Hermopoli urbe ubi ut aiunt nocte aduentus eius omnia comminuta sunt idola ... SPIRITALITER: Fuga Iesu in Egyptum significat Christum ad gentes iturum diabolumque; usque dicam: pater loquitur ad filium: Esto in gentibus donec omnes credant ... Tunc Herodes ... quoniam dilusus, potentes enim contempti iracundi fiunt. Iratus est ualde ... additur autem ualde quia a magis inlusus. Mittens: hic apparet quia lingua regis gladius est. Omnes pueros: more leonis qui de ore eius lapso agno totum deuorat gregem. In omnibus: in campis .xx. ut aiunt .c. pueri in unoquoque campo. A bimatu: regis iniqua malitia loco et tempore omnes antecedit quia non solum in Bethleem sed in omnibus finibus eius et non solum xii dierum/p.39/ uel unius anni sed duorum annorum pueros occidit ... id est, a puero duorum annorum usque puerum unius noctis. Sed queritur cur sub hoc tempore filii occisi sunt. Nouit rex iniquus et subtilis quia regi et deo nascenti possibile est et utrum in breui tempore crescens oculis omnium quasi unius anni uel duorum puer appareret an crescenti uim in paruitatem corporis celaret et ideo sub hac conditione temporis occidit siue quia magi annum natiuitatis domini aduenerunt et per annum alterum diu eos expectans ubi, dilusum se conperit, iratus, occidit pueros .ii. annorum'.

The correspondence of idea and many phrases between our sermon and this commentary gives me some confidence to suggest that a similarly-close correspondence in such a long passage will not be found elsewhere, although the variation in name of the town Hieropolis, Hermopolis, suggests that the composer of the Pembroke-type collection did not see the Orléans manuscript. Neither name, of course, equates the 'etymology' ciuitas solis, which should be Heliopolis, and such a lack of equation could confirm that our composer has conflated passages from two different sources, since the name does not appear in Vienna 940 and the meaning does not appear in Orléans 65 (62).

Two more commentaries, on this occasion on Genesis, appear to have been used. As introduction to the Omelia in Parasceuen de Passione Domini (no. 30) our composer notes (Pembroke fol. 65v l.4) that his readers should first enquire how the human race and the world was formed in the beginning and in what manner it fell afterwards in sin, and again, how it was redeemed and restored through the grace of God. The first section is obviously based on selected verses from Scripture in Genesis caps. 1, 2 and 3 up to Adam's disobedience and fall, but the echoed Scriptural verses are sometimes explained. Two such explications are verbally close to Pseudo-Bede, In Pentateuchum Commentarii, expositio in primum librum Mosis (PL 91, 189 seq), which certainly includes ideas found elsewhere in anonymous texts with definable insular influences. Pembroke 25 fol. 65v ll.8-16 reads:

'Duas igitur res ante omnem diem et ante omnem tempus condidit deus, angelicam uidelicet creaturam, et informem materiam, quę quidem ex nichilo facta processit, qui autem uiuit in aeternum, secundum materiae substantiam, creauit omnia semel, (B, J: secundum distinctionem (B: districtionem) uero specierum per sex dierum alternationem formata sunt. In eo autem quod dicit creauit omnia semel,) nihil non simul factum in omnibus creaturis reliquit non omnia uero ex nihilo condidit deus, sed quedam fecit ex nihilo, quedam ex aliquo; ex nihilo angelos et informem materiam et animas, ex aliquo hominem et ceteras mundi creaturas'.

Cf. Pseudo-Bede, PL 91, 191:

'Proinde duas restante (sic) omnem diem et ante omne tempus condidit, angelicam videlicet creaturam, et informem materiam; quamvis enim omnia simul facta sunt: Qui enim, inquit Salomon, vivit in aeternum, creavit omnia simul (Ecclesiasticus 18,1) ... Itaque non omnia ex nihilo fecit Deus, sed quaedam ex nihilo, quaedam ex aliquo, condidit Deus. De nihilo mundum, et angelos et animam; ex aliquo hominem et pecora, et caeteras creaturas'.

Also, Pembroke 25 fol. 66r ll.4-5 reads:

'Faciamus hominem ad imaginem et similitudinem nostram (Genesis 1, 26), id est, in aeternitate et moribus, et presit (Genesis 1,26), his omnibus'.

Cf. Pseudo-Bede, PL 91, 201:

'Alii uero inquirunt in quibus interior homo imaginem Dei et similitudinem teneat, id est, in aeternitate et in moribus, secundum Origen'.

Four more passages of explication are verbally close to explanations which are still unpublished, and need some description. A commentary on the earlier chapters in Genesis is extant in a volume now bound as two manuscripts, Paris BN lat. 10457 and lat. 10616, together with Isidore, Liber de Natura Rerum, and, at present in Paris 10616, some comments on problems of Scripture presented as questions by a Discipulus to a Magister. The two-manuscript volume was 'written doubtless at Verona by an expert scribe of the time of Egino, Bishop of Verona between 796 and 799, who died at Reichenau in 802' (CLA V (1950), no. 601). Bernhard Bischoff (no. 3 in McNamara pp.103-04) noted the commentary, at present in Paris 10457, as having Irish influence but the questions and answers in Paris 10616 are more important for explications in Pembroke 25.

i.   Pembroke 25 fol. 66r ll.17-20:

'Operabatur quidem in paradyso non pro necessitate sed pro diliciosa uoluntate, et custodiebat sibi ipsi paradysum ne eum peccando amitteret'.

Cf. Paris 10616 fol. 114r (the manuscript is tightly bound; letters in brackets below are covered in the margins):

'Quid [o]perabatur Adam in paradi[so] [a]ut unde illum custodiebat cum neque fur neque latro tunc ullus erat? Magister: Operabatur in paradiso non per necessitate sed pro [d]ilitiosa uoluptate. Custo[d]iebant autem sibi ipsi pa[r]adisum ne eum peccandum [a]dmitterent'.

ii. Pembroke 25 fol. 66v ll.18-23:

'... et statim aperti sunt oculi eorum (cf. Genesis 3,7). Hieronimus dicit: Numquid antea caeci erant aut a deo sine oculis creati sunt non utique sed ad bonum non ad malum apertos oculos habebant. Sed tunc aperti sunt ut uiderent quia nudi essent, intelligentes bonum et malum post mandati transgressionem'.

Cf. Paris 10616, fols. 116r-116v:

'Discipulus: [Q]uid est quod dicitur de Adam [et] Eua cum comedissent aper[t]i sunt oculi eorum numquid [p]rius ceci erant aut a deo [s]ine oculis creati sunt? Magister: [H]abebant utique tunc oculos [se]d ad bonum non ad malum [a]pertos ante illa enim pre[u]aricationem et uidere ui[d]ebant et cum tamen [n]udi essent male se, id est, [p]er concupiscentia non ui[d]ebant postquam uero/116v/de arbore illa unde commederunt in eo dicuntur eorum oculi cum se tu[r]piter concupiscendo uide[re] caeperunt'.

iii. Pembroke 25 fol. 67r ll.16-26:

'Hieronimus ait: Quomodo autem non est mortuus Adam dum comedit ex ligno, de quo dixerat ei dominus: In quocumque enim die comederis ex eo, morte morieris (Genesis 2,17)? Quattuor enim sunt genera mortis. Prima enim mors est cum deus propter peccatum relinquit animam. Secunda cum anima relinquit corpus. Tertia dum [J: cum] anima post mortem corporis in inferno dampnatur. Quarta cum post resurrectionem caro simul et anima in poenis cremabantur aeternis. Mortuus est tunc Adam secundum hanc primam mortem, quam diximus, recedendo a deo'.

Cf. Paris 10616 fol. 115r-115v:

'Quomodo non est mortuus dum comedit? Magister: [Q]uattuor sunt genera mor[t]uorum. Prima cum deus [p]ropter peccatum reliquit [a]nimam. Secunda cum anima/115v/reliquid corpus. Tertia cu[m] anima post mortem corpor[is] in infernum damnatur. Quarta cum post resurre[c]tione (sic) caro simul et anima cremabunt. Mortuus est ergo tunc Adam secundum ha[nc] primam mortem, quam di[xi]mus, recedendo ad (sic) deo'.

iv. Pembroke 25 fol. 67r l.26 - 67v l.8:

'Sic enim a deo creati sunt ut possent semper immortales uiuere si tamen preceptum dei seruassent et si uoluissent (J: noluissent; B omits: et si uoluissent) eius uerba contemnere possent/67v/utique mori. In arbore uero illa qualiscumque fuerit preceptum dei [J: domini] intelligendum est; in obseruatione enim [B: eius] precepti scientia erat [J: erit] boni, in transgressione uero precepti scientia erat [J: erit; B omits: boni ... erat] mali. Serpens autem tunc sicut nec [J omits] modo loqui non poterat sed per eum diabolus locutus est, nesciente ipso serpente quid loqueretur, sicut et nunc diabolus per demoniacos loquitur cum ipsi nesciunt quid loquantur'.

Cf. Paris 10616 fol. 117r-117v:

'Discipulus:/117v/Mortale corpus an inmortale primis omnibus (sic) creatu[r]? Magister: Sic ad (sic) deo creata ... ut possint si uellint sempe[r] uiuerent si tamen dei p[re]cepta seruassent et si uo[lu]issent eius uerba contem[ne]re possint utique mori'.

Cf. Paris 10616 fol. 114v:

'In arb[o]re uero illa qualiscumque fuerit preceptum dei intellegendum est; in obseruation[e] precepti scientiae erant bo[n]i, in transgressione scientiae erant mali'.

Cf. Paris 10616 fol. 115v - 116r:

'Discipulus: Loquebatur tun[c] serpens quando primis h[o]mines seduxit, aut scieb[at] quid loqueretur? Magister: Serpens tunc sicut nec mo[do] loqui non poterat sed per diabulus locutus est, nesciente ipso serpente qui[d]/116r/loqueretur, sicut et tunc diabolus per demoniacos loqui[t]ur cum ipsi nesciant quid [lo]quantur'.

It is clear that our composer saw explications such as these in Paris 10616, but probably not in this manuscript in which the questions are not assigned to Hieronimus, as in two Pembroke passages nos. ii and iii, and also because in passage i Paris 10616 reads: <u>dilitiosa uoluptate</u> for Pembroke (and all MSS): <u>diliciosa uoluntate</u>. The Pembroke composer may have seen the comments as questions and answers, however, if we allow the hint of a question in Pembroke for passage iii. It is difficult for me to say whether the commentary in Paris 10616 had Irish/insular features since no Hiberno-Latin scholar has considered it in detail. It may be said that insular writers favoured the question-and-answer form for teaching; they also favoured numbered lists; but, obviously, neither of these modes of presentation is their sole prerogative. One hint, however, given by passage iii on the four kinds of death, may point to a theme which, at present, is found in texts with insular features.

The theme there on the four kinds of death is presented in another text of Pseudo-Bede, <u>Quaestionum super Genesim ... Dialogus</u> (PL 93, 270), and, verbally as Pseudo-Bede, in Angelom of Luxeuil, <u>Commentarius in Genesin</u> (PL 115, 133), and, in different words, in Pseudo-Augustine <u>Sermo</u> 171 (PL 39, 2074). All these, however, are verbally quite different from the Paris 10616 and Pembroke 25 presentations. But a comment on Matthew 2, 20 (on those who were <u>defuncti</u> when the Christ-child returned from Egypt) within a commentary on Matthew in Paris BN lat. 12021 is similar in word to the passages quoted. On fol. 5v we read:

'Quia quatuor genere (sic) sunt mortis. Prima quando deus propter peccatum relinquid anima[m]. Secunda quando anima relinquid corpus. Tertia cum post mortem corporis in infernum damnetur (sic). Quarta cum post resurrectionem corporis cum caro et cum anima in infernum tormenta patiuntur'.

This commentary (Paris 12021) has not yet been considered by Hiberno-Latin scholars, but its phraseology often has correspondence with that in Pseudo-Jerome, <u>Expositio Quatuor Evangeliorum</u>, in many of its brief chapters, although it adds material, as on the four kinds of death. Paleographers indicate that the manuscript originated in Brittany and it also contains a text of the <u>Collectio Canonum Hibernensis</u> (Wasserschleben p.LXVII no. 3). The connections of this one theme, but also the manuscript (Paris 10616) in which the questions on Genesis are now extant, at least hint at the questions having an insular connection.

Apart from such comparatively sizeable passages it also appears that our composer recorded individual explications which persist in insular-influenced exegesis, and themes most closely connected with insular works and/or with collections of sententiae found in manuscripts from Irish/Anglo-Saxon spheres of influence on the Continent.

Within item 13 (in die Theophaniae) the composer draws together a number of significations for the gifts of the Magi. Pembroke 25 fol. 24r l.10-24v l.1.reads:

'Quid significant haec munera nisi animam et corpus et spiritum per quae si inmaculate (B: immaculata illa) offeramus (B: offerimus) deo placere ualeamus (B: ualemus). Tria sunt ergo munera pretiosa quę obtulerunt magi domino in die ista (J: isto) et habent in se diuina misteria; per tus (B, J: thus) enim deus, per aurum rex regum et dominus dominantium, per myrram simplex humanitas (J: simplicitatem humanis) designatur. Iterum, per aurum sapientia et splendor eloquii, per thus oratio munda, per myrram mortificatio uitiorum signatur. Ideo tria hec munera accepit Iesus ab unoquoque magorum quia trinus est unus est, trinus est enim (J omits) in personis et unus in substantia, significans quod tria munera ab unoquoque homine exiguntur, id est, recta cogitatio et locutio bona et opus perfectum. Idcirco autem, myrrha inter dona reputatur Christi quia ungentum (B, J: unguentum) pretiosum est et optimum quo corpora defunctorum solent ungeri ut imputribilia perseuerent, et ideo ex ipso unctum est corpus Iesu ne putresceret in morte quam uoluntarie pro nostra redemptione et salute suscepit, sicut de eo et omnibus sanctis eius propheta testatur dicens: Pretiosa est in conspectu domini mors sanctorum eius (B omits: eius) (cf. Psalm 115, 5)'.

Sections of this passage are abstractions from a sermon as in the text of Munich Clm. 6233, fols. 131r - 131v, (which is used largely for the end of the Pembroke item), as:

'Munera ista maiorum (for: magorum) fidem gentium que anima et corpore et spiritu saluandę sunt ... ' and: 'Mirra uero in donis Christi reputatur unguentum pretiosum et bonum quo corpora defunctorum unguentur et imputrabilia perdurant indicium mortalitatis et mortis eius quam uoluntariae pro nostra redemptione et salute suscepit, sicut de eo et de omnibus sanctis eius propheta testatur dicens: Pretiosa est in conspectu domini mors sanctorum eius (cf. Psalm 115, 5)'.

Two explications are found in Gregory, Homilia 10 in Evangelia. 6 (PL76, 1112-13), i.e. per thus deus etc., and: per aurum sapientia etc., and can be regarded as commonplace, although both are presented in Pseudo-Jerome on the Gospels (PL30, 554, 555). The explication as Trinity is also found in Pseudo-Jerome (PL30, 554) but also in Pseudo-Augustine Sermo 136 (PL39, 2014), and a wide-ranging study would be needed to demonstrate that this explication is either distinctively or persistently insular. Only one such detailed study, relevant to the explications here, has been done to my knowledge, that in which Patrick Sims-Williams argues that 'recta cogitatio et locutio bona et opus perfectum' is an Irish triad (Ériu 29 (1978), pp. 78 - 111). Obviously he does not consider our example, but would appear to have read everything in print, and indicates (p.82) that, while the triad 'thought, word and deed' is not an Irish invention, it 'must be classed with the 'Irish symptoms' identified by Bischoff'.

Other themes, not necessarily explications, have been studied, which appear to persist in insular texts. Pembroke 25 Item 1 (for Advent) presents the theme of the seven gifts of the Holy Spirit exemplified in the patriarchs, beginning on fol. 4r 1.20:

'Iste septiformis spiritus, qui in patriarchis diuisus est, adunatus quidem in Christo permansit. Igitur in Adam spiritus sapientię fuit ... spiritus intellectus fuit in Noe ... spiritus consilii fuit in Abraham ... spiritus fortitudinis fuit in Isaac ... spiritus scientiae fuit in Iacob ... spiritus pietatis fuit in Moyse ... spiritus timoris Domini fuit in David ... Hęc omnia carismata spiritus sancti septiformis in Christo Iesu aeternitaliter permanserunt qui fons est et origo illorum, dei sapientia et dei uirtus'.

The identification of gift with individual patriarch is consistent over a number of anonymous or pseudonymous collections (although attached scriptural citations vary) including Pseudo-Bede, Collectanea (PL94, 553), Pseudo-Alcuin, De septem sigillis (ed. Matter, Traditio 36 (1980),pp. 115, 116), Pseudo-Isidore, Liber de Numeris (McNally VII.1), Catechesis Celtica, Vat. Reg lat. 49 fol. 3r, and a number of early ninth-century manuscripts noted by McNally in his dissertation (pp.108-09) on the Pseudo-Isidore Liber de Numeris. As McNally says (p.109): 'wenn nicht direkt irischer Ursprung, so doch wenigstens Zusammenhang mit irischer Exegese uermuten'.

A less extensive study has been undertaken for a theme, which often has no enumeration in sermons, initially by T. D. Hill (see bibliography sub nom.) who named it 'The Seven Joys of Heaven', although in three early Latin collections with insular connections, Pseudo-Bede Collectanea, Catechesis Celtica, and Pseudo-Isidore Liber de Numeris, it is numbered, and, as in the Liber (McNally, Diss. p.116) it is named: 'Septem sunt miracula quae non inueniuntur in saeculo'. As Anglo-Saxonists have illustrated (see a collection of information in Bazire-Cross, Rogationtide pp. 11-12 and notes 39-43) the presentation of a list of 'x without y' to describe the delights of heaven, was common in Latin texts under insular influence, in Old English prose, for the poet Cynewulf, and in certain Pseudo-Augustinian sermons. In the last case the use of the theme may point to an insular influence when the manuscript tradition of such sermons is delineated. In the Pembroke-type collection and in those Old English texts which use the theme, insular influence, in my view, is indicated.

Other statements appear within the Pembroke-type collection, which at this stage may hint, but that only without more detailed study, at an 'insular-influenced' presentation by our composer. But I think it necessary to call the attention of others to what may be termed 'oddities' which are unlikely to have originated in orthodox and named patristic works. These 'oddities' are miscellaneous and are so presented.

The second item for Epiphany (no. 14) describes the three other manifestations of Christ associated with this festival, the miracle of the five loaves and two fishes, the wedding at Cana and Christ's baptism in Jordan. Verbal echoes of Latin works indicate that our author drew on the relevant Scriptural narratives, on a sermon as now in Munich Clm. 6233, on Pseudo-Augustine Sermo 136 for Epiphany, and on antiphons (see list of sources above). One statement however, deriving from Munich Clm. 6233, is unusual to say the least. Pembroke 25 fol. 25r l.24 reads:

'Et fecit uinum de aqua, id est,. cl. modios, et mutauit speciem aquę conuertens in colorem et saporem (J: soporem) uini'.

Munich Clm. 6233 fol. 131v-132r reads:

'in hac die fecit Iesus uinum de aqua,. cl. modios, ut refertur, mutauit elimento aquae et conuertit in colorem et saporem uini'.

If I have understood this statement, is this a miracle as in Scripture? One recalls explication of Scriptural statements in anonymous commentaries which often lean towards rationalism (and mediaeval common-sense), here perhaps (but why?) to avoid an explanation of the supernatural. As Archbishop Trench, Notes on the Miracles of Our Lord (Dublin, 10th ed., 1874), remarked (p.113) and then carefully explained: 'The conditions under which the miracle was accomplished are all, as Chrysostom long ago observed, such as exclude every suspicion of collusion'. Against such orthodoxy the statement in Munich 6233 and Pembroke 25, indeed, appears odd.

Within the narrative on the Maccabees (item 47) we find some confusion of naming which is paralleled, and naming which I have not seen elsewhere, from only one name in Scripture. Pembroke 25 fol. 109r l.4 records: 'Haec sunt autem nomina illorum, Eleazarus et Felicitas et septem filii eius, Dardanus, Dardianus, Antiochus, Mentonius, Anchius (B: Ancius), Anchialus (B: Ancialus), Heubresius'. Eleazarus is, of course, not the father of the seven brothers (II Maccabees cap.6) and the mother and sons are not named in II Maccabees cap.7. A transfer has named the mother from the saintly mother Felicitas who also had seven sons (BHL 2853-55), and whom Gregory praised, without naming the sons, in his Homilia 3 in Evangelia (PL76, 1086 seq.). The transfer has an analogue in the Pseudo-Isidore, Liber de Numeris VII.36, in McNally's typescript edition: 'Septem fratres, filii Felicitatis, de quorum triumphys et cruciatibus in Machabeis scriptum est'. But, as yet, no parallel has come to eye for the sons' names. As we know the Irish named and described the Magi (Bischoff in McNamara pp.91-92). Perhaps they also named the Maccabees.

An unusual hagiographical narrative may also have an Irish origin. Within the item for Michael the Archangel (no. 55) is a story of a contest between Michael and a tangible (as opposed to the Apocalyptic) dragon. The salient points are that an immensely huge, flame-spewing dragon terrified inhabitants in the southern part of

Asia. In answer to their prayer for help, God sent the archangel, in the form of a bird, to fight and eventually kill this dragon. The inhabitants had to cut up the dragon into parts which were carried 'per .xii. iuga bouum' and thrown into the sea. A church was then built in which the claws of St. Michael as a bird still appear on the stone 'quasi in caera mollissima ... omni tempore'. A detailed discussion and edition of this story has appeared in Magister Regis: Studies in honor of Robert Earl Kaske ed. A. Groos et al. (Fordham U.P., New York, 1986). Briefly however we may say that this is a rare story found elsewhere in the manuscript Vat. Reg. lat. 703B (saec XII, Caen) which also contains books of the ecclesiastical history of Ordericus Vitalis. The story in the manuscript derives from that in the Pembroke-type collection for reasons presented in the paper. Another text of the story is presented in abbreviated form in Vat. Reg. Lat. 542 (saec. XII) within a legendary, in which our story is an 'epilogue' to a narrative of the Apparitio S. Michaelis in Monte Tumba. This summary account indicates that the composer of the Pembroke-type narrative used, but did not create, the story. The story of Michael and the dragon is also known and adapted in the Irish vernacular collection of the Leabhar Breac (ed. Atkinson), and we may note that stories from earlier Hiberno-Latin texts are often transmitted in later Irish vernacular pieces.

But none of this information is distinctive evidence of Irish origin for the story. When, however, I sent the Irish vernacular text for Atkinson's translation to be considered by my Celticist friend, R. L. Thomson, together with an edited text of the Pembroke Latin item, he commented on the Irish, but also on the Latin of the opening phrase of the account, Pembroke 25 fol. 127v l.11:

'Hanc quoque inmensam et ammirabilem in dextrali parte Asiae fecisse legimus uirtutem. Draco enim ingens mirae magnitudinis montem quendam altum occupans in illis regionibus uenit, cuius flatus flamiuomus quantoscumque in giro suo tangi potuisset omnes interficiebat'.

He asked rhetorically: 'Can we take dextralis 'southern' as a sign of insular origin? The careful Clare Stancliffe would do so. Commenting on Catechesis Celtica,

Vat. Reg. Lat. 49, in the volume <u>Ireland in Early Mediaeval Europe</u> she notes (p.24): 'the author uses certain Latin words and phases that are distinctively Irish/Celtic. For instance, 'north' and 'south' are rendered by <u>sinistralis</u> and <u>dextralis</u> ... '. In the company of these scholars who are familiar with Celtic Latin, we should say that the creator of the phrase 'in dextrali parte Asiae' was a Celt or one familiar with Celtic Latin usage, and if the phrase was part of the original writing of the narrative on Michael, that account probably originated in the insular area.

One final point cannot be part of the argument above. When I first commented on it orally, I said in joke that this must be Irish, but the Irish present were only politely amused. Nevertheless it should be revealed as a noteworthy association of information. Within item 30 (<u>de Passione Domini</u>) our composer narrated the story of creation to the expulsion of Adam and Eve, in order to explain that 'diabolus regnabat in mundo' until Christ's Advent and sacrifice. His narrative is based on recognisable verses from Genesis caps. 1 - 3, but with insertions. Most of these additions have been discussed above in relation to recognisable commentaries. One insertion is without analogue, in which a statement on Eve and the forbidden fruit is sandwiched within phraseology from Genesis 3, 6, Pembroke 25 fol. 66v l.13:

'Credidit igitur mulier suggestioni serpentis et, quia bonum erat lignum ad uescendum et pulchrum oculis, tulit de fructu illius (cf. Genesis 3, 6) sinistra manu, et idcirco breuior est (B adds: sinistra manus) humano generi quam dextera quia illa extensa est ad malum, et comedit deditque uiro suo (Genesis 3, 6)'.

We may expect ascetic exegetes to choose Eve's <u>sinister</u> hand, but only tailors in modern times are truly conscious of the fact that right arms in physically active right-handed people are often longer than their left. Can this be an example of Irish medieval rationalisation?

The argument above for insular influence on the Pembroke-type collection is, obviously, most firmly based on demonstrated contacts with works of named insular writers, and on echoes of passages of anonymous and pseudonymous collections of <u>sententiae</u>, of groups of sermons or individual sermons, and of commentaries, all of which reveal insular symptoms, but, in support of these more firmly-demonstrable links, also on presentation of themes which may not have originated in the insular area but persisted in writings with insular features, and on the slight use of Celtic Latinisms, which probably were accepted within given passages, but presumably made sense to our composer. Those who are not familiar with the insular Latin material may abstract as inconclusive certain proposed contacts, particularly from among the individual themes and suggested Celtic Latinisms. I am fully aware of the tentative nature of some suggestions, but even if most of such proposed contacts are negated, enough remains to suggest that our composer had access to writings created by insular writers or under insular influence.

The date and place of origin of the Collection

Evidence of contact with insular texts and with themes and ideas which persist in such texts indicates that the collection was composed in a house which had access to such books. In view of the traffic of people and books between the British Isles and the Continent in the eighth and ninth centuries, also that none of our extant manuscripts is the archetype, and that these manuscripts are both English and Continental, it is impossible to say, however, whether our collection was composed in the British Isles or at some centre on the Continent where insular influence was apparent.

A tantalizing hint, however, is offered in the Pembroke 25 manuscript alone which, if taken, might identify a house through which the collection passed or in which it might have originated. Item 75 in Pembroke is a sermon for one confessor, the source of which is a sermon attributed to Maximus of Turin, on Eusebius of Vercelli, and obviously popular since it was the choice for the feast both in the Roman homiliary of Alanus of Farfa and in the collection of Paul the Deacon. Such general sermons were sometimes made specific by the insertion of a name of a particular confessor at the beginning. This is the case in Pembroke item 75 which begins, at fol. 151r l.5: 'Ad sancti ac beatissimi istius patris nostri cubƀ, cuius hodie festa celebramus, fratres karissimi, laudes ...'; a phrase which clearly echoes the source: 'Ad sancti ac beatissimi istius Patris nostri laudes, cujus hodie festa celebramus ...' (PL 57, 417), with the notable exception of the abbreviated insertion: cubƀ. Neither of the two other manuscripts which contain Pembroke item 75, St. John's 42 and Balliol 240, record the word, although otherwise both echo the Pembroke phrase verbatim. The abbreviation is clearly for a proper noun, a name, but its expansion is puzzling, and was, I think, to Henri Barré also since he omitted the word in his record of the incipit (Homéliaires p.24). Expert consultants, however, favour an expansion to Cudberct, identified as the well-known confessor Cuthbert of Lindisfarne. It may be interesting that Cuthbert was revered at Bury in the eleventh century, but it is disappointing that the abbreviation was not for the name of a traceable abbot of the house in which our collection was composed.

It is not possible to narrow appreciably the limits of the date of composition. If we had only the manuscripts of the Latin collection the terminus ad quem, at present, would be the date of the earliest manuscripts, Chartres BM 25 (44), reputedly about 1000 A.D., and Canterbury Cathedral Addit. 127/12, within the early years of the eleventh century. But vernacular derivatives from the Pembroke-type collection in the Vercelli Book indicate that the Latin collection was available somewhat earlier. N. R. Ker, Catalogue of Manuscripts containing Anglo-Saxon (Oxford, 1957), p.460, dated the Vercelli manuscript as saec. X^2. It is also clear from a comparison of vernacular variant texts with relevant sermons in the Vercelli Book and the Latin texts from which the vernacular writing is derived, that, on occasions, the Vercelli pieces offer incorrect readings. This information indicates that the exemplars in Old English were available before the date when the Vercelli manuscript was written. With regard to this additional evidence the terminus ad quem of the Latin collection would be within the second half of the tenth century.

Source-analysis allows a consideration of the terminus a quo, although a little more discussion is needed than when Henri Barré first described the collection. He noted (Homéliaires p.17) the use of Amalarius, De ecclesiasticis officiis (composed towards 820 A.D), in items 16 and 31, and we have added that Hrabanus Maurus, De Clericorum Institutione (written under the abbacy at Fulda of Eigil who died in 822 A.D) was abstracted for items 22, 31, 32, 48, 78 - 88 and perhaps for item 43. Barré (p.17 and note 60) also remarked on the use of the anonymous sermon Legimus in ecclesiasticis historiis (items 56-63, now as one sermon) which he attributed to Helisachar of Saint-Riquier who died between 833 and 840 A.D. (Revue Bénédictine 68 (1958) pp.211-12). Barré's attribution depends solely, and thus doubtfully, on a single ascription in an eleventh-century manuscript. But earlier unassigned texts of the sermon suggest that it may have originated somewhat earlier. These manuscripts are Munich, Bayerische Staatsbibliothek Clm. 6314 (saec. IX 2/4) from Freising, and

Verona, Biblioteca Capitolare XCV, written there during the time of Archbishop Pacificus who died in 844 A.D., (on these manuscripts see Traditio 33 (1977) pp.102 and 135 respectively). Since neither of these two manuscripts is the exemplar, and their presence indicates that copies had been made in centres in different countries after 825 A.D. and before 844 A.D.,we might possibly assume that the exemplar originated nearer the beginning than the end of that second quarter, approximately at the time when the named books of Amalarius and Hrabanus Maurus became available.

Our present study has added one other fact which now needs considering, the identification of the collection called Catechesis Celtica as a source for three items (26, 27 and 29) in our collection. Earlier scholars had indicated that items in Catechesis Celtica drew on Pascasius Radbertus, Expositio in Matheo Libri XII (860-863 A.D.) and De corpore et sanguine Domini (written in the 830s and revised by 863 A.D.), but Jean Rittmueller (Peritia 2 (1983), pp.185-214 at 201-02) has given adequate evidence, at least for one item in Catechesis Celtica which she analyses, that Pascasius Radbertus himself had drawn on earlier Hiberno-Latin material, known also to the compiler of the Catechesis Celtica series. Bernhard Bischoff had also noted the transmission of insular themes and ideas in the work of Pascasius Radbertus (in McNamara pp. 92-93, 114, 158 note 106) and the recent CCSL edition of Pascasius Radbertus on Matthew, within vol. LVIB (Index Auctorum), records the influence of anonymous commentaries, some with 'Irish symptoms'. If we also accept the hint indicated above that the Pembroke-type collection drew on a variant manuscript of the sole extant manuscript of Catechesis Celtica in Vat. Reg. lat 49, even the proposed date of that single manuscript obviously has no bearing on the distinguishing of a terminus a quo for the Pembroke-type collection.

In view of the inconclusive evidence for dating the anonymous sermon Legimus and individual items within the Catechesis Celtica collection, except that Pascasius Radbertus was not a source for these, it would seem more prudent, at present, to rely on the use of dateable books by named authors and to indicate the terminus a quo as after 822 A.D. when Hrabanus Maurus had certainly written his De Clericorum Institutione.

The collection and its influence.

This Latin collection, extant as a whole or in part in five English manuscripts from the eleventh to the fourteenth century, may make fair claim to popularity if we recall the probable loss or destruction of English manuscripts in later centuries. That popularity of the Latin text is confirmed here by its use in the sermons of Anglo-Saxon writers. But, since the collection was copied, or separate items abstracted, also in three Continental manuscripts, possible discovery of more Latin manuscripts should not be precluded with the fuller cataloguing of library holdings, nor illustration of use in sermons of other European vernaculars.

The collection is extant in a fourteenth-century Anglo-Latin manuscript (Balliol 240) so readers of Middle English sermons may also care to glance at it, especially since Helen Spencer (Mediaeval Studies 44 (1982), pp.271-305), has already demonstrated (p.274) that William de Montibus, Chancellor of Lincoln Cathedral from 1191 until his death in 1213, used Pembroke item 22 for Lent (printed by Spencer pp.283-291) as basis for a sermon in his series, known as the Collectio 'Filius matris'. William, indeed, read more widely in the Pembroke-type collection, as an extension on his base source reveals. An enumeration of the three reasons why the day of a man's death is concealed, followed by an ubi sunt passage (ll.61-71, Spencer pp.284 and 286), is adapted directly from Pembroke item 89 (among the general sermons at the end of the collection) fol. 167r ll.9-22. As Spencer stated (p.276): 'The Latin Filius matris cycle enjoyed some standing in the later Middle Ages, being copied well into the fifteenth century', and was translated into the English vernacular in the late fourteenth and fifteenth centuries. Obviously, the Pembroke-type collection had influence on various routes.

It is particularly important, however, for Old English anonymous sermons, probably being second in influence only to the Carolingian homiliary of Paul the Deacon, from which it differs in content and purpose. In the main the items copied whole by Paul the Deacon are exegeses on Scriptural pericopes for the feasts of the liturgical year and the Common, but for the reading-pieces of the Pembroke-type collection the sources used are mainly narrative or precepts of advice from 'popular' writers whose aim is to instruct the faithful in basic tenets of the faith and behaviour, without involvement in the distinctions of theological argument. Such a sermonary would be more useful for moral sermons, or for thematic insertions into such sermons. This is how items from the collection were used in Old English, although the main derivatives were assigned to periods of special observance or days of festival.

At present eight Old English sermons used items from the Pembroke-type collection, and, as will be argued below, two others echoed themes found in the verbal form of Pembroke items. The eight sermons which have clear derivative passages are: Vercelli Homilies III, XIX, XX, XXI, Tristram III, Assmann XI, XII, Belfour VI; the two arguable derivations of thematic material are in Brotanek II and Fadda I (see full discussions below, and for titles of editions see bibliography II A above).

As a result of discovery of direct source for some prose items in the Vercelli Book, two general points may be made about its compilation:-

i. The vernacular codex was not compiled until after the 820s, the earliest date for the writing of the Pembroke-type collection. Other vernacular items, not dependent on this Latin collection, could, obviously, have been composed earlier than that date.

ii. Differences of readings between items in the Vercelli Book and those in variant manuscripts for those items compared with the Latin source confirm that, on occasion, the Vercelli scribe made errors and that he copied from sermons already in the vernacular.

On the basis of the discovery, Dr. Scragg and I have discussed the possibility of assigning Vercelli Homilies XIX, XX, XXI to one author as Paul Szarmach speculated (Old English Homily p.248), although with caution, and as Karl Jost (Wulfstanstudien pp.178-182), proposed common authorship for Assmann XI, XII and Brotanek II. Jost's proposal is discussed below, but Scragg and I agree that simple access to items in the Pembroke-type collection is not, in itself, a sufficient reason for such claim of common authorship for the named items in the Vercelli Book. Some grouping of another kind has been proposed for the Vercelli pieces to suggest that the one scribe of the codex copied groups of items from different exemplars and collected these in his compilation. For those items dependent on the Pembroke-type collection, Scragg (Anglo-Saxon England 2 (1973), p.195) and Celia Sisam (in the introduction to the facsimile edition, pp.40-44) agree that Vercelli III drew on a different exemplar from the group consisting of Vercelli XIX, XX and XXI, which reveals common scribal features. Such studies of scribal habit, are, however, different from investigation of authorial style and choice of vocabulary such as that initiated by Karl Jost in his analysis of the Wulfstan canon. Such a study has not yet been attempted for the groups in the Vercelli Book. When an analysis is made of Vercelli XIX, XX, XXI, to which Tristram III might be added (see discussion of this sermon below) to discern common features, if so, in distinction, at least, from other anonymous prose items in relevant manuscripts, it will be possible to consider the suggestion of common authorship of the group. The analysis could well be progressive, and, perhaps, conclusive, if linked with previous studies of scribal habit and, as here, of source-study.

The Latin and Old English Texts

Editorial Procedure

As noted in the preface, the Latin texts are presented as a reading edition for vernacular specialists whose concern is with the meaning, but not form, of the Latin phrases and words. The editions below present the base text, Pembroke 25, with minimal emendation, normally in relation to variant readings from other manuscripts and/or the text of a direct source, if relevant. Such emendations are demarked within square brackets. Meaningful variant readings are recorded, but not spelling variations normally, or transpositions of words within phrases. Scribal corrections to the base text are not normally distinguished, but may be recorded in the textual notes in relation to variant readings and the need for an editorial decision. Abbreviations in the base text have been silently expanded. Punctuation, with capitalization, has been modernised for easier reading, although punctuation of the base text has been considered, and once noted where this affects the meaning of the vernacular derivative.

Sigla for the individual manuscripts are conveniently the different initial letters of the present designation of these manuscripts, since the Paris manuscript, containing selected items from the Pembroke-type collection, has not been seen. The Grenoble MS. texts abbreviate and adapt the relevant Pembroke-type items, and readings from this manuscript have been recorded only for Pembroke item 93 (source for Vercelli Homily XX), which otherwise is extant only in Balliol MS. 240.

Also as noted in the preface, the Old English texts have been taken from the most up-to-date editions. In the case of items from The Vercelli Book the considered typescript edition of Donald G. Scragg has been used, but line references are given to Paul E. Szarmach's recent printed edition. Dr. Scragg has had the advantage of seeing the Pembroke 25 manuscript. Hildegard Tristram's edition of the Ascension Day sermon (her no. III) presents manuscript punctuation, but this has been modernised, and a few editorial changes have also been made from consultation of the manuscript, as recorded in the introductory essay to this section.

Lexicographers who wish to abstract equivalents from the Latin and Old English texts below should consult relevant printed editions for record of variant readings in other vernacular manuscripts.

Vercelli XIX

The discussion of Vercelli XIX by Bazire-Cross pp.6-15, now needs modification, obviously, to attribute some of the adaptation of ultimate sources to the composer of the Pembroke-type collection rather than to the writer of the vernacular sermon. But many of the earlier deductions still stand and readers are referred to that introduction. Close verbal echo, on occasions, and echo of significant detail demonstrate that the composer of the Old English sermon used three separate items (nos. 36, 38, 40) of the Pembroke-type collection, in two of these cases in contrast to ultimate sources. Some argument is needed to suggest that he recalled briefer passages from two other items (nos. 1, 42), and also had access to popular 'insular' material. For the three clear cases, selective illustrations are sufficient.

1.   Item 36 (Pembroke no. XXXV, fol. 83v, printed below).

(a)   After the long introduction, concluding with the story of Adam's fall and the subsequent power of the Devil over man, the Old English composer considers the Rogationtide festival, and records what would be a puzzling statement, if only the Old English text were available: 'These Rogation-days ('gangdagas') are compared with many holy men, but it is too long for us to narrate all that' (ll.54-55). This, at least, is a rare comparison, and unknown elsewhere to me, but Vercelli XIX (ll.48-49) adds Ascension Day as a fourth to the group of three Rogation-days, and Pembroke 25 item 36 (ll.4-31) includes a lengthy comparison of the four days with four perfect men, Noah, Abraham, Moses and Christ, also with the four evangelists, and for good measure, the cross. Without the Latin even the immediate Anglo-Saxon audience might have been puzzled.

(b)   Earlier, Bazire-Cross (p.10) wrote of the narrative of Jonas in Vercelli XIX as a story told 'with free and varied reference to the ideas of Jonas chapters 1-3 inclusive'. These additions and changes are made by the Latin composer of Pembroke item 36, e.g.

(i)   In Scripture Jonas <u>descendit ad interiora navis et dormiebat</u> (Jonas 1, 5) but in Old English: 'þa gereste he hine on anum ende' (l.93), approximating to the Latin: in pupe nauis dormientem (ll.49-50).

(ii) In Scripture the Lord sent ventum magnum and tempestas magna (Jonas 1, 4); in Old English, 'þa onsende God mycelne ren and strangne wind and grimme yste on þa sæ, swa þæt þæt scip ne mihte naþer ne forð swymman ne underbæc' (ll.94-96), equating emisit deus pluuiam magnam et uentum ualidum et procellam acerbissimam in mare, ita ut ipsa nauis nec ante nec retro ...natare poterat (ll.45-47).

(iii) In Essays and Studies (for the English Association) ed. Kenneth Muir (London, 1974), pp.84-97 at pp.93-97, I argued that critics and translators had overlooked a problem in the poem known as Resignation (l.100) 'hwy ic gebycge bat on sæwe'. In relation to the phrase 'him þær scip gebohte' (l.91), in the then unpublished Vercelli XIX, and the Vulgate text: dedit naulum ejus (Jonas 1, 3), I suggested that the phrase in the poem and prose text meant 'to pay the fare' thus indicating the extreme poverty of the poetic speaker who could not do this. Our new source may confirm the unrecorded idiom since it is clear that Vercelli XIX closely echoes Pembroke no. 36 for the section and most probably here: 'him þær scip gebohte' now echoes: dantem eis nabulum (l.44).

(iv) In our earlier essay (p.10) Miss Bazire and I commented on a problem of textual variation in Old English, in which Vercelli XIX notes that God took away from Nineveh 'þæt fyrene clyne ... þe ofer þa ceastre wæs on þam genipe hangiende' (l.112), but two later manuscripts substitute 'egeslice fyr' for 'fyrene clyne'. Accepting the old rule of textual criticism of the difficilior lectio, we regarded 'fyrene clyne' as the original reading, as it now certainly is, the whole phrase echoing massa ignea iam supra eam in nube pendebat (l.39).

2.   Item 40 (Pembroke no. XXXVIIII, fol.91r, printed below).

The short section on Mamertus of Vienne and the origin of the Rogationtide observances in Vercelli XIX differs largely in detail from the traditional accounts, as was discussed and illustrated in Bazire-Cross pp.10-11. There we speculated that some influence came from a story about the institution of the major litanies by Gregory the Great, recorded among the Homiliae Subdititiae as no. 97 (PL 94, 499) by Pseudo-Bede. That speculation may remain for the Latin item, but now Vercelli XIX takes its account from the Pembroke-type collection, as illustrated below. I merely note one similarity here. Vercelli XIX records that so great was the pestilence that: '[þa] þe oðre to eorðan bæron þæt sume hie feollon deade ofer þæs deadan byrgenne þe hie þonne byrgdon and sume hamweard be wege forðferdon' (ll.120-122), approximating to ut illi homines qui illos mortuos ad sepulturam portabant aut super sepulchrum aut in via mortui, cadebant (ll.40-42).

3.   Item 38 (Pembroke no. XXVII, fol.87v).

As noted in the list of sources above, Pembroke item 38 is based solely on Caesarius Sermo 207 but with additions and with variant readings from Morin's printed text.   Where Szarmach (Traditio 26 (1970), pp.319-20) indicated, and Bazire-Cross (pp.9-10) developed, the links between Vercelli XIX and Caesarius 207, the Pembroke item is an intermediary. Two extracts of all three texts presented below (Extract 1) demonstrate this fact.

It is now clear that the composer had access to three of the five items (36-40) for Rogationtide in the Pembroke-type collection, and thus reasonable to assume reading of other items where verbal echo or similarity occur between a passage of Vercelli XIX and a Pembroke sermon. On that assumption I suggest that the English composer read Pembroke item 1 (fols. 3r-3v) for his presentation of the Creed on the Trinity as the opening paragraph of the sermon (ll.1-9), although the Latin extract cited below (Extract 2) from fol. 3r is based on Caesarius Sermo 3 on the Creed. The Latin phrase from fol. 3v, however, which was obviously echoed by the Anglo-Saxon, is not in Caesarius's sermon.

As illustrated in Extract 3 below, the description of Adam's trials on earth after his disobedience, which is recorded in Vercelli XIX, is found also in the Pembroke manuscript at fol. 67r (and also at fol. 3v) especially the phrase uixit Adam in labore et erumna; cf. 'Adam lifde on þysse worulde on geswince and on yrmþe', (ll.37-38).

Also the precise number of years he spent in infernum, 5228, (although a common figure, Bazire-Cross pp.7-8), noted in Vercelli XIX (ll.39-40),is the figure chosen in Pembroke fol. 80r. These ideas appear to be taken by the Anglo-Saxon from a fuller reading of the Pembroke-type collection.

Another common theme probably came from such general reading. This has been called 'The Seven Joys of Heaven' by T. D. Hill who first identified it, although early Latin examples added by Bazire-Cross (pp.11-12 and notes) named the theme 'wonders not found in this world'. The theme became a formulaic sequence of alternatives of 'x without y' to express the delights of heaven and the absence of earth's trials (Bazire-Cross, ibid). The formulaic presentation is made in item 25 (at fol. 52v) and in two general sermons at the end of the Pembroke collection (no. 89 at fol. 166v; no. 91 at fol. 171r), but the words of Vercelli XIX (ll.136-38) are found almost verbatim at the end of Pembroke item 42, for Ascension Day, fols. 96v-97r (see Extract 4 below).

The Seven Joys theme is found commonly in 'insular' texts or in pseudonymous texts which have not yet been assigned places of origin, and, in relation to other non-scriptural comments in Vercelli XIX, Bazire-Cross pp.7-8 noted some details found elsewhere in other Hiberno-Latin texts. One was the specification of the 'tree of life' as a 'fig-tree', the other was the statement that Eve's formative rib came from Adam's left side, for which a parallel from a commentary in the so-named 'Reference Bible' was quoted from one manuscript, Vat. Reg. Lat. 76 fol. 54v: Cur de costa et non de alio osse. Ideo quia costa prope sit ad cor ubi est dilectio. That, we thought, was a hint that the rib was on the left side near the heart. But I now know that Vat. Reg. Lat. 76 has omitted a clearer statement found in other manuscripts of the 'Reference Bible'. These are Paris BN lat. 11561 and Munich Clm. 14276 (Bischoff I A in McNamara p.97). The text (Paris fol. 17v col. 1; Munich fols. 28r-28v) reads: De quo latere facta est Eua? De sinistro latere quia ibi deest una costa in memoriam eius operis.

The identifications of new sources and explications of minor ideas in this sermon, do not change the views expressed in Bazire-Cross (p.12) that 'the homilist has his audience and his purpose firmly in his mind, adapting and moulding the material to that end of the need for penance and obedience to God's commands'. Instead, however, of drawing from several books the composer relies largely on the Pembroke-type collection from whose individual items he selects his two major narrative examples, the story of Jonas, and the description of the trials of Mamertus's congregation, as also minor passages, but the presentation is fluently handled.

Item 36 fol.83v XXXV. Omelia in Rogatione: feria ii.

Scitis, fratres karissimi, quod istos quattuor dies cum summa
diligentia custodire debetis, in grandi humilitate, in patientia, in caritate,
in castitate, in puritate, in uigiliis, in ieiuniis, in orationibus, in
aelimosinis, in omni bonitate, et in dilectione dei et proximi. Comparantur

5   enim isti quattuor dies quattuor uiris perfectis, id est, Noe, Abrahe, Moysi et
Christo. Ideo Noe primum comparantur quia ips[e], iubente domino, arcam in
figuram aecclesię in qua nunc omnes homines per baptismum saluantur
i[n]struere cepit per quam octo homines cum suis animalibus ex mundis et
immundis, delente diluuio terram, saluati sunt. Abrahę autem quia ipse sine

10 lege nulloque precepto ammonente integram fidem primum seruauit et [in]
deum patrem mundi conditorem toto corde credidit. Et ideo trinitatem
sanctam in hospitio suscipere meruit cui postea dictum est a domino: Erit
semen tuum sicut stellae caeli et arena quę est in littore maris (cf. Genesis
22,17). Moysi uero quia ipse populum Israel de Aegypto uenientem per mare

15 rubrum, siccis pedibus, et per uias desertas, domino iubente, deduxit. Et ideo
pro sua pietate qua deum semper pro [po]pulo supplicabat totam legem digito
dei in monte Sinai scriptam suscepit et dominum facie ad faciem uidit. Ideo
autem Christo, filio dei, certissime compara[n]tur quia sicut ille post multa

84r mirabilia quę in hoc mundo peregit et post / 84r / multas inuidias a Iudęis sibi
20 inlatas et post passionem resurrectionemque suam coram apostolis in cęlum sua

---

4. J omits: in, before: dilectione. 6. P: ipsa; B, J, R: ipse. 8. P: is struere;
B, J, R: instruere. 9. B, P, J: terram; R: terrea. 9. J omits: ipse, before: sine.
10. J omits: primum, before: seruauit. 10. R: ad; B, P, J omit: in. 16. P:
propulo; B, J, R: pro populo. 17. P, J, R: dominum; B: deum. 18. B omits:
certissime. 18. P: comparatur; B, J, R: comparantur.

Vercelli XIX, Scragg (Szarmach 70, 51-53); cf. Latin 1-4.

We hie sceolon healdan on mycelre eadmodnysse and on myclum geþylde and on soðre lufe and on eallre clænnesse lichoman and sawle and on godum wæccum and nytwyrðum and on fæstenum and on halgum gebedum and on ælmesdædum and on eallre godnesse and on lufe Godes and manna.

Vercelli XIX, Scragg (Szarmach 70, 54-55); cf. content of Latin 4 seq.

Manegum haligum mannum þas gangdagas syndon wiðmetene, ac us is lang þæt eall to gereccanne.

N.B. V XIX S.70,48-49, regards Rogationtide as 4 days (including Ascension Day).

SOURCES FOR LATIN

No sources have been identified except for obvious reference to Scriptural story.

potentia ascendit, et multos secum educens ad dexteram dei patris, sedit per

diuinitatem in excelsis. Ita nos per ieiunium et orationem et aelymosinam et

alia bona opera quę in his diebus agimus, ab omnibus abluimur peccatis, et ad

deum in mansionibus regni caelestis absque macula transferimur. Et iterum

25 comparantur quattuor aeuangelistis qui humanitatem Christi et diuinitatem

eius in quantum potuerunt dulci sermone narrauerunt, per totum mundum

predicantes. Et iterum comparantur cruci in qua saluator mundi pependit

pro salute humani generis, quia sicut diabolus, humani generis inimicus, per

crucem Christi iugulatus est et damnatus, ita his quattuor diebus per

30 inuocationem dei nominis in helymosinis et ieiuniis et orationibus ab omnibus

depellitur Christianis.

Sciendum est quoque, fratres karissimi, quod isti quattuor dies habent

nomina, id est, Rogationes et Triduanas et Lętanias et Ascensionem domini.

Et ideo Rogationes dicuntur eo quod rogauit dominus Ionam prophetam ut iret

35 in Niniuen ciuitatem magnam ad predicandum in ea et ad conuertendum

populum eius, ignorantem deum. Ionas autem non ausus est ire ad eam;

putabat enim quod nolebant conuerti ad deum propter iniquitates et

impietates suas, et ipsa ciuitas quadraginta adhuc dies habebat in spatium

84v / 84v /et tamen massa ignea iam supra eam in nube pendebat ut succenderet

40 eam si non relinqueret prauitatem suam, quia dominus iratus erat ualde

---

21. P, J, R: sedit; B: sedet. 27. R ends at: predicantes. 28. B omits: humani
generis, after: salute. 30. B, J omit: nominis. 36. J: ignorante domino.

Vercelli XIX, Scragg (Szarmach 71, 84-89); cf. Latin 34-40.

Uton nu gehealdan georne þis fæsten, neah þam þe hit awriten is on
haligum bocum þæt þa fæston þe þurh þæs witigan lare to Gode gecyrdon, and
þæt fæsten swa fæston swa him wisode se [witega se] wæs haten Ionas.   Be
ðam is on bocum awriten þæt God þurh haligne gast hine het faran to sumere
mærre ceastre seo wæs Niniue haten, and þær sceolde bodigean Godes bebodu.
Ac for þam þe ðæt folc wæs awyrged and æbreca, he him swiðe ondred and
þæder faran ne dorste.   For ðam þe God wæs swiðe yrre þære ceasterleode,

contra eam.

Quam ob rem Ionas putans latere posse a conspectu domini fugere uoluit et, inueniens nautas nauigantes ad aliam regionem, rogauit eos ut secum ducerent eum, dantem eis nabulum. Triduanae autem ideo dicuntur eo quod, introeunte Iona propheta in nauem, emisit deus pluuiam magnam et uentum ualidum et procellam acerbissimam in mare, ita ut ipsa nauis nec ante nec retro propter Ionæ inoboedientiam natare poterat. Qua propter nautae, timentes timore magno, miserunt sortem ut scirent de cuius reatu hęc acciderant, et cecidit sors super Ionam prophetam, in pupe nauis dormientem. Et ammirati sunt quod cecidisset sors super seruum dei et a somno suscitantes eum narrauerunt ei hęc omnia. Et ipse iam, intelligens presentiam domini effugere nullo modo posse, permisit se mitti in mare et ipsi cito miserunt eum. Et ingens coetus, uelociter ueniens, glutiuit eum et fuit in uentre eius tribus diebus et tribus noctibus. Et postea, deo gubernante, depulsus est in patriam, ad quam mittebat eum dominus, et euomuit eum uiuum super ripam maris (cf. Jonas caps. 1&2).

Et ipse quidem intrauit Niniuen, ciuitatem magnam itinere dierum trium, et predicauit in ea ita ut ipse rex, una cum exercitu suo, in deum caeli toto crederet corde, et ieiunium dierum trium a maiore usque ad minorem esse preciperet, et surgens de solio suo et abiciens a se uestimentum suum regale,

---

45 . P , J: emisit; B: misit . 51. J omits: iam . 52 . P , B: domini; J: dei .
52 . P , J: mitti; B: mittere . 55 . P , B: ad quam; J: ad quod . 57 . P: intrauit; J: in; B: intrauit in .

Vercelli XIX, Scragg (Szarmach 71, 89-104); cf. Latin 42-57.

ða wolde [he] for þi Godes bebodu forfleon. Ac him com to cyððe þæt [he] hie forfleon ne meahte. He þeah on fleame wæs, oð he to sæ becwom, and him þær scip gebohte, and mid þam scipmannum him þohte ofer sæ to seglgenne. Ac he ne mihte, swa he gemynt hæfde, Godes willan forfleon. Ac sona swa he wæs in agan on þæt scyp, þa gereste he hine on anum ende, and þa sona swa þa menn þe on þam scipe wæron ut on þære sæs dypan gesegled hæfdon, þa onsende God mycelne ren and strangne wind and grimme yste on þa sæ, swa þæt þæt scip ne mihte naþer ne forð swymman ne underbæc, for unhyrsumnesse þæs witigan þe Ionas wæs haten. Þa for þam þa ondredon þa scipmen him swiðe þearle, hluton him þa betwynan for hwylces hiera gyltum him swa getimod wære. And þa behluton hie hit sona to Iona[m] þam witigan, and he his nan þing nyste. Ða wundrodon hie sona þæt se hlyt ofer þone Godes þegn gefeoll. Awrehton hine þa of slæpe and rehton hit him eall, and he þafode þæt hine man wearp ut on þa sæ, þa he ongiten hæfde þæt he nahwar God forfleon [ne] meahte, and hie him fore gebædon. And hine sona an mycel hwæll forswealh, and he wæs on him þry dagas and .iii. niht and syððan, eal swa hit God wolde, seo sæ þone fisc ferede oð he com to þam ilcan eðle þe he ær on bodian sceolde, se witega, and hine þærut of him aspaw ofer þære sæstaðe.

Vercelli XIX, Scragg (Szarmach 71, 105-108); cf. Latin 58-60.

And he ða sona on þreora daga fyrste þurhfor þa mæran and þa myclan burh, and bodode on þære Godes bebodu, swa þæt se cyng þære ceasterware mid hire on God gelyfde on eallre heortan, and he bebead þæt hie ealle fram þam yldestan oð þone gingestan þreora daga fæsten healdan sceoldon. And he aras of his cynesetle and him fram his cynereaf ofawearp

85r et induens se sacco et sedens / 85r / in cinere, clamauit et dixit: Homines et

iumenta, boues et peccora non gustent quicquam nec pascantur et aquam non

bibant. Et operiantur saccis homines et iumenta clament ad dominum in

fortitudine, et conuertatur uir a uia sua mala et ab iniquitate, que est in

65   manibus eorum.   Qui[s] scit si conuertatur et ignoscat deus et reuertatur a

furore irę suę et non peribimus?   Et uidit deus opera eorum, quia conuersi

sunt de uia sua mala, et misertus est populo suo dominus deus noster. Et sic

tota ciuitas, ab omni plaga quę in ea futura erat per predicationem Ionae

prophetę, cunctis ad deum toto corde clamantibus et man[ibus] ad caelum

70   extendentibus, salua facta est (cf. Jonas cap. 3).

Hęc itaque, fratres karissimi, in omni angustia tribulationum nostrarum

imitari debemus, incipientes a principibus quorum iniquitate corruit populus

et quorum iterum ęquitate aedificatur patria et quorum clementia roboratur

regnum ut simul ab omnibus saluemur peccatis. Laetanię uero ideo dicuntur

75   quia grandis lętitia est populum fidelem in unum audire dei precepta et

relinquere mala et unanimiter ad aecclesiam uenire et deum colere et

diligere et eius mandata seruare et sequi, nudis uestigiis, reliquias sanctorum

cum magna humilitate.

Hoc quoque intelligendum est, fratres karissimi, quod in his iiiior diebus

80   nulla opera mundialia facere, sed ieiunare et orare et aelimosinam dare et

---

62-63. B omits: boues . . . iumenta. 64. B omits: uir. 65. P: qui; B, J:quis.
69. P, B: manus; J: manibus. 72. P, B: imitari; J: inimitari. 74. P, J: Laetanie,
Letanie; B: Letania. 74. B omits: uero ideo. 80. J omits: et orare.

Vercelli XIX, Scragg (Szarmach 71, 109-116); cf. Latin 61-70.

and hine mid hæran ymbscrydde and to Gode georne cleopode mid eallre þære burhware. And he bebead ærest þæt ægðer ge þa menn ge ealle þa nytenu þe hie ahton sceoldon þry dagas and þreo niht on an fæstan. And hie ða swa dydon, and him ða God his mildheortnesse [for]geaf and him fram þæt fyrene clyne adyde þe ofer þa ceastre wæs on þam genipe hangiende, þæt sceolde forniman ealle þa burhware and forbærnan binnan feowertigum dagum butan hie to Gode gecyrran woldon. Ac hie dydon swa him to donne wæs, gecyrdon to Gode ælmihtigum, and he him sona his mildheortnesse forgeaf, swa he symle deð ælcum þara þe he ongyt þæt him on eallum mode to gecyrreð.

N.B. For the 'fyrene clyne' 'þe ofer þa ceastre wæs on þam genipe hangiende', cf. Latin 1.39: massa ignea iam supra eam in nube pendebat.

pacem a deo petere homines fideles debere. Ideo autem ascensiones domini dicuntur, quia dominus noster Iesus Christus, post magnam uictoriam et

85v postquam alligauerat / 85v / diabolum in infernum deorsum, uidentibus apostolis de monte Oliueti ascendit in caelum et sedit ad dexteram dei patris

85 omnipotentis, inde uenturus iudicare uiuos ac mortuos, id est, iustos et peccatores, in cuius dextrali parte nos, in die iudicii collocati, caelestium bonorum mereamur esse consortes, eodem domino nostro Iesu Christo donante, cuius oboedientia redemti sumus; cui est honor et imperium et potestas una cum patre et spiritu sancto per infinita secula seculorum. Amen.

---

83. J omits: et postquam. 84. P, J: sedit; B:sedet. 85. P, J: ac; B: et. 87. J omits: esse. 88. P, B: cui; J: cuius.

Item 40 fol. 91r XXXVIIII. Item alia.

Oportet nos, fratres dilectissimi, annuntiare uobis quomodo dies
sanctificati ac uenerabiles sunt, in quibus a uitiis et peccatis possumus nos
mundare si cum bono animo et bona uoluntate hoc ieiunium uoluerimus
implere, non solum autem abstinentia carnis, sed etiam ab omnibus uitiis.
5   Quid enim proficit ieiunare et abstinere a carne et uino nisi cessemus a uitiis
et peccatis?

Nos enim legimus quia dominus per spiritum sanctum iussit Ion[e]
prophete populo Nineuitarum prędicare; sed, quia ipse populus impius et
sacrilegus erat et malignus, timuit illuc ire, sed iterum ammonitus est per
10   spiritum sanctum, et perrexit in Nineuen ciuitatem magnam, et tunc
91v   predicauit ibi quod a domino iam dictum erat quod / 91v / ciuitatem et
populum illum post dies .xl. perderet et deleret de terra propter eorum
malitiam. Sed mox ut audiuit rex uerbum domini per prophetam, uestiuit se
cilicio, et sedit in cynere, et iussit populum suum ita indui ut illis tribus
15   diebus nec homines, nec iumenta, nec boues, nec pecora gustarent quicquam
nec pascerentur, et aquam ne biberent, et quando uidit deus tantam
afflictionem et tantam conpunctionem et eorum lacrimas, quia conuersi sunt
de uia sua mala, misertus est populo suo et dimisit illis peccata sua.

Aduertite ergo, fratres, si populus impius et idolis seruiens tam cito
20   potuit mitigare iram dei, quantomagis nos fideles Christi, qui de suo sumus

---

1. P, J: dilectissimi; B: karissimi. 1. P: quod modo; B, J: quomodo. 2. P, J:
possumus; B: possimus. 3. P, J: mundare; B: emundare. 4. J omits: etiam ab. 7. P,
B: enim;   J: autem. 7. P: Ionae; B, J: Ione. 9. P, J: ammonitus; B:
ammotus. 16. P, J: pascerentur; B: pascentur. 16. P: ne; B, J: non.

SOURCES FOR LATIN

No sources have been identified except for scriptural references.

sanguine redempti et sui sumus filii uocati, poterimus ab eo impetrare ut dimittat nobis peccata [no]stra, si bono animo istud triduanum ieiunium impleuerimus. Cognoscat ergo unusquisque Christianus pro certo quia quando famis aut mortalitas hominum siue peccorum, siue siccitas aut nimia

25   pluuia, siue tempestas aut qualiscumque tribulatio, uel persecutio a malis hominibus fiunt, non de alia parte ueniunt super nos nisi propter nostra peccata, quia precepta dei non custodimus. Propter hoc autem mittit deus in nos flagella, non ut pereamus sed ut conuertamur ad eum et emundemur, quia omnipotens deus nullam rem sub cęlo tantum amat quantum animas

30   hominum. Ideo dixit Iesus in euangelio: Nolo mortem peccatoris sed ut magis conuertatur a culpa et uiuat (cf. Ezekiel 18,32; 33,11).   Isti igitur dies sanctificati sunt per ieiunium triduanum ante ascensionem domini nostri Iesu Christi, sicut illi tres dies quadragesimæ ante pascha; sed illi tres dies

92r   tristitiam passionis Christi significant / 92r /,   isti uero letitiam
35   resurrectionis et gloriose ascensionis eius ad cęlum nobis demonstrant.

Multi autem homines querunt quare istis tribus diebus in hoc tempore ieiunamus. Nos enim legimus quod a sancto Mamerto, Uienensium ciuitatis ępiscopo, hęc consuetudo primum initiata est quoniam in eius tempore mortalitatem magnam populus suus pertulit, et infirmitas grauissima super

40   suam plebem euenit, et talis fuit illa mortalitas ut illi homines qui illos

---

22. P: uestra; B, J: nostra. 27. P, B: quia; J: qui. 28. P, J: conuertamur; B: reuertamur. 30. J omits: Iesus; B: dominus. 32. J omits: sunt. 33. B omits: dies. 37. P, J: enim; B: autem. 37. P: uienensium;   B: uienentium; J: uienentii. 40. P, J: suam; B: suum. 40. B omits: ut illi homines qui illos mortuos; inserts as correction at bottom margin: quod uiuentes qui corpora mortuorum.

Vercelli XIX, Scragg (Szarmach 71, 117-120); cf. Latin 37-40.

Eac we ræddon on halegum bocum þæt on sumere ceastre þe wæs Uienna
haten, on þære wæs sum bisceop se wæs nemned Mamertus.   Be ðam is
awriten þæt ðæt folc þe he bewiste wearð þearle mid færlicum deaðe
fornumen, and swa mycel wearð seo untrumnes and se færlica deað ofer eall
þæt folc þe [he] bewiste þæt [þa]

mortuos ad sepulturam portabant aut super sepulchrum aut in uia mortui, cadebant.   Ideoque supradictus Mamertus sanctus episcopus rogauit uenire omnes uicinos episcopos qui in Gallia illo tempore erant, et uoce lacrimabili ad illos dixit: Ieiunemus ergo, fratres, ut discedat a nobis hǫc mortalitas,

45   quia si deus omnipotens illo populo Nineuitarum, qui idolis seruiebat, per ieiunium et orationem et lacrimas et gemitum misertus est, quantomagis nobis, qui Christiani sumus, et in baptismo diabolo et omnibus pompis et operibus eius rennuimus, et deum patrem omnipotentem et filium et spiritum sanctum credimus, miserebitur et dimittet crimina et facinora nostra.   Et

50   statim ut illi episcopi et ille populus hoc ieiunium, cum bono animo, unanimiter impleuerunt, ira dei et omnis mortalitas ab ipso populo discessit, et recuperata est sanitas in eis.   Propter hanc causam illi sancti patres in unum constituerunt ut in isto tempore tribus diebus omnis populus Christianus in partibus Galliarum hoc ieiunium cum humilitate et oratione et aelymosinis

55   cǫlebrarent.

Et ideo rogo et ammoneo uos, fideles Christi, ut in istis diebus ieiunium et orationem et aelymosinam, cum bona uoluntate, adimplere faciatis, et a cybo uel potu usque ad horam nonam abstineatis, nisi quem i[n]firmitas

59   ieiunare non permittit.   Discamus ergo humilitatem per quam deo

92v   appropinqua[re] possumus, / 92v / ante deum nos humiliemus ut in nobis

---

41. P: mortuos; J: homines. 46. J omits: est. 57. P, B: orationem; J: orationibus. 58. B adds: a, before: potu. 58. P: imfirmitas; B, J: infirmitas. 60. P: appropinquaque; B, J: appropinquare. 60. P, B: possumus; J: possimus. 60. P, J: ut; B: et.

Vercelli XIX, Scragg (Szarmach 71, 120- 72, 129); cf. Latin 41-54.

þe oðre to eorðan bæron þæt sume hie feollon deade ofer þæs deadan byrgenne þe hie þonne byrgdon and sume hamweard be wege forðferdon, swa þæt nan þara þe oðerne to eorðan bær ham mid þam life ne com. Þa bæd se bisceop Mamertus ealle þa bisceopas þe on ðam earde wæron mid wependre stefne þæt hie ealle and hira folc þry dagas fæston and bædon hira dryhten þæt hie ealle alysde fram þam myclan and þam færlican deaðe. And hie ða ealle swa dydon, and gesetton þa him betwinan þæt man a syððan sceolde þas þry gangdagas healdan fullice mid fæstenum and mid ælmessylenum and mid cyricsocnum and mid eadmodlicum gange and mid reliquiasocnum and mid eallum godum weorcum. And hie sona æt Gode geearnodon ece hæle and þæs færlican deaþes afyrrednesse.

habitet dei uirtus. Respuamus superbiam quia per illam mirabilis angelorum creatura cedidit de cẹlo sicut scriptum est: Deus superbis resistit, humilibus autem dat gratiam (cf. James 4,6; I Peter 5,5). Timeo autem, fratres, et dolet me quia multos in uobis uideo, tam uiros quam feminas, qui istos dies

65   non pro humilitate sed propter uanam gloriam et superbiam colunt, quia quantum plus pretiosa uestimenta habere possunt, semetipsos ornant et induunt se, et diliciosa sibi conuiuia prepar[a]nt, et ebrietatem sectantur, et non pro dei timore nec amore, sed pro sua misera exaltatione, in unum conueniunt, et dum plus debuerant sua peccata ieiunando, orando, et ad

70   aecclesiam ueniendo plangere, magis crescunt in sua misera exaltatione et uanitatibus huius mundi.   Tale enim ieiunium reprobat deus sicut per prophetam dicit: In diebus ieiunii uestri inuenietur uoluntas uestra, et omnes debitores uestros repetitis (cf. Isaias 58.3).   Quale autem ieiunium diligit?   Iterum per prophetam dicit: Hoc est magis ieiunium quod elegi (cf.

75   Isaias 58,6): Frange esurienti panem tuum, et egenos uagosque induc in domum tuam; si uideris nudum, uesti eum, et carnem tuam ne despexeris (cf. Isaias, 58,7). Et si uideris uiduas et orfanos oppressos a malis hominibus in quantum potes adiuua eos et defende, et mortuos sepeli, et infirmos uel in carcere positos uisita, et de bonis tuis eos refice.   Et si tunc clamaueris ad

80   dominum exaudiet te deus et dicet tibi: Iuxta te sum (cf. Isaias 58,9);

---

61. P, J: respuamus; B: respuemus.   66. P, B: semetipsos; J: semper ipsos.   67. P, J: induunt; B: induant.   67. P: preparent;   B, J: preparant.   68. J omits: timore nec.   68. P, J: misera; B: miseria.   70. B omits: misera.   71. P, J: enim; B:autem?. 72. P, J: uoluntas; B: uoluptas.   74. B omits: magis.   76. P, B: uesti; J: operi; Isaias: operi.   79. B omits: eos.

quoniam misericors est dominus deus supplicantibus et diligentibus se quibus promisit claritatem ęternam.   Rogationes autem ideo dicuntur quia illis diebus debet unusquisque homo rogare deum ut dimittat illi peccata commis[s]a.   Caueat autem ne falsum iudicium propter aurum et argentum

85 iudicet licet rogando dimittat illi deus peccat[um] quia scriptum est: In quo enim iudicio iudicaueritis iudicabitur de uobis (cf. Matthew 7,2) quoniam qui misericors non fuerit ipse misericordiam non consequetur (cf. Matthew 5,7),

93r et qui / 93r / bene iudicauerit in hoc seculo, melius iudicabitur de illo in uita eterna.   Sic et rapaces caueant, qui res alienas per malum ingenium et per

90 potestatem tollunt, quia in infernum sine fine cruciabuntur.   Periurium nullus faciat quia scriptum est: Periurii et rapaces regnum dei non possidebunt (cf. I Corinthians 6,10). Furtum nullus presumat facere, quia fures et latrones deus non amat.   Homicidium nullus homo presumat facere, quia maximum et primum peccatum est sicut scriptum est: Cain, primus homicida, per inuidiam

95 occidit Abel fratrem suum, et qui illud facit non uenit ad poenitentiam nisi ieiunando et plorando et abstinendo grandi abstinentia et pleniter pęnitendo. Adulterium fugite quia scriptum est: Adulteros deus iudicat (cf. Hebrews 13,4).   Cauent potentes huius seculi quod scriptum est: Quia potentes potenter tormenta patientur (cf. Sapientia 6,7). Considerate autem omnes

100 communiter. Ubi sunt parentes uestri quos aliquando habuistis in hoc

---

82. J omits: eternam. 84. P: commisa; B, J: commissa. 85. P: peccatis; B, J: peccatum. 88. P, J: de illo; B: illi. 88. P, B: uita eterna; J: uitam eternam. 90. P, B: infernum; J: inferno, after correction. 91. P underpoints a second: faciat, after: quia. 91. P, J: periurii; B periuri. 94. P: Cain; B: Caym; J: Caim. 96. B adds: orando, after: ieiunando. 98. P, B: quod;   J: sicut. 99. P: patientur; J: pacientur; B: patiuntur.

seculo, et nunc non apparent, et si bona non fecerunt in uita sua, in infernum cum diabolo et sociis eius cruciantur?   Quid illis adiuuat purpura aut diuitiae temporales aut aurum aut argentum uel res pauperum quas per malum ingenium et potentiam tulerunt?   Quid illis adiuuat eorum superbia

105 aut luxoriosa conuiuia uel crassitudo et pulchritudines aut possessiones uel diuitiᶒ huius seculi? Numquid cum illis in infernum descenderunt?   Non quidem, sed hᶒc omnia in hoc seculo dimiserunt, et ipsi sine ulla consolatione cruciantur in flammam ignis.

　　　Ideo rogo et ammoneo uos, fratres karissimi, ut in istis diebus ad

110 aecclesiam dei ueniatis cum omni humilitate et mansuetudine, cum reuerentia et suauitate ieiunantes et orantes, ut pius et misericors deus nobis et uobis pacem pariter tribuat.   Famem a nobis tollat;   infirmitates et egrotationes auferat;   pluuiam, quando necesse fuerit, donet;   serenitatem

93v cᶒli donare dignetur;   peccata dimittat; / 93v / crimina indulgeat; reᶜ[s] et

115 peccatores ab omni uinculo peccatorum absoluat;   omnes iniquitates deponat; fidem rectam confirmet;   spem certam fideliter sperare faciat;   iustitiam amplificet; castitatem mentis et corporis concedat;   omniumque bonorum operum in nobis uirtutem inmittat;   supra haec autem omnia caritatem perfectam in cordibus nostris perfundat,   prestante domino nostro Iesu

120 Christo qui cum eo et spiritu sancto uiuit et regnat per infinita secula seculorum. Amen.

---

102. J: angelis, underpointed to delete before: sociis. 102. P, B: eius;   J: suis. 105. P: luxoriosa; B: luxuriosa; J: luxuria. 107. P, B: ipsi sine ulla; so J after correction. 110. B omits: omni. 114. P: reo; B, J: reos. 116. P, B: sperare; J: spirare. 118. P, B: uirtutem;   J: unitatem. 118.   J adds: habentem before: caritatem. 119. P, B: nostris, J: uestris.

Extracts.

1. Item 38 fol.87v XXXVII Alia in iiii feria in Letania Maiore.

Extract fol.88r ll.17-24:-

Consurget enim ille cum sua infidelitate, tu autem surge cum fide; ille pugnat
superbia, tu humilitate; ille exhibet luxuriam, tu castitatem; approhendit (B, J:
apprehendit) ille nequitiam, tu tene iustitiam; ille ingerit iracundiam, tu
sectare patientiam; ille inmittit auaritiam, tu exerce misericordiam; ille
ammonet gulam, tu contine abstinentiam.

Source: Caesarius 207.1 (Morin, II 829):-

Consurgit ille cum infidelitate, tu surge cum fide; ille pugnat cum superbia, tu
cum humilitate; ille exhibet luxuriam, tu retine castitatem; adprehendit ille
nequitiam, tu iustitiam tene; ille ingerit iracundiam, tu sectare patientiam; ille
inmittit avaritiam, tu exerce misericordiam; ille gulam, tu abstinentiam; ille
malitiam, tu bonitatem.

Vercelli XIX, Scragg (Szarmach, 70, 56-61):-

Se deofol dæges and nihtes winnð ongean us mid his geleafleste; uton we winnan
ongean hine mid geleaffulnesse. He winnð mid ofermodnesse; uton we ongean
mid eaðmodnesse. He us gegearwað galnesse; uton we ongean clænnesse. He
gegripð manfulnesse; uton we ongean rihtwisnesse. He us on bebringeð
yrsunge; uton we fylgean geþylde. He us on asent gytsunge; uton we began
mildheortnesse. He us myngað to gifernesse; uton þær ongean gehealdan
forhæfednesse.

N.B. Where Caesarius and P25 <u>differ</u> at Caesarius: ille gulam, tu abstinentiam.
P25: ille ammonet gulam, tu contine abstinentiam.
V XIX reads: He us myngað to gifernesse; uton þær ongean gehealdan
forhæfednesse.

Extract fol.88v ll.24-28:-

Credimus enim quod uos uelut apes prudentissimas (B, J: prudentissime) ad aluearium suum uoluntarie festinatis (J: festinetis) ad aecclesiam dei ut dulcedinem spiritalis mellis ex diuinis lectionibus fideliter pergustetis.

Source:-   Caesarius 207.2 (Morin, II 829-30):-

Magis enim de vestra devotione confidens credo vos velud apes prudentissimas
ad alvearium Christi fideliter festinare, ut dulcedinem spiritalis mellis ex divinis
lectionibus possitis accipere.

Vercelli XIX, Scragg (Szarmach, 70, 62-64):-

Eall we sceolon efestan to Godes templum swa swiðe swa ða bion doð to hira hyfe, to þam þæt we magon getreowlice onbyrgean þa swetnesse þæs gastlican huniges of ðam godcundum rædingum (variant: larum).

N.B. Where Caesarius and P25 <u>differ</u> at Caesarius: ex divinis lectionibus possitis accipere.

P25: ex diuinis lectionibus fideliter pergustetis.

V XIX reads: we magon getreowlice onbyrgean...of ðam godcundan rædingum.

2.   Item 1 fol.3r   I.   Incipit omelia in quarta dominica ante natale domini.

Extract fol.3r ll.2-10:-

Primum omnivm oportet nos memorari (B: memorare), fratres karissimi, et recitare de deo ueraciter, et loqui caeli ac terrae conditore et omnium que in eis sunt, quem trinum in personis credere debemus;   alia est enim persona patris, alia filii, alia spiritus sancti, et unum in maiestate et in potestate et diuinitate, confiteri.   Deus est enim pater, deus filius, deus et (R omits: et) spiritus sanctus.   Non tres tamen depromimus sed unum deum dicimus et fatemur, quia in hac trinitate nihil prius aut posterius, nihil maius aut minus, sed totę tres personę coeternae sibi sunt et coaequales.

Extract fol.3v ll.4-6:-

...a quo omnia, per quem omnia, in quo (B: quem) omnia, facta sunt, uisibilia et inuisibilia, quę nullus mortalium per omnia edicere ualet.

Vercelli XIX, Scragg (Szarmach 69, 1-9):-

Men ða leofestan, us gedafenaþ ærest þæt we gemunen and gereccen be Gode ælmihtigum, þe geworhte heofonas and eorðan and ealle gesceafta, þone we sculon gelyfan þrynlicne on hadum and anlicne on spede; oðer is soðlice se had ælmihtiges fæder, oðer is ælmihtiges suna, oðer ys ælmihtiges haliges gastes. And þeahhwæðere we sceolon andettan anne God on mægenþrymme and on mihte and on godcundnesse for þam se fæder ys ece God and se sunu is ece God and se haliga gast ys ece God.   Ealle þry, se fæder and se sunu and se haliga gast, wæron æfre efenece and æfre beoð, and hie þry an God syndon. Fram þam, [and] þurh þæne and on þam syndon geworhte ealle þa þinc þe gesewene syndon and ealle þa þe ungesewene syndon, þa ne mæg nan eorþlic man ealle asecgan.

3.   Item 30 fol. 65v XXVIIII . Omelia in Parasceuen de Passione Domini.

Extract fol. 67r ll.6-16:-

Dixit quoque deus: Ecce Adam quasi unus ex nobis factus est, sciens bonum et malum. Videte ne forte sumat de ligno uitae (B, J add: et comedat) et uiuat in aeternum (cf. Genesis 3,22). Eiecit ergo dominus deus Adam de paradyso ut operaretur terram de qua factus est et collocauit eum ante paradysum uoluptatis (cf. Genesis 3, 23). Quandiu enim abstinuit mansit in paradyso, ut autem manducauit statim expulsus est. Et factum est omne tempus quo uixit Adam in labore et erumna super terram anni .d cccc.xxx. et mortuus est (cf. Genesis 5,5) et descendit in infernum et omne humanum genus post illum N.B. Quandiu... illum, almost verbatim as fol. 3v usque ad aduentum domini.

Item 34 fol. 79v XXXIII . Item alia de Resurrectione Domini.

Extract fol. 80r ll.7-10:-

Inde (Christ at Harrowing of Hell) eripuit primum hominem Adam qui per quinque milia ducentos uiginti et octo annos propter suas culpas in infernum (J: inferno) detinebatur.

Vercelli XIX, Scragg (Szarmach 70, 35-39):-

Ac hit him wearð biterlice forgolden on hyra life ge eac æfter, ægðer ge him ge eallum mancynne þe him fram cwom, oð ures drihtnes tocyme. Nigon hund wintra and þritig wintra Adam lifde on þisse worulde on geswince and on yrmþe, and syððan to helle for, and þær grimme witu þolode fif þusend wintra and [twa hund wintra and]eahta and .xx. wintra.

4.   Item 42 fol.95v XLII. Item alia in eodem die (in Ascensione Domini).

Extract fol. 96v l.28-97r l.4:-

...ubi premium perpetuum, ubi manna celeste, (B adds: ubi) uita sine morte, iuuentus / 97r / sine senectute, lux sine tenebris, gaudium sine tristitia, pax sine discordia, securitas semper uiuendi sine timore mortis...ubi est beatitudo angelica et felicitas perpetua.

Vercelli XIX, Scragg (Szarmach 72, 136-138):-

þær is ece med, and þær is lif butan deaðe and geoguð butan ylde and leoht butan þystrum and gefea butan unrotnesse and sybb butan ungeþwærnesse and orsorhnes butan deaþes ege to lybbenne, and þær is ece gesælignesse...

Vercelli XX

Many years ago, within his survey of the Vercelli Book, Max Förster (Morsbach Festschrift pp.81-82) briefly noted the source for the body of this sermon as Alcuin De Virt. caps. 27-34 (recte 35), and, accepting this identification, Bazire-Cross (pp.25-26) commented on the relationship of the vernacular text with Alcuin's tract, there with reference to their own line-numbering, but equating Szarmach's edition (1.50-G 1.33) which will be noted here. The facing Latin and Old English texts below now illustrate clearly however that a text of Pembroke item 93 was the immediate source for the section of Vercelli XX. The presentation of the Latin text of this Pembroke item notes readings from the other full text of the sermon in Balliol 240 (B) and, where possible, from the abbreviated and selective text in Grenoble 278 (470) (G), together with some readings from Alcuin's tract (A) as printed only in Migne's Patrologia Latina.

Some points, however, should be made to confirm or correct the earlier comments of Bazire-Cross (pp.25-26), and to illustrate the connection. There Bazire-Cross noted examples of the Anglo-Saxon's excellent Latinity. For the gerundial forms there illustrated Vercelli XX now closely translates the Pembroke item e.g. on avarice: 'seo is swiðlic grædignes, ægðer ge welan to hæbbenne ge to gehealdenne' (ll.70-71), cf. est nimia cupiditas habendi uel tenendi diuitias (ll.29-30) (Pembroke and Vercelli XX omit Alcuin's acquirendi, cap. 30); on anger: 'grædignes teonan to wr[e]canne' (Szarmach 1.79 reading: wyrcanne (MS.) for: wr[e]canne), cf. cupiditas ulciscendi iniuriam (1.37) (an adaptation of Alcuin, cap. 31: ulciscendi cupiditas, injuriarum memoria). The technical word tumor (1.36) and unusual word abrupta (1.43), accurately translated by the author of Vercelli XX (ll.78 and 85 respectively), are taken directly from Alcuin into the Pembroke item (Bazire-Cross p.26).

Perhaps more interesting, however, were the comments made by Bazire-Cross (p.26) to indicate that the original Anglo-Saxon did not use 'a Latin sequence of words which correspond exactly to those in the edition of Migne's Patrologia Latina'. The examples there chosen now identify the use of the intermediary. Differences from Alcuin in PL were noted: fornication was overcome 'þurh soðe lufe' (1.68), not per castitatem (Alcuin, cap. 29), but now per caritatem (Pembroke 1.27, and all manuscripts); the cardinal virtue, fortitude, is described as 'micel miht þæs modes' (1. G 23) not magna animi patientia (Alcuin, cap. 35), but now magna animi potentia (Pembroke 1.87 etc.). There also appeared to be a different sequence of words from those of Alcuin to define virtus in the Old English, in which adjectives qualified different nouns. Now compare a text, punctuated as in P, B, with the Old English, in contrast with Alcuin, cap. 35:

Pembroke 11.78-80:

> quid sit uirtus animi, habitus nature, decus uite, ratio morum, pietas cultus diuinitatis, honor hominis, (B: meritum) eternae beatitudinis.

Vercelli XX:

> þæs modes mægen is se gyrla þæs gecyndes and seo arfæstnys þæs lifes and þæt gescead þæra þeawa and seo arfæstnys and se biggeng þære godcundnysse and se wurþmynt þæs mannes and seo geearnung þære ecan eadignysse. (11. G 14-17, but the text as Scragg below).

Alcuin cap. 35:

> Virtus est animi habitus, naturae decus, vitae ratio, morum pietas, cultus divinitatis, honor hominis, aeternae beatitudinis meritum.

One speculation by Bazire-Cross (p.26) is now inaccurate. On vainglory, Vercelli XX says: 'of ðyses leahtres wyrttrum byð acenned . . .' (1.103) but Alcuin, cap. 34 has: ex cujus vitii radice . . . germinare videntur. Bazire-Cross assumed a scribal error for the Latin germinare and proposed generare, little suspecting a thorough adaptation and substitution as in Pembroke 1.62: ex huius autem uitii radice nascitur.

Another definable source for Vercelli XX was brilliantly forecast by Joan Turville-Petre (Traditio 19 (1963), pp.51-78) when she postulated 'a lost penitential homily' as a Latin source, from an analysis of vernacular derivatives, including Vercelli homily III (see item 22 of the collection in the list of sources), and referred also (p.56, and variously within the paper) to Vercelli XX. Although the Latin item 22 had not yet been found and printed by Helen Spencer (Mediaeval Studies 44 (1982), pp.283-291) Bazire-Cross indicated 'a probably single Latin source' (p.26) for what is now Szarmach ll.29-45 and Bazire-Cross pp.32 l.35-33 l.1. The passages from the source, Pembroke item 22, are printed below as Extract 1, with note of differences from the ultimate Latin source, the Collectio Canonum Hibernensis (but, admittedly, in the insufficient modern edition) and placed facing the Old English passages from Vercelli XX. The only extra point to note is the indication there that the composers of Vercelli III and XX drew independently on the Latin sermon in the Pembroke-type collection.

Bazire-Cross (p.27) also noted 'a small linking passage between the extract on fasting and almsgiving and the extracts on the sins' (Szarmach, ll.46-49). This now derives from the opening words of Pembroke item 93, as printed below. And taking up a hint from Turville-Petre, Bazire-Cross (p.27) also illustrated echo of ideas found in Caesarius of Arles Sermo 207, although many of these ideas could be found elsewhere in presentations of the Rogationtide observances. We should now recall that Caesarius 207 would be the most easily available source for a composer already using the Pembroke-type collection since that sermon is the base for item 38.

There may now be more contacts between Vercelli XX and other items in the Pembroke-type collection. Bazire-Cross (p.28) referred to 'a reminiscence of the 'Joys of Heaven' motif' in the concluding lines of Vercelli XX. Four pairs of phrases presented in the 'x without y' formula, 'lif butan deaðe ... wlite butan awendednesse' (ll.112-113), equate such phrases in Pembroke item 25 fol.52v, within a longer passage from the Latin which was certainly translated for Vercelli XXI (Szarmach p.87 ll.204-208) and is printed as Extract 4 in illustration of Vercelli XXI below. But also a larger sequence in Vercelli XX, ll.110-114 ('nu we eaðe magon ... gaste'), which includes the phrases of the 'x without y' formula, is verbatim as Brotanek II fol. 169b ll.13-20 in Old English. The relationship between the Latin and the three Old English extracts, or the Old English sequences to one another, may become clearer when a full linguistic analysis and comparison is completed.

Finally, Donald Scragg has suggested to me that Vercelli XX ll.23-28, on giving of tithes, could have been adapted from a passage in Pembroke item 52 <u>Omelia in iiii</u>^{or} <u>Tempora</u>. Extract 2, printed below, demonstrates the similarity of idea and some echo of word, together with the near-citation of the same two Scriptural testimonies, from a collection known to the composer of Vercelli XX.

Clearly now Miss Bazire and I must now withdraw our statement (Bazire-Cross p.25) that Vercelli XIX and XX 'differ in attitude to their definable literary sources', and look forward to a full linguistic analysis which may indicate that the two sermons were written by the same man.

Item 93 fol. 173r XCIII. Predicatio bona de VIII vitiis idemque virtvtibus.

Precauere nos oportet semper, fratres karissimi, octo uitia principalia que assidue animas hominum iugulant, deum offendunt, et diabolo placent, atque ad infernum trahunt nisi cito subuenerit uera poenitentia dura atque perfecta.

5 Spiritale siquidem est primum uitium quod est superbia, de qua dicitur: Initium omnis peccati superbia (Ecclesiasticus 10,15), quae regina est omnium malorum, per quam angeli ceciderunt de caelo in demones, quae sepe fit ex contemptu mandatorum dei. Fit etiam, quando attollitur mens de operibus bonis dum meliorem se esse per haec aestimat aliis. Ex ipsa uero nascitur

10 omnis inoboedientia, et presumptio et contentio et heresis et arrogantia atque alia mala, sed haec omnia uera humilitas uincere potest.

Corporale est secundum uitium quod est gula, quae est intemperans cybi et potus uoluptas, per quam primi parentes humani generis paradisi felicitatem perdiderunt, et in hanc erumnosam uitam deiecti sunt; ubi omnis

15 homo per peccatum nascitur, per laborem uiuit, et per dolorem moritur. Que tribus modis regnare uidetur in homine, id est, dum homo horam canonicam et statutam gulae causa anticipare cupit, aut exquisitione cybos sibi preparari

173v iubet magis quam necessitas corporis, / 173v / uel sue qualitas persone exigat, vel si plus accipiat in edendo uel bibendo propter desiderium

20 intemperantie suae, quam sue proficiat saluti. De qua nascitur inepta

---

1. P, B: octo uitia principalia; G: de octo uiciis principalis. 2. P, G: iugulant; B: uigilant. 2. P: deum; B, G: deo. 3. P, B: subuenerit; G: superuenerit. 6. G omits: superbia. 6. G adds: et radix, after: est. 7. P, B, A: quam; G: quem. 7. P, B: in demones (not A); G: in demones uersi sunt. 7. P, B: quae sepe fit; G: que incipit; A: quae fit. 9. G omits: per haec. 9. P, G: uero; B: enim. 12. P, B, A: quam; G: quem. 15. P, B, A: per peccatum nascitur, per laborem uiuit; G: per laborem nascitur. 16. P, A: regnare; B: regenerare; G: erogare. 16. B inserts: ante, before: horam. 17. P, B, A: gulae; G: regule. 17. P, B, A: causa; G: cause. 17. P, G: preparari; B: prepari; A preparare. 18. P, B, A: qualitas; G: equalitas. 19. P, B, A: edendo; G: erendo. 20. P, G, A: quam; B omits.

Vercelli XX, Scragg (Szarmach 78, 46-49); cf. Latin 1-4.

Utan nu, men þa leofestan, georne ægðer began ætgædere, ge fæstenu ge ælmysdæda, and uton us georne scyldan wið þa ehta heafodleahtras þe singallice manna sawla wundiað and God geæbyliað and deoflu gegladiað and on helle gebringað ælcne þara þe hie oð hira ytemestan dagas begað.

Vercelli XX, Scragg (Szarmach 78, 50-55); cf. Latin 5-11.

Se forma heafodleahtor ys ofermodignes, seo ys gecweden cwen eallra yfela. Þurh ða feollon englas of heofonum on helle and to deoflum gewurdon. And heo ys gecweden angin ælcere synne, seo byð oft uppasprungen of f[o]rhogunge Godes beboda. And þonne þæt [mod] byð uppahafen be godum wurcum, þonne se mann wenð and teleð hyne sylfne rottran þonne oðerne. Of þære byð soðlice acenned ælc unhyrsumnes and geþristlæcung and geflit and gedwyld and gylp and oðere manega yfelu. Ac þas mæg seo soðe eadmodnes ealle oferswiðan.

Vercelli XX, Scragg (Szarmach 78, 56-62); cf. Latin 12-20.

Þonne ys se oðer heafodleahter gecweden gifernes, seo ys ungemetigende gewilnung ægðer ge ætes ge wætes. Þurh þa, þa forman magas mennesces cynnes forspildon heofona rices gesælignesse and wurdon aworpene on þis earmlice lif, on þam byð ælc mann þurh synne acenned, and þurh geswync he leofaþ, and þurh sar he swylt. Seo byð gesewen þrym gemetum on þam menn rixiende, þæt ys þonne þæt se man wile ær rihtre tide hys willon mete þicgan and dryncas drincan and mare lufað on ægðerum þara þonne hyt ænig gemet sie. Of þære bið acenned ungescead

---

SOURCES FOR LATIN

5-11.   Alcuin, De Virt. cap.27 (PL 101, col.633), with omissions and adaptation.
12-20.   Alcuin, cap.28, with omissions and adaptation.

l̦etitia, scurilitas, leuitas, uaniloquium, inmunditia corporis, instabilitas mentis, ebrietas, libido et alia mala qu̦e per ieiunia et abstinentiam optime uincuntur.

Tertium uitium est fornicatio qu̦e est omnis corporalis immunditia; de

25 qua nascitur c̦ecitas mentis, inconstantia oculorum atque corporum, ioca, petulantia, et omnis incontinentia, odium mandatorum dei, et neglegentia uitae futur̦e et alia multa, qu̦e tamen uincitur per caritatem et continentiam et recordationem ignis aeterni [et timorem presentie dei].

Quartum uitium est auaritia qu̦e est nimia cupiditas habendi uel tenendi

30 diuitias, pestis quidem inexplebilis est, sicut hydropicus, qui quanto plus bibit tanto plus illi sitis addita crescit, sic et auaritia quanto magis habet tanto plus disiderat.   Cuius genera sunt inuidia, furta, latrocinia, homicidia, mendacia, iniqua iudicia, contemptus ueritatis et caetera multa, quae uero uincitur per timorem dei et fraternam caritatem et per opera misericordie.

35 Quintum uitium est ira per quam nemo potest habere maturitatem consilii sui;   de qua pullulat tumor mentis, rixae, contumeliae, indignatio, blasphemia, sanguinis effusio, homicidia, cupiditas ulciscendi iniuriam, quae autem uincitur per patientiam et longanimitatem, et per rationem intellectualem, quam deus inserit mentibus hominum.

40 Sextum uitium est accidia qu̦e deo famulantibus multum nocet quia

---

22. P, B, A: ieiunia; G: ieiunium. 23. P, B: uincuntur; G: uincere potest; A: uincitur. 25. P, B, A: inconstantia; G: instantia. 26. P, B, A: neglegentia; G: neglegentie. 27. P, B, A: continentiam; G: largitatem. 28. B adds: et timorem presentie dei, after: aeterni; cf. A: et timorem praesentiae sempiterni Dei; G omits: et recordationem ... dei. 29-34. G omits section on auaritia. 29. B omits: uel tenendi. 30. P, A: inexplebilis; B: implebilis. 30. P, A: quanto; B: quando. 35. P, B, A: maturitatem; G: naturitatem. 36. P, B, A: pullulat; G: polluat. 37. P, B: blasphemia; A, G: blasphemiae, blasphemie. 38. P, A: rationem; B: orationem; G: racionalem. 39. G omits: hominum. 40. P, B, A: deo; G: dei.

Vercelli XX, Scragg (Szarmach 78, 62-64); cf. Latin 21-23.

bliss and sceandlicnes and leohtbrædnes and idel spræc and lichoman unclænnes and unstaðolfæstnes modes and druncenes and galnes and oðere manega yfelo unatellendlice. And þonne mæg seo beon selest oferswiðed þurh fæsteno and þurh forhæfednesse.

Vercelli XX, Scragg (Szarmach 78, 65-69); cf. Latin 24-28.

Þonne ys se þridda heafodleahter gecweden forlyr, þæt ys eall lichamlic unclænnes. Of ðam [þið] acenned modes blindnes and eagena unstaðulfæstnes and idele plegan and wrænnes and eall u[n]forhæfdnes and hatung Godes beboda and gymeleast þæs toweardan lifes and oðere manega. Þæt byð ðeahhwæðere oferswiðed þurh soðe lufe and þurh gehealdsumnesse and þurh gemynd þæs ecan fyres and þurh ege Godes andweardnesse.

Vercelli XX, Scragg (Szarmach 78-79, 70-76); cf. Latin 29-34.

Þonne ys se feorða heafodleahtor gecweden gytsung, seo is swiðlic grædignes, ægðer ge welan to hæbbenne ge to gehealdanne, and heo ys witodlice ungefyllendlic cwyld. Eall swa wæterseoc mann þam wyxt togeiht þurst þæs ðe swiðor þe he swiðor drincð, swa byð se gytsienda man swa he mare hæfð swa he mare gewilnað. Þære gytsunge cynnreno syndon anda and stala and sceaðunga and mannslihtas and leasunga and unrihtwise domas and soðfæstnesse forhogung and oðere manega yfelo. Seo byð soðlice oferswiðed þurh Godes ege and þurh [broðera] soðe lufe and þurh mildheortnesse wuruc.

Vercelli XX, Scragg (Szarmach 79, 77-81); cf. Latin 35-39.

Þonne ys se fifta heafodleahter gecweden yrre, þurh þæt ne mæg nan mann habban fullþungennesse hys geþeahtes. Of ðam sprytt modes toðundennes and saca and teonan and æbylgð and yfelsacung and blodes agotenes and mannsliht and grædignes teonan to wr[e]canne. Þæt byð soðlice oferswiðed þurh geðyld and þurh þolomodnesse and þurh andgytlic gescead ðe God onasæwð on manna modum.

Vercelli XX, Scragg (Szarmach 79, 82-83); cf. Latin 40.

Þonne ys se syxta heafodleahtor gecweden sleacnes, seo derað þearle foroft þam þe Gode þeowgean willað,

---

SOURCES FOR LATIN

21-23. Alcuin, cap.28.   24-28. Alcuin, cap.29 with omissions and adaptation.
29-34. Alcuin, cap.30 with omissions and adaptation.   35-39. Alcuin, cap.31 with omissions and adaptation.   40. Alcuin, cap.32 (PL 101, col.635) with omissions and adaptation.

mens otiosa per omnia discurrit.   Haec est enim que maxime monachos

174r   excutit de cellula in seculum, et de regulari conuer- / 174r / -satione eicit

eos in abrupta uitiorum.   De qua nascitur somnolentia, pigritia boni operis,

instabilitas loci, peruagatio de loco ad locum, murmuratio et inaniloquia et

45   alia multa.   Quae tamen uincitur per studium lectionis, et per assiduitatem

boni operis atque per desiderium futurę premiorum beatitudinis.

Septimum uitium est tristitia.   Duo enim sunt genera eius: unum

salutiferum, et alterum pestiferum.   Tristitia quidem [salutaris] est quando

de peccatis suis animus peccatoris contristatur; alia est tristitia huius seculi

50   que mortem operatur animae. In bono opere proficere non ualet, sed animum

perturbat, et sepe in disperationem mittit, et caetera.   Ex ipsa enim nascitur

malitia, rancor animi, pusillanimitas, amaritudo, in qua etiam presentis uitę

nulla est dilectatio, quae uero uincitur letitia spiritali et spe futurorum et

consolatione scripturarum.

55   Octauum uitium est uana gloria, dum enim homo appetit in bonis suis

laudari uanum est gloriari, et non deo dat honorem nec diuinę imputat gratiae

quicquid boni facit, sed quasi ex se habeat, dum homo nichil absque dei gratia

habere   oterit boni, sicut ipsa ueritas discipulis ait: Sine me nihil potestis

facere (John 15,5);   et apostolus inquit: Quid habes quod non accepisti?   [Si

60   autem accepisti,] quid gloriaris, quasi non acceperis?   (I Corinthians 4,7).

---

42. P, B: cellula; G: cellulas; A: cella.   42. G adds: et, before: eicit.   43. P, B, A:
abrupta; G: obruta.   44. P, B: ad locum; G, A: in locum.   46. G omits: per, before:
desiderium.   48. P, A: alterum; B, G: alium.   48. P: et uirtutis; B, G, A:
salutaris.   49. P, B, A: contristatur; G: tristet.   49. B reads: est, twice.   50. P: in
bono opere proficere non ualet; B, G: et nihil in bono opere proficere ualet; A: quae
nihil . . . ualet.   51-54. G omits: Ex ipsa . . . scripturarum.   56. B omits: uanum est
gloriari; not in Alcuin.   56. G omits: deo.   56. P, B, A: honorem; G: honore.   57. P,
B, A: sed; G: et.   56. P, B, A: diuinae, diuinę; G: diuicię.   57. P, B, A: habeat; G:
exhibeat.   59. P omits: si autem accepisti, as in B and Scripture; G: si accepisti. This
citation is an addition to Alcuin.

Vercelli XX, Scragg (Szarmach 79, 83-89); cf. Latin 41-46.

forðam þæt mod geondscrið geond eallo þing. Þis is se leahtor þe swiðost munecas utanytt of hyra mynstrum on worulde, and hie utawyrpð of hira regullican drohtunge on leahtra seaðas. Of þære byð acenned slapolnes and sleacnes godes weorces and unstaðolfæstnes stowe and worung of stowe to stowe and murcnung and idele spræca and oðere manega yfelo. Seo byð þeahhwæðere oferswiðed þurh þone bigang þære rædinge and ðurh þa singalnesse þæs godan weorces and þurh þa gewilnunge þæra meda þære toweardan eadignesse.

Vercelli XX, Scragg (Szarmach 79, 90-97); cf. Latin 47-54.

Þonne ys se seofeða heafodleahter gecweden unrotnes. Þonne syndon soðlice twa cynnryno unrotnesse, an halwendlic and oðer cwylmberendlic. Ðonne witodlice [is] seo unrotnes halwendlic þonne þæs synnfullan mannes mod byð geunrotsud for his synnum. Ðonne is oðer, men ða leofestan, ðysse worulde unrotnes, seo gewyrcð deað þære sawle, and heo ne mæg nan þing on godum worcum fromian, ac heo gedrefeð þæt mod and on orwennesse oft ðæs mannes mod gebrincð. Of þære byð [soðlice] acened yfelnes and modes angsumnes and wacmodnes and byternes, on þære ne byþ nan gelustfullung þy[se]s andweardan lifes. Seo byð soðlice oferswiðed of gastlicre blisse and of hyhte þæra toweardra goda and of haligra gewrita frofre.

Vercelli XX, Scragg (Szarmach 79, 98-103); cf. Latin 55-59.

Ðonne ys se eahtoða heafodleahter gecweden idel wuldor. Þæt is witodlice idel to wuldrigenne þonne se mann gegyrnð þæt he beo hered on his godum and ne sylð Gode nanne wyrðment, ne hit ne geteleð to godcundre mihte swa hwætt swa he godes deð, ac eall swylc he hit of him sylfum hæbbe, þonne se mann ne mæg nan þing godes habban butan Godes gife, swa swa he sylf his leorningcnihtum sæde: 'Ne mage ge nan þing butan me don.'

SOURCES FOR LATIN

41-46.   Alcuin, cap.32.
47-54.   Alcuin, cap.33 with omissions and adaptation.
55-59.   Alcuin, cap.34, with omissions, adaptation, and addition of citation
          from I Corinthians.

Quapropter qui gloriatur, in domino glorietur; quia nihil sine donante deo boni habere poterit.   Ex huius autem uitii radice nascitur iactantia, arrogantia, indignatio, discordia, cupido, simulatio boni operis, cum de se homo uult laudari quod se agere nescit.

65   Cuius morbi medicina est recordatio diuinae bonitatis, per quam omnia bona nobis conlata sunt, quae habere uidemur, et perpetua ipsius dei

174v   caritas, / 174v / in cuius laudem omnia agere debemus, quicquid in hoc seculo operamur, et magis desiderare a deo laudari in die retributionis ꬲterne, quam a quolibet homine in huius transitoriꬲ uitae conuersatione.

70   Hꬲc sunt, fratres karissimi, octo uitia principalia cum exercitibus suis quꬲ cotidie pugnant contra humanum genus.   Hi sunt bellatores diaboli, fortes contra homines qui, deo auxiliante, facile uincuntur a bellatoribus Christi per uirtutes sanctas.   Primum enim superbia uincitur per humilitatem, gula per abstinentiam, fornicatio per castitatem, auaritia per

75   largitatem, ira per patientiam, accidia per instantiam boni operis, tristitia mala per lꬲtitiam spiritalem, uana gloria per caritatem dei, et per multas alias uirtutes quae sunt prudentia, iustitia, fortitudo, temperantia.

Primum igitur quꬲrendum est quid sit uirtus animi, habitus naturꬲ, decus uitꬲ, ratio morum, pietas cultus diuinitatis, honor hominis, [meritum]

80   ꬲternae beatitudinis. Cuius partes sunt, ut diximus, quattuor principales:

---

66. P, B, A: conlata, collata; G: conlaudata. 66. G adds: et, before: habere. 66. P, B: et perpetua; G, A: etiam et perpetua. 67. G adds: est, before: caritas. 67. G ends at: debemus, adds benediction. 72. P: homines; B: hominem. 78-80. Text punctuated as P, B; contrast A. 79. P, A: diuinitatis, B: unitatis. 19. P: ut seruitium; B, A: meritum.

135

Vercelli XX, Scragg (Szarmach 79, 103-105); cf. Latin 62-64.

Ðonne soðlice of ðyses leahtres wyrttrum byð acenned boiung and gylp and æbylð and ungeðwærnes and gifernes and licettung godes wurces, þonne se mann wyle þæt beo be him gehered þæt he furþon don ne cann.

Vercelli XX, Szarmach 79, 105-G3; cf. Latin 65-69.

Þonne ys þære adle læcedom gemynd þære godcundan godnesse, þurh ða us synt ealle god forgyfene þe we on þysse worulde syndon gesewene to hæbbene, and seo ece soðe lufe þæs sylfan Godes, on þæs lofe we sceolon don swa hwæt swa we on þisse worulde wyrcað, and ma we sceolon gewilnian þæt we syn fram Gode geherede on þam dæge þæs ecan edleanes, þonne fram ænigum men on þisse drohtnunge þises gewitendlican lifes.

Vercelli XX, Scragg (Szarmach 79-80, G4-G12); cf. Latin 70-77.

Ðis syndon, men ða leofestan, þa ehta heafodleahtras mid heora herum þe dæghwamlice ongean mancyn winnað. And hi synd swiðe strange deofles cempen ongean mennisc cynn, þa beoð eaðelice, Gode gefultumigendum, fram Cristes cempum feohtendum þurh halige mægenu oferswiþed. [Ærest soðlice seo ofermodignys byð oferswiþed] þurh eadmodnysse and seo gyfernyss byð oferswiþed þurh forhæfednysse, and þæt forlyr þurh clænnysse, and seo gytsung þurh rumgyfolnysse, and þæt yrre þurh geþyld, and seo sleacnys þurh anrædnysse godes weorces, and seo yfele unrotnys þurh gastlice blisse, and þæt idelwuldor bið oferswiðed þurh Godes [clænnysse and þurh manega] oðre mægnu, þæt synd snoternysse and rihtwisnes and strengð and gemetung.

Vercelli XX, Scragg (Szarmach 80, G13-G17); cf. Latin 78-80.

Þonne is ærest witodlice ælcum menn georne to secenne and to smeagenne hwæt si þæs modes mægen. Þæs modes mægen is se gyrla þæs gecyndes and seo arfæstnys þæs lifes and þæt gescead þæra þeawa and seo arfæstnys and se biggeng þære godcundnysse and se wurþmynt þæs mannes and seo geearnung þære ecan eadignysse. Þis syndon þa mægenu þæs modes. Þonne syndon þa fyrmestan mægenu and þa healicestan dælas þære ecan eadignysse, eall swa we ær sædon,

---

SOURCES FOR LATIN

61-77.   Alcuin, cap.34.
68-80.   Alcuin, cap.35.

N.B. Vercelli XX has a leaf missing. Szarmach supplies material from Cambridge, Corpus Christi College 162 art.36, (his manuscript G.). Scragg's edited text (as above) differs in places.

prudentia, iustitia, fortitudo, temperantia. Prudentia est rerum diuinarum humanarumque, prout homini datum est, scientia, in qua intelligendum quid cauendum sit homini, uel quid faciendum, et hoc est quod in Psalmo legitur: Diuerte a malo et fac bonum (Psalm 33,15). Iustitia est animi nobilitas,

85 unicuique rei propriam tribuens dignitatem. In hac diuinitatis cultus, et humanitatis iura, et iust [a] iudicia, et aequitas totius uitae conseruatur.

Fortitudo est magna animi potentia et longanimitas, et perseuerantia in bonis operibus, et uictoria uitiorum genera. Temperantia, est totius uitȩ modus, ne quid nimis homo uel amet, uel odio habeat, sed omnes uitȩ huius uarietates

90 considerata temperet diligentia. Haec uero in fide et caritate nimis

175r obseruantibus aeternȩ gloriȩ ab ipsa ueritate, id est, ab Iesu / 175r / Christo, premia pollicentur. Nulla enim melior est prudentia quam ea qua deus secundum modulum humanȩ mentis intelligitur et timetur et futurum eius creditur iudicium. Uel quid iustius est quam deum diligere eiusque mandata

95 custodire, per quem, dum non fuerimus, creati sumus et postea a seruitute diabolica liberati fuimus, qui nobis omnia quȩ habemus perdonauit? Et quid hac fortitudine melius est quam diabolum uincere, et omnes eius sugestiones et omnia aduersa mundi pro dei nomine fortiter tolerare? Nobilis autem uirtus est ualde temperantia, per quam omnis honor uitȩ huius inter homines

100 constat; ut omnia in quacumque causa homo temperanter cogitet, loquatur, et

---

81-83. B omits: rerum . . . faciendum; blank space in MS. 86. P: et iusti; B: iusta; A: et justa. 90. P, A: considerata; B: considerat. 92. B omits: ea qua; P as A. 96. B adds: in, before: nobis. 99. B omits: per quam; P as A.

Vercelli XX, Scragg (Szarmach 80, G17-G26); cf. Latin 81-90.

snoternys and rihtwisnes and strengð and gemetegung. Þonne is seo snoternys gecweden ingehyd, swa swa hit mannum geseald is ægðer ge godcundra þinga ge menniscra, on þam is to ongitenne hwæt þam men si to warnigenne oððe hwæt to donne, and þæt is awriten on þam sealme: 'Gecyr fram yfele and do god'. Þonne is seo rihtwisnys gecweden þæs modes æðelnys, on þære byð gehealden se biggeng þære godcundnysse and þa gerihtu þære mennisclicnysse and efne ealles þæs lifes. Þonne is seo strengð micel miht þæs modes and langsumnys and þurhwunung on godum weorcum and sigor ongean eallra leahtra cynrenu. Þonne is seo gemetegung ealles þæs lifes gemet, þe læs þe ænig man to þearle hwæt lufige oððe on hatunge hæbbe, ac seo besceawode geornfulnyss gemetegað ealle þa missenlicnyssa þises lifes.

Vercelli XX, Scragg (Szarmach 80, G26-G33); cf. Latin 92-98.

And witodlice nis nan snoternyss bætere þonne seo þe God bið onagiten æfter mennisces modes gemete and ondræd bið, and his towearda dom gelyfed byð. Hwæt is us rihtwislicre þonne we God lufion and his bebodu gehealdon - þurh þone, þa we næron, we wæron gesceapene and syððan we wæron alysede fram deoflicum þeowdome - se us forgeaf ealle þa þing þe we habbað? Hwæt is us bætere toforan ælcere middangeardlicre strengðe þonne we oferswiþon helle deofla and stranglice wiðstandan for Godes naman eallum heora larum and ealle wiðerwerde þing þises andweardan middaneardes?

SOURCES FOR LATIN

81-100.   Alcuin, cap.35.

agat cum consilio salutis suae. Hęc enim sunt leuia et suauia deum diligenti,
qui ait: Discite a me, quia mitis sum, et humilis corde; et inuenietis requiem
animabus uestris. Iugum enim meum suaue est, et onus meum leue (Matthew
11,29-30). Nonne melius est et beatius deum diligere, qui est aeterna

105 pulchritudo, aeterna dulcedo, aeterna suauitas, ęterna fragrantia, ęterna
iocunditas, perpetuus honor, indeficiens felicitas; quam huius seculi amare
species pulchras, dulces sapores, sonos suaues, odores fragrantes, tactus
iocundos, et honores atque felicitates transitorias, quae omnia uelut uolatilis
umbra cito recedunt et transeunt, et decipiunt amantem se, et in aeternam

110 eum mittunt miseriam. Qui uero deum et dominum fideliter amat, et
indesinenter colit, mandata perseueranter implet, caelestem cum angelis dei
gloriam et claritatem aeternam perpetualiter possidere dignus efficietur.

Prestante domino nostro Iesu Christo cui est honor et imperium et
potestas cum patre et spiritu sancto per omnia secula seculorum. Amen.

---

101. B omits: Hęc . . . suauia; blank space in MS. 101-102. P, A: deum diligenti qui
ait; B: quia deum diligent qui ait. 108. P, A: transitorias; B: transitorie. 108. B
omits: quae, before: omnia. 109. B omits: et transeunt; blank space in MS; P as
A. 109. P, A: amantem se; B: amatores. 110. B omits: eum mittant miseriam; blank
space in MS; P as A. 110. B omits: uero; P as A. 111. B adds: et eius, before:
mandata. 114. B adds: una, before: cum. 114. P: omnia; B: infinita.

101-112. Alcuin, De Virt. cap.35.

Extracts.

1. Item 22 fol.42v XXII. Omelia in Dominica ii in Quadragesima.
Extract fol.44v ll,4-11:-

Post haec congrue sequuntur ieiunia, de quorum laudatione (B,J: laudibus) dicit Isidorus: Ieiunium est res sancta, opus celeste, ianua regni celestis, forma futuri seculi, quod qui sancte agit, deo coniungitur, mundo alienatur, spiritalis efficitur. Per hoc prosternuntur uitia, humiliatur caro et diaboli temptamenta uincuntur. Hieronimus dicit: Ieiunium castigat corpus, refrenat uitia, incitat uirtutes from <u>Collectio Canonum Hibernensis</u> 12.3 (ed. p.34): ieiunium...uirtutes .

fol.45v ll.8-20, 23-27:-

Ad extremum sequitur de elimosina, que est plenitudo et perfectio bonorum operum (J omits: operum), de cuius laudibus ait Agustinus: Aelimosina est res sancta, auget presentia, demit peccata, multiplicat annos, nobilitat mentem (J: mentes), dilatat terminos, mundat omnia, liberat a morte et a poena, iungit angelis, separat a doemonibus, murus est inexpugnabilis circa animam, demones expellit, inuiat angelos in auxilium. Hieronimus dicit: Aelimosina penetrat celum, precedit dantem, pulsat ianuam regni, excitat angelum in obuiam, deum conuocat in adiutorium from CCH 13.2 (ed. pp.38-39): aelimosina...adiutorium .

...Tria sunt enim genera aelimosinarum. Una corporalis: aegenti (B: egenis) dare quicquid poteris. Altera spiritalis: dimittere ei a quo lesus fueris. Tertia: delinquentem corrigere et errantes in uiam reducere ueritatis. [from Alcuin, <u>De Virt.</u> cap 17, PL 101, 626].

<u>Comparison of base text (P) with Latin source.</u>

Passage 1. 2. est; CCH omits.
3. celestis; CCH omits.
3. seculi; CCH omits.
3. deo; CCH: domino.
4. per hoc; CCH: per hoc enim.
4. et; CCH omits.
6. refrenat; CCH jejunium refrenat.

Passage 2. 3. est; CCH omits.
4. omnia; CCH: omnia et reliqua usque ubi ait.
4. a morte et; CCH omits.
5. est; CCH omits.
6. in auxilium; CCH omits.
8. angelum; CCH: angelos.

Vercelli XX Scragg (Szarmach 78, 29-34):-

Fæsten and ælmessylen sceolon æghwylcum Cristinum menn ætgædere fyligean, forðam þæt fæsten ys halig þing, and hit is heofonlic weorc, and hit is duru ðæs heofonlican rices, and hyt ys hiw þære toweardan worulde, and se byð Gode geþeodd se ðe hyt haliglice deð, and he byð geelfremed fram middangerde, and he byð gastlic geworden. Þurh þæt beoð leahtras afyllede, and þæt flæsc byð geeadmett, and þurh þæt beoð deofles costunga oferswiðede, and hyt framað swiðe myclum for Gode þam þe hyt willindlice fæst.

Vercelli XX Scragg (Szarmach 78, 35-45):-

And seo ælmessylen ys gefyllednes and fulfremednes eallra goda, and heo ys halig þing, and heo geycð þa andweardan, and heo gewanaþ synna, and heo gemænigfylt gear, and heo geæðelað þæt mod, and heo tobræt gemæro, and heo aclænsað eallo þing, and heo alyst fram deaþe and fram witum, and heo geþeodeð þone mann þe hy begæð Godes englum, and hine ascyreð fram deoflum, and heo ys unoferwinnendlic weall ymb þa sawle, and heo framadrifð deoflu, and englas togelaðað on fultum, and heo þurhfærð þone heofon, and heo forestepð þone syllendan on heofona rices wuldre, and heo cnyst heofona rices duru, and heo awecð englas ongean, and heo tosomne gecigeð dryhten ælmihtigne on fultum þam þe hie luflice and rumodlice dæleð. Þreo cynn syndon ælmesdæda: an is lichomlic, þæt man þam wædliendan to gode sylle swa hwæt swa man mæge; oðer is gastlic, þæt man forgife þam þe oðerum ænig yfel deð eall þæt he him to wite; þridde is þæt man þa dweliendan on soðfæstnesse weg gelædde.

N.B. i. Both of these Old English passages differ in word from Vercelli III (Förster, 63-64 and 68-70, respectively). Thus the Old English of Vercelli III and Vercelli XX derive from the Latin passage (and probably variants of this) and not from each other in Old English.

ii. In passage 2, J. omits: operum, cf. V XX: ealra goda; and N.B. V III: ealra goda weorca as P.

2. Item 52 fol. 122r LII. Omelia in iiii[or] Tempora.
    Extract fol. 123r ll.10-17:-

Reddite ergo primum, fratres karissimi, decimas fructuum uestrorum quos dominus deus, de quacumque arte uobis dederit, ... et aelimosinas quoque pauperibus de nouem partibus, prout unicuique deus dederit, largius erogate, quia aelimosina a peccato et a morte liberat (cf. Tobias, 4, 11) et sicut aqua extinguit ignem, ita aelimosina (B omits; a peccato ... aelimosina) emundat peccata (cf. Ecclesiasticus 3, 33).

Vercelli XX Scragg (Szarmach 77, 78, 23-28):-

Ac utan symle of eallum þam godum þe us God her on worulde læne hym þa teoðunga don eadmodlice; þonne tiðaþ us dryhten þe rumodlicor þara nigon dæla. And utan georne of ðam nigon dælum Godes þearfum ælmessan dælan, forðan seo ælmessylen alyst þone synfullan mann fram synnum and fram deaþe (cf. Tobias 4, 11), and swa swa wæter adwæscit fyr, swa adwæscit seo ælmessylen þa synna of manna gehwyclum þe h[y] rumodlice dæleð (cf. Ecclesiasticus 3, 33).

Vercelli XXI

Paul Szarmach (Old English Homily pp.248, 250-52) has briefly considered the structure of Vercelli XXI, and almost all the sources indicated below have been found by others. But Donald Scragg has asked me to print whole items and extracts from the Pembroke-type collection and to discuss the content of the sermon as an aid to his forthcoming edition of the Vercelli prose for the Early English Text Society. We have had a rewarding exchange of information. After I had argued the importance of the Latin collection for the understanding of the background of Vercelli XIX and XX, and other anonymous Old English homilies, at Leeds in March 1984 (and at Kalamazoo in May 1984), I gave Dr. Scragg a print-out of a microfilm of Pembroke MS 25. Within a short time he had recognized the contacts between Vercelli XXI and a number of items within the Latin collection from his intimate knowledge of the Vercelli sermons.

These new discoveries by Scragg, together with illustrations by earlier scholars (noted in Szarmach's edition p.83 and pp.88-90), suggest that the whole homily was created as a fluent fusion of mnemonic lists and passages, probably collected and noted in preparation by the composer, yet with the obvious purpose that a congregation should retain at least some of the words and ideas within those memorable lists. Some even of those few sections without source at present may also have derived from written works, in view of the demonstration which is now possible, referring to Szarmach's already-printed edition.

The Anglo-Saxon composer begins forcefully (ll.1-3) with the two prime commandments of the New Testament: Love God and neighbour, which are presented in three gospels, the Old English phrases being nearest to Mark 12, 30 and 31, but they are a close echo of the citations which begin Pembroke item 91 (printed in full below) since another Old English passage was translated from this Pembroke sermon.

The attributes of the Lord are then enumerated in a list of names (ll.4-7), (eighteen in all) within this world: life, health, hope, etc, and within the future world: glory, bliss, peace, etc. A similar list of attributes, but with different names, occur at the end of Bazire-Cross Homily 3 (pp.53-54), but neither of the lists have sources, at present.

Our composer now (ll.8-11) admonishes his audience to learn humility and to shun pride, with a translated abstraction from Pembroke item 40 ll.59-63 for Rogations (printed above for Vercelli XIX) within the paragraph immediately following the description of Mamertus of Vienne's institution of the festival which was used by the composer of Vercelli XIX.   The Old English words echo the Latin, including the part-quotation of the Epistle of James 4, 6 (as I Peter 5, 5): <u>Deus superbis resistit, humilibus autem dat gratiam</u> cf. 'God symle þam ofermodigum wiðstent, and he sylð þam eaðmodu[m] gyfe' (ll.10-11).   He then warns the mighty by echoing <u>Sapientia</u> (Wisdom) 6, 7: <u>Potentes autem potenter tormenta patientur</u> cf. 'þæt þa rican swa mycle maran witu þoliað' (ll.12-13), reminding these powerful and rich of their future if they do not do God's will in this world.   That warning is extended to everyone with a list of the wretched sinners (ll.16-19) (twelve in all) abstracted verbatim in translation from Pembroke item 24 (for the fourth Sunday in Lent), as printed in Extract 1 below. These will go to hell unless they are converted before their death (ll.19-22).

Szarmach (p.88) has suggested tentatively that part of the following section (ll.26-37) on the value and the methods of almsgiving 'seems to be indebted in a general way to two passages from Caesarius of Arles in <u>Sermo</u> 158 and 199'.   There is now some further support for an ultimate link with <u>Sermo</u> 199, apart from details noted by Szarmach, since phrases from two items for Rogationtide, nos. 39 (based on Caesarius <u>Sermo</u> 208) and no. 40 ll.5-6 (used for Vercelli XIX), are translated within the whole section (ll.23-37), and <u>Sermo</u> 199 is a partial base for Pembroke item 21 for another period of especial penance, the first Sunday in Lent.   The English preacher begins (ll.23-25) with a rhetorical question for the wealthy abstracted from Pembroke no. 40 ll.5-6 (printed above for Vercelli XIX): 'What profits any man to abstain unless he also cease from vices?'. The problem of the poor man, who does not know what to give, is then answered with a citation of Isaias 58, 7: Break your loaf etc., and the ubiquitous need for almsgiving is further exemplified with the gift of the drink of water. Another short list (ll.33-35), ultimately from Caesarius <u>Sermo</u> 208, but probably from its presentation in Pembroke item 39 (Extract 2, printed below) allows the preacher to tell his audience to pray for God's mercy, and 'among other good works give alms', 'Because alms-giving frees the sinful man from sins and from death', (ll.36-37, echoing Tobias 4, 11).

Szarmach's proposed links with the two sermons of Caesarius looked, to me at first, somewhat tenuous, being citations of Isaias 58, 7 and Tobias 4, 11 in Sermo 158; and Isaias 58, 7 and Matthew 10, 42 (and Mark 9, 40), on the cup of cold water, in Sermo 199. But I am now inclined to accept a recall of Sermo 199, obviously via its abstraction for Pembroke item 21, but also because of the citation of Isaias 58, 7 and the adaptation of the Scriptural cup of water as minimal almsgiving of a poor man. This use in Sermo 199, Pembroke no. 21 and in Vercelli XXI is quite different from that in its Scriptural context (Matthew 10, 42; Mark 9, 40). Influence from Sermo 158, which is not used in the Pembroke-type collection, is, in my view, less likely, especially since the citation of Tobias 4, 11 is found also in Vercelli Homily XX (Szarmach, p.78 l.26).

The next section (ll.38-44), a long list of twenty items, presents the 'ways of God' as Christian acts and attitudes. This list is translated verbatim from the final paragraph of the general sermon, Pembroke item 91 ll.48-54 (printed in full below), entitled Predicatio bona omnibus Christianis, with the omission of one Latin item: studium scientiae legis dei, and the addition of one in Old English at the end: 'his willan wyrcað oð hira endedæg' (l.44).

Then follows an admonition: 'Let us now clothe and adorn our souls with good works and with virtues', which introduces yet another sequence, here enumerating twelve virtues of the soul (ll.45-65). The list is translated from the concluding section of the general sermon, item 90 l.81 seq. (printed in full below). For this theme, however, we now know an ultimate source and can demonstrate that a text of Pembroke no. 90 was an intermediary for Vercelli XXI. In his edition (p.88) Szarmach referred to Paulinus of Aquileia's Liber exhortationis cap. 23 (PL 99, 218-19) although commenting that this 'may not . . . be the ultimate source'. A footnote in PL against

Paulinus's tract cap. 20 (PL 99, 211) however, notes that Paulinus caps. 20-45 are found in Pseudo-Basil, Admonitio ad Filium Spiritualem (PL 103), and cap. 23 of Paulinus compares with Pseudo-Basil cap. 2 (PL 103, 686). Although the Admonitio is not among Basil's authentic works it was written certainly before the seventh century when Defensor composed his Liber Scintillarum and abstracted aphorisms from the Admonitio (see the edition by H. M. Rochais (CCSL, CXVII.1, Turnhout, (1957), Index scriptorum p.245). Paulinus, one of Charlemagne's group of scholars at the end of the eighth century, obviously drew on Pseudo-Basil, and may now be left aside, since Paulinus cap. 23 omits virtues within the list of Pseudo-Basil cap. 2, which are also in Pembroke item 90 and Vercelli XXI. Charles Wright has also indicated to me a certain popularity for the Pseudo-Basilian chapter by noting that it appears among sententiae diversae in Munich, Bayerische Staatsbibliothek, Clm. 19410 pp.20-21 (saec. IX med.) and I have also seen it in Munich, B.S., Clm. 14364 fols. 38r-38v (saec. IX[1]) in a similar miscellaneous collection of themes and aphorisms. Like Paulinus, however, both extracts omit items in their copying from the list as in Pseudo-Basil. Nevertheless they can be cited as variant texts in a comparison between Pseudo-Basil, Pembroke no. 90 and Vercelli XXI. In comparison with Pseudo-Basil, Pembroke 90 adds a brief introduction, Conemur ergo nos indui et solerter ornari animarum uirtutibus, numbers the virtues, has one more than Pseudo-Basil (no. 12), and changes individual words, some of which are significant for the Old English of Vercelli XXI. These are:-

i. a pusillanimitate declinare (no. 2) cf. Ps.-B.: ab impatientia declinare;

ii. iram prohibere (no. 7) cf. Ps.-B: animae iram cohibere;

iii. odium exsecrari (no. 8) cf. Ps.-B.: invidiam exsecrari;

iv. omnem uoluptatem carnis mente abicere (no. 10) cf. Ps.-B.: omnem voluptatem carnis subjicere menti.

Pembroke no. 90 also adds a conclusion: Hae (B: haec) sunt duodecim uirtutes quibus animae iustorum induentur in die iudicii fulgentes ante conspectum domini; and then has a slight echo of Pseudo-Basil: Has ergo uirtutes optinere poterimus si terrenis rebus celestia preponamus. Vercelli XXI obviously echoes both the introduction and concluding words of Pembroke no. 90 (which are extensions and variation on Pseudo-Basil) although itself extending the introductory words of Pembroke no. 90. The numbering of the virtues, and the addition of a twelfth virtue clearly derive from Pembroke 90, whose composer rather clumsily added the twelfth virtue to balance a preceding list of the 'twelve abuses of the world', since it seems to reflect but oppose the first virtue. With some differences of individual words from Pseudo-Basil, noted above, Vercelli XXI follows Pembroke no. 90 at iram prohibere, 'forhæbbe fram yrre'; at odium exsecrari, 'onsceonige hatunge'; at omnem uoluptatem carnis mente abicere, 'aweg aweorpe of ðam mode ealne þone yflan luste þæs lichaman flæsces'. But the writer of Vercelli XXI seems to cavil at the sense of a pusillanimitate declinare of Pembroke no. 90, as an antithesis of patientiam sectari, with his 'forbuge ælc unriht yrre'. The Vercelli XXI phrase, however, does indicate that the Anglo-Saxon did not see the Pseudo-Basil ab impatientia declinare, which makes appropriate sense as an antithesis and would have been translated, if seen. There are, however, brief extensions in the Vercelli sermon, e.g., a neat antithesis for the third virtue ('forfleo ælce unclænnesse'), which is not extant in any of the Latin lists named above, and seeming rejection of words of metaphoric content, as for the fourth virtue: et omnia caduca calcare (Ps.-B. etc.), contrast, 'forseo ealle gewitendlicu þing', and for the fifth virtue: Tumorem superbiae abominari (obominari) (Ps.B., Munich Clm. 14364, Pembroke no. 90) but superbiam abominari (Paulinus, Munich Clm. 19410) cf. 'onscunige ofermodignesse'. Nevertheless a text, not necessarily among those extant or known, of the Pembroke-type sermon was the direct source for the original of Vercelli XXI.

Now the Vercelli composer adapts slightly but follows closely a section from Pembroke item 34 De Resurrectione Dei ll.38-67 (printed in full below) for the next paragraph (ll.67-96). Parts of the relevant passage in the Latin sermon are based on Caesarius Sermo 57.3 (Morin I, 252) for the description of Christ's beneficial deeds and sacrifice for us, and on Pseudo-Augustine Sermo 136.6 (PL 39, 2015) for the admonition to give holy gifts of the listed virtues in return. But the Pembroke sermon is the intermediary, notably at the addition after mortis faucibus nos eripuit ll.41-42 (from Caesarius) of et diabolum cum suis satellitibus in infernum deorsum suppressit. Et non solum nos redimit cf. 'and hu he ðone deofol on helle mid his wæggesiðum ofþrihte. And na þæt an þæt he us þanon alysde' (ll.72-73). For the record of our gifts to God, Pembroke no. 34 ll.49-52 extends the Pseudo-Augustinian list greatly, to twelve items, all of which are translated in Vercelli XXI (ll.78-80), but accepts the Pseudo-Augustinian summation ll.52-53 with a little change of word, accurately reflected however in Vercelli XXI (ll.81-82). But Pembroke no. 34 ll.57-60, followed by Vercelli XXI (ll.83-96), continues by bidding the congregation to hold all these virtues firmly in mind, to consider the health of their souls and not to forget the precepts through which Christ promised the Kingdom of heaven, 'Be merciful' etc. (Luke 6, 36), 'Blessed are the merciful' etc. (Matthew 5, 7), 'Blessed are the pure (clean) in heart' etc. (Matthew 5, 8) (cited in full in Pembroke no. 34, cf. Vercelli XXI ll.87-89). The reward is then presented in Vercelli XXI, security on doomsday, and invitation to the heavenly banquet with the patriarchs, if, however, we give alms, do penance and perform the works of mercy, named as: caring for the hungry, thirsty, naked and strangers. The only change of note between Vercelli XXI and Pembroke no. 34 is a reversal of the description of the reward on doomsday and afterwards, and the proviso of the good deeds.

Earlier scholars had noted parallels between Vercelli XXI Uton eac . . . forgifen hæfð (ll.67-75) and Pseudo-Wulfstan ed. A. S. Napier (Berlin, 1883), Sermon XXX, pp.144 l.29-145 l.9 (see Szarmach, edition p.89), but D. G. Scragg (Anglo-Saxon England 6 (1977), pp.197-211) has argued convincingly that Napier XXX is 'a homily in which virtually every sentence is taken from earlier writings' (p.210), and specifically that the noted passage in Napier XXX derives from an Old English passage as available in Vercelli XXI (Scragg p.198).

From the end at doomsday, our composer recalls (l.97 seq.) the beginning for his audience, that, as descendants of Adam, they are mortal, will become dust, but from earth they will arise on doomsday to reveal their deeds to the Lord. They will be 'earme oððe eadige' (l.101) as they have merited in this world. They should protect themselves against vices and sins (named in a short list, ll.107-08) and especially against pride, the worst of all, exemplified in the fall of the angels. 'Beset with torments in the burning hell, they knew the better with whom they strove' (ll.113-14). So let us follow virtuous ideas and do virtuous deeds because they bring the righteous soul to the happiness above on the last day.

The whole section (ll.97-121) is sprinkled with brief lists, variant doublets, antitheses, and echoing alliterations. Two passages, indeed, have been noted as 'poetic', one (ll.99-101) by Angus McIntosh (Proc. British Academy (1949) p.141, note 29), the other (ll.114-19) having a close parallel in the poem known as An Exhortation to Christian Living (see Szarmach edition p.89). The assumption has been that the prose sections derive from earlier poems. That may be, but the derivation may equally well have been from the prose to the verse, as may be illustrated by the extant texts of Vercelli XXI and the Exhortation.

Vercelli XXI (ll.114-19) reads:

'Ac uton beon eaðmode and ælmesgeorne and wise on wordum and on dædum eac, and uton bliðum mode on haligum hige wæccan lufian and gebedum fylgian on þisse hwilwendan tide oftust þeah symle þær we ænlype beon. For þan þæt halige gebed and seo hluttre lufu Godes ælmihtiges and seo ælmessylen þe man for Gode gedeð and eac oðera feala godra weorca geglengaþ and gebringað þa soðfæstan sawla on blisse and on wuldre on þære uplican eadignesse . . . .'

This passage translates into understandable prose of clear intent:

'And (but) let us be humble and zealous in alms, and wise in words and also in deeds, and, with a happy mind in holy thought, let us love vigils and, most often in this passing time, be attentive (Bosworth-Toller Dict. s.v. 'fylgian') to prayers although we may always be alone there (then), because holy prayer and pure love of Almighty God and the alms which are done for God, and also many other good works, adorn and bring the righteous souls to happiness and glory in the blessedness above (on high)'.

But not all the statements of the prose are as clear in the verse. The prose commands persistent not merely public prayer, but the verse reads:

and gebedum filige

oftost symle   þær þu ana sy.

(and be attentive to prayers most often, always, where (when) you may be alone), where either a contradiction or a tautology is forced by the demands of the rhythm ('oftost symle'). The prose directs all the virtuous acts towards God who will reward the righteous soul, but the verse weakens the persistent direction by adding to love of God, also 'of men' ('Godes and manna'), again to accede to the requirements of rhythm in a line which lacks alliteration. Once it appears, the versifier (if not a scribe) has left a dangling half-line: 'and eac oþera fela'. Finally, 'on dædum eac' (prose) goes more logically with 'wis(e) on wordum' (prose and verse) than 'and wæccan lufa' (verse), here to fulfil the need of alliteration. I suspect that the listing, and sometimes alliterating, prose has been turned with a little difficulty into verse, not that the prose is a 'dilution' of the verse.

Now the Old English composer of the exemplar of Vercelli XXI uses an abstract of a vernacular presentation, first of the events and horrors of Doomsday (ll.122-179), then of the aftermath of death of the sinner (ll.180-186) and finally an admonition to look to the needs of the soul by leaving vices and performing good deeds (ll.187-196). Although there are slight changes, and some omissions of phrases and words, the passage in Vercelli XXI: 'Men þa leofestan . . . þæt yrre God witnie', (ll.122-196) is parallel to Vercelli II (ed. Förster) p.44 l.1-p.52, l.107, which forms the bulk of the latter sermon. There may even be a little more contact between the two vernacular sermons, since ten of the Vercelli XXI list of fourteen necessary virtues (soðfæste . . . gehyrsume', ll.199-200) are found in Vercelli II (ed. Förster) p.53 ll.139-142. Within his survey of the anonymous homilies (Anglo-Saxon England 8 (1979)) Scragg has recalled the connection (indicated in Förster's edition of Vercelli II) and stated (p.232) that the section in Vercelli XXI 'is a slightly modernised version of Vercelli II, drawn from a copy without some of the errors and omissions of the latter' (i.e. the copy in Vercelli II).

The section first (ll.122-137) records the terrifying sights and sounds of

Doomsday which are also found in other vernacular versions of that   Day of Judgement, here: the roaring flames throughout the world; the loss of light of sun, moon and stars; the bloody Cross in the heavens; the terrifying and awe-inspiring countenance of the Lord as when he was abused by the Jews; the weeping sinners; the four angels blowing trumpets at the four corners of the earth at the resurrection of destroyed bodies; the Lord showing his countenance and wounds to the sinful but a whole body to the righteous (as in Vercelli II, but this is a certain omission from Vercelli XXI); the Jews seeing the crucified Lord; the judging of every man according to former deeds. Three such sermons with descriptions of Doomsday were discussed in Bazire-Cross (Homilies 3, 10, 11) and all the themes as in Vercelli XXI were illustrated within those discussions at pp.41-43, 127, 137-38 with footnotes. These themes were well-known to Latin and Anglo-Saxon homilists, and had varying origins.

Then follows (ll.138-146) a sequence of phrases begun with the orator's exclamations, 'Hwæt!, Eala!, Eala hwæt!' (twice), to remind the sinner what to fear: his wandering from the sight of the Lord to Hell, the devil Antichrist and the tortures as reward for the sinner's deeds, and Doomsday here presented, not unusually (see Bazire-Cross pp.41-42), as a sequence of names ('yrmðe dæg, earfoðnessa dæg' etc.) based on, but extending and varying, the Dies Irae sequence (Sophonias 1, 15-16). The next sequence of nearly fifty phrases (ll.147-172) describing what 'is revealed for us on that day' (l.146) has caused some problem for the editors. Förster for Vercelli II, and Szarmach for Vercelli XXI, print the sequence as verse, but A. S. Napier (Wulfstan (Berlin, 1883), Sermon XL, p.186 l.1 seq.) presented a similar, but somewhat different, sequence as prose. The similarities between Napier's printed passage and those in Vercelli II and XXI are, however, so consistent that undoubtedly all three derive ultimately from the same original, whatever the relationship of each is to the other. In order to present the sequence as verse, however, both Förster and Szarmach had to assume omission of phrases in their respective texts, which they added from the other texts. Lists such as this are notoriously susceptible to omission, but also addition, and there is no certainty that the exemplar of, in our case, Vercelli XXI, had a phrase which is proposed for insertion. No order of logic or of description exists, which might allow some control. The lists could fall into rhythmic pairs, as heard, because most items are adjective plus noun, or noun plus descriptive genitive, but one pair (l.147) does not alliterate, one pair substitutes rhyme for alliteration (l.160), and one phrase dangles without a pairing (l.172); four more phrases are also alone if the emendations by Szarmach are disallowed (ll.151, 155, 165, 167). No doubt the original composer wanted the total of the sequence to have its effect in a rolling but jumbled list of the horrors of Doomsday (fire appears four times, ll.151, 161, 167, 171, and 'se hata scur' l.154 has the same effect as 'se fyrena ren' l.162). Where the rhythms and alliterations are there, they are heard, but the prime intention was to produce a seemingly endless list. Omissions, additions and repetitions of idea were less important.

The list has the required overwhelming and numbing effect but the preacher yet continues (ll.173-186) that the sinners could wish that they were never born, or were turned into dumb beasts; the world with all its treasures could not compensate for heaven being covered. Lo! we do not dread what we see daily, our neighbour die, when the body decays in the cold earth for worms to eat. For the sinner comes a wretched division of body and soul and departure into eternal hell-torments, iterated in yet another list mainly in alliterating pairs (ll.183-185).

So let us be mindful of our soul's need; leave vices (presented in an extensive list, ll.188-191); let us love the Lord and our neighbour; let us (again!) do works of mercy: 'be merciful to poor men, strangers and sick' (l.194); suffer blithely the one who sins against us and forgive him 'in this holy time' (l.196), so that God does not punish us with his wrath; let us not despair though we have sinned, but ask for his grace and mercy, do his will and be virtuous (in a list of fourteen items, ll.199-200), have caritas between us, hasten to the heavenly kingdom and earn it here while we can.

Now, at last, (l.203) our composer is ready to conclude his lengthy sermon with the reward for the good, an enumeration of the delights of heaven. This description again exemplifies his predilection for lengthy lists, and clearly indicates his methods of preparation. The final passage (ll.203-216) is a collocation of phrases from no less than four concluding passages from sermons in the Pembroke-type collection. Donald Scragg noted three of these, but as soon as I realised the common factor in the method it was easy to pick up the fourth. The sequence; 'leoht ealles leohtes ... ælcum ende' (ll.203-204) is based in order on the ending of Pembroke item 50, fol. 119v (Extract 3 printed below) with little adaptation, with some omissions, and with one difference where a scribal miscopying is indicated in the two Latin manuscripts which contain the suspect phrase. Pembroke fol. 119v reads: 'ubi claritas angelorum et claritas sanctorum', whereas Vercelli XXI has : 'þær is seo ece torhtnes eallra engla, þær is swete lufu eallra haligra'. One suspects a repetition of word in error in the Latin and that the Vercelli XXI composer saw <u>caritas</u>, <u>charitas</u>. Relevantly, such a Latin error is attested in another Old English sequence which also translates (and extends) the Latin list. A sermon for Lent in the Bodley MS. Junius 85, 86 (ed. A. M. L. Fadda, <u>Nuove Omelie Anglosassoni</u> p.25 ll.251-254) reads 'ðær bið leohtes leoht and willa ðæs leohtes and þær bið ece gefea and þer biþ seo ece ar . . . ac ðær bið blis butan ænde'. The translation of <u>fons luminis</u> as 'willa (with analogical nominative) ðæs leohtes' (see Extract 3) indicates access to a Latin phrase which is not translated in Vercelli XXI, and 'haligra lufu' indicates an original Latin reading <u>caritas sanctorum</u>.

Then immediately follows another sequence (ll.204-208), one of the examples of the 'Seven Joys of Heaven' theme (with extension) within the Pembroke-type collection, this time from Pembroke item 25, fol. 52v (Extract 4 printed below), in a verbatim translation. At this point Vercelli XXI adds a few phrases which are not from the Pembroke-type collection: 'þær hie næfre leofe . . . nihte æfter nihte' (ll.208-210), but soon returns, now to Pembroke item 18 fol. 113v (Extract 5 printed below), to enumerate the kinds of holy men who live with Christ (ll.210-212), with some kinds omitted, and two kinds added: 'þa eaðmodan and þa facenleasan' (l.212). Finally (ll.213-216) our preacher turns to the end of Pembroke item 42 ll.69-74 (for Ascension Day) which is printed in full below to illustrate one source of Tristram Homily III. The Latin passage begins <u>Quem laudant angeli</u>, and ends with the benediction, the Old English omitting some Latin phrases and adding a little of its own.

Here ends a vernacular sermon from a diligent abstractor who could not resist a desire to overwhelm with words.

Vercelli XXI, which is extant as a complete sermon only in this manuscript, has no title assigning it to a feast-day or a festival-time, but some miscellaneous evidence can be gathered which allows a speculation. The first hint is a phrase in XXI which is an extension on the parallel passage in Vercelli II. Where the latter sermon (ed. Förster p.52 l.105 seq.) reads 'Ond þeah ure hwylc wið oðerne gegylte . . . forbere he him þæt liðelice, þe læs him God þæt yrre witnige', Vercelli XXI ll.195-96 reads 'bliðlice', for 'liðelice', but inserts a phrase after 'bliðlice': 'and 'forgyfe on þysse halgan tide', by this indicating that the sermon was for a time of high festival, not one quando uolueris.

Vercelli XXI was apparently copied with XIX and XX from one exemplar since they 'form a distinct group' and probably came from 'a late West Saxon collection' (Scragg, Anglo-Saxon England 2 (1973) pp.194, 205). As Bazire-Cross (pp.xviii-xix) noted, both Vercelli XIX and XX were entitled as for Rogationtide in the other manuscripts which contain these sermons although they, like XXI, are without title in the Vercelli Book. Also both contain information appropriate to that special period of observances, as Bazire-Cross indicated in their discussion of the sermons (pp.9-11, 27-28). Now, of course, use of an immediate source, the Pembroke-type collection, further demonstrates that Vercelli XIX and XX were for the Rogation Days. As illustrated above, Vercelli XIX draws on three (36, 38, 40) of five items in Pembroke entitled for Rogationtide, and Vercelli XX appears to have used item 38 (from Caesarius Sermo 207) for its opening paragraph.

In content Vercelli XXI may appear to be less specifically or traditionally for this period. It does, however, translate passages from the Pembroke-type collection items 39 and 40 for Rogationtide, although such passages could be used for any time of especial penance, and other sources are item 24 for Lent, item 34 (in effect for the Easter period) and items 90 and 91 among the general sermons. Its largest abstraction, however, is the description of the events of Doomsday, but such a topic is sometimes in order for sermons within Rogationtide. Within the collection of Rogationtide homilies by Bazire-Cross are three which feature the terrors of the last days: no. 3 in which the composer has used a version of the Apocalypse of Thomas and added material of his own (see pp.41-43), no. 10, drawing on Caesarius Sermo 57 de die iudicii with other traditional material from scripture and commentary (see pp.126-128), and no. 11 (see pp.136-138). For such a topic within Rogationtide Caesarius of Arles (or his manuscript copyists) offers a precedent. His Sermo 157 on the Gospel passage: 'Come blessed, receive the kingdom' (Matthew 25, 34), apparently is assigned to the third rogation day in antiquioribus codicibus (Morin, II 641) and is an admonition of the Judgement, including the need for the works of mercy, and the famed rejection: Discedite a me maledicti (Matthew 25, 41). Caesarius merely discussed the situation and the need to beware and prepare for the day, but the scene is there for other writers to describe within the period of festival.

The varied strands of evidence displayed here appear to assert that the 'holy time' specified in Vercelli XXI could well have been Rogationtide.

Item 90 fol.168r XC. Predicatio de principibus et populis.

Doctorum est omnes cum modestia ammonere quęcumque debeant
agere, illorum est humiliter audire ortamenta doctrinę quę illorum procedat
ex ore; sacerdotum est quę non licet fieri prohibere, populorum est non facere.

168v   Primum igitur pre omnibus ammonendi sunt /168v/ principes, quibus
5   dictum est: Diligite iustitiam qui iudicatis terram; seruite domino in
bonitate et in simplicitate cordis quęrite illum; quoniam inuenietur ab his qui
non tæmptant illum, apparet autem eis qui fidem habent in eum, peruerse
enim cogitationes separant a deo (Sapientia 1, 1-3, but as Gildas).

Hoc Gildas, commemorans in Ormesta Britanniae, explanat dicens: Hoc
10   unum testimonium si toto corde seruaretur, sufficeret ad corrigendos patrię
duces. Nam si dilexissent iustitiam, diligerent utique fontem et quodammodo
originem totius iustitie [deum].

Iterum ammonendi sunt principes de his que conueniunt eis; unicuique
enim principi septem conueniunt: primum deum timere, ueritatem cum
15   misericordia iudicare, humilem fieri in bonos et fortem esse in malos,
pauperes reficere, aecclesiam dei defendere et semper adiuuare, inter
propinquos et alienos similem esse [in] iudicium et semper caueant quod
dominus per prophetam dicit: Per me reges regnant (Proverbs 8,15) et per me
obtinent imperium. Ac si aperte diceret: Nisi a me adiutorium postulauerint
20   nichil ualent, propheta testante: Nisi dominus custodierit ciuitatem, frustra

---

2. P: doctrine; B: doctor.   7. B omits: autem.   12. P: domini (abbrev.); B, Gildas:
deum. 17. B adds: in, before: iudicium.

5-12.   Gildas, De excidio Britonum cap.62, 2-4 (ed. Winterbottom p.117), with
            rearrangement.
14-19.   cf. Collectio Canonum Hibernensis (CCH.) 25,15 (ed. p.81). Ideas
            and some verbal echoes, some differences.

uigilat qui custodit eam (cf.Psalm 126,1).

Iterum considerare debent ut in semetipsis dignitatem nominis sui semper custodiant; nomen enim regis hoc in se retinet, ut subiectis omnibus rectoris officium procuret.

25   Rex ergo a regendo dicitur; et ideo considerare debet qualiter alios corrigere poterit, si proprios mores, ne iniqui sint, non corrigit.

Iniquitas enim regis iniqui pacem populorum rumpit, offendicula regno suscitat, terrarum fructus demit, seruitia populi impedit, carorum mortes

29 praeparat, hostium cursus in prouincias concitat, undique bestias

169r / 169r / quadrupedum delacerationi prouocat, potestates aeris ad nocendum suscitat, terrarum fecunditatem marisque ministeria prohibet, f[ul]mina succendit, arborum flores exurit, fructus immaturos deicit, et non solum presentis imperii faciem sibi ipsi suff[us]cat sed etiam in filios et nepotes, ne regni hereditatem obtineant, obscurat.   Propter piacula enim iniquorum

35 regum, Saul, Cyroboae, Achab et ceterorum similium, semina eorum extinxit deus ne regnarent in mundum.

Iterum boni reges gaudeant quia eorum bona opera patriam aedificant.

Iustitia enim ueri regis et iusti principis haec est: Neminem iniuste iudicare, aduenis et uiduis et pupillis defensorem esse, furta cohibere,

40 adulteria emendare et [si] necesse est punire, decantatores et impudic[o]s et

---

23-24. B omits: ut . . . procuret. 26. P, CCH: ne iniqui; B: nequi. 27. P, CCH: offendicula; B: offendiculo. 29. P, CCH: concitat; B: incitat. 31. P, B: flumina; CCH: fulmina. 32. P, CCH: succendit; B: succedit. 33. P, B: suffocat; CCH: suffuscat. 40. P: et; B: et si. 40. P; impudicus; B, CCH: impudicos.

22-24.   cf. CCH. 25, 3 (p.77). Adaptation but some verbal echoes.
25.   A commonplace etymology e.g. Augustine, De Civitate Dei V, 12; Isidore, Etym. IX.3,1; Sent. III,48.
25-26.   cf. CCH. 24,3 (p.77). Some echoes.
27-36.   cf. CCH. 25,3 (p.77). Rather close in word.
38-40.   cf. CCH. 25,4 (p.77). Some variation and omission.

[h]istriones non nutrire, impios et gentiles de patria pellere, parricidas et periurantes uiuere non sinere, ecclesias dei semper defendere, pauperes elemosinis alere, iustos super regni negotia ministros constituere, seniores et sapientes et sobrios consiliarios habere, magorum et auguriorum

45 superstitionibus non consentire nec intendere, patriam fortiter et iuste contra aduersarios defendere, per omnia in deo confidere, de prosperitate mundi animum non eleuare, et cuncta aduersa patienter ferre, fidem catholicam in deo semper habere, et filios suos impie agere non sinere, certis horis orationibus insistere, ante horas congruas et canonicas cybum non summere,

50 ad aecclesias dei certis temporibus in solemnitatibus conuenire et diuinas lectiones humiliter audire, et nichil ibi de uanitatibus huius mundi disputare, sed cum puro corde et conscientia bona, absque ira et indignatione, humiliter

169v / 169v / ad domum redire.

Iustitia ergo ueri regis et iusti principis pax populorum est, et stabilitas

55 regni, cura languorum, gaudium hominum, temperies aeris ad utilitatem, serenitas maris, terrę fęcunditas, solacium pauperum, hereditas filiorum, spes futurę beatitudinis, abundantia segetum, fęcunditas arborum, et lętitia hominum.

Igitur considerandum est regibus et ueris principibus quod alibi legitur:

60 Prosperitas regni regis est in misericordia et exaltatio nominis eius in

---

41. P, B: pistriones; CCH: histriones. 52. B omits: humiliter. 58. P: hominum; B: omnium. 59. P: quod; B: quia.

41-49.   cf. CCH. 25,4 (p.77).   Some variation and omission.
54-58.   cf. CCH. 25,4 (pp.77-78).   Some variation and omission.
60.   cf. CCH. 25,4 (p.78).

largitate et longitudo dierum eius in uero iudicio.   Sicut Salomon ait: Misericordia et ueritas custodiunt regem et roboratur clementia thronus eius (Proverbs 20,28).

Ammonendi quidem sunt principes de his omnibus ut sint sublimes,
65   modesti, humiles, cunctis affabiles, et sint omnia in omnibus.

Item ammonere debemus populum ut sciant se seruos esse dominorum et subiecti fiant, sicut apostolus ait: Serui obedite dominis uestris carnalibus (cf. Ephesians 6,5).   Et iterum: Serui, subditi estote omni ordinationi humanae propter deum, siue regi, quasi grad[ui] precellenti, siue ducibus, tamquam ab
70   eo misis ad uindictam malefactorum, et ad laudem bonorum (cf. I Peter 2, 13-14). Item ammonendi sunt ut honorem dominis impendant: non tantum bonis sed etiam discolis (I Peter 2,18).   Haec est enim uoluntas dei in Christo Iesu.

Post haec ammonendi sunt omnes ut simul caueant duodecim abusiones
75   quę in mundo sunt; id est: sapiens sine operibus, senex sine religione, iuuenis sine oboedientia, diues sine elemosina, femina sine pudicitia, dominus sine ueritate, Christianus contentiosus, pauper superbus, rex iniquus, episcopus neglegens, plebs indisciplinata, populus sine lege.

79   Oportet nos, fratres karissimi, haec precauere ne confusi sine ex-
170r   / 170r / -cusatione in die iudicii inueniamur ante tribunal Christi.

---

69. P: grad; B, CCH: gradui.   79. B adds: aut, before: sine.

61-63.   CCH. 25,4 (p.78) .
67-68.   CCH. 24,2 (p.75) for quotation.
68-70.   CCH. 24,4 (p.76) for quotation.
71-72.   cf. CCH. 24,2 (p.75) for quotation.
75-78.   cf. chapter headings in Ps.-Cyprian, De duodecim abusivis saeculi (ed. Hellmann; also PL 4,947-60, PL 40,1079-88), but variously presented as a list, e.g. Ps.-Bede, Collectanea (PL 94,545).

Conemur ergo nos indui et solerter ornari animarum uirtutibus.

Prima enim uirtus animae est diligere deum et odire illa que non diligit deus.

Secunda est patientiam sectari et a pusillanimitate declinare.

Tertia est castitatem tam corporis quam anime custodire.

85 Quarta est uanam gloriam contemnere et omnia caduca calcare.

Quinta est humilitatem studere et tumorem superbie obominari.

Sexta est ueritatem amplecti et omne mendacium fugere.

Septima est iram prohibere et furorem reprimere.

Octaua est pacem diligere et odium exsecrari.

90 Nona est ab omni stultitia declinare et diuinam sapientiam amplecti.

Decima est omnem uoluptatem carnis mente abicere.

Undecima est auaritiam spernere et uoluntariam paupertatem assummere.

Duodecima est caritatem dei habere et proximi et non solum amicos in deum

sed etiam inimicos propter deum diligere.

95 Hae sunt duodecim uirtutes quibus animae iustorum induentur in die iudicii

fulgentes ante conspectum domini.

Has ergo uirtutes optinere poterimus si terrenis rebus caelestia
preponamus; ubi est manna caeleste et aeterna premia, ubi est uita angelica
et celestis gloria, ubi est beatitudo angelorum cum Christo regnantium, ubi
100 est lucida lux et securitas sempiterna et regnum caeleste sine fine, ubi
pascuntur sancti in aeterna gloria per infinita secula seculorum. Amen.

---

86. P: obominari; B: abhominari; Ps.-Basil: abominari. 95. P: hae; B: haec. 98. P: preponamus; B: preponent. 99. B adds: iustorum, before: angelorum.

82-96.   cf. Ps.-Basil, Admonitio ad Filium Spiritualem, cap.II (PL 103,686) for the first eleven of these twelve virtues. I suspect that the twelfth was added by our writer to match the twelve abuses. Note that the twelfth extends and adapts the first virtue.

97-98.   For the first phrase cf. Ps.-Basil cap.II.

Vercelli XXI, Scragg (Szarmach 84, 45-67) cf. Latin 81-98:-

Men ða leofestan, uton us nu ymbscrydan and gefrætuwian mid godum
weorcum and mid mægenum urum sawlum on þyssum andweardan life, þy
læs we beon on ðam toweardan dome fram Gode and fram eallum his
haligum werede aworpene, and deoflum betæhte and besencede on helle
witum. Þæt fyrmeste mægen þære sawle ys þæt we lufien urne ecan God of
eallre ure heortan and of eallre sawle and of eallum mægene, and þæt we
hatien ealle þa þing þe he ne lufað. Þonne ys þæt oðer mægen þære sawle
þæt man fylige geþylde and forbuge ælc unriht yrre. Þonne ys þæt þridde
mægen þære sawle þæt man gehealde clænnesse ægðer ge lichoman ge sawle
and forfleo ælce unclænnesse. Þonne is þæt feorðe mægen þære sawle þæt
man forhycge idel wuldor and forseo ealle gewitendlicu þing. Þonne is þæt
fifte mægen þære sawle þæt man bega eaðmodnesse and onscunige
ofermodignesse. Þæt syxte mægen þære sawle ys þæt man lufie soðfæstnesse
and forfleo ælce leasunga. Þæt seofoðe mægen þære sawle ys þæt se man
hine forhæbbe fram yrre and fram hatheortnesse. Þæt eahtoðe mægen ys
þære sawle þæt man lufie sybbe and onsceonige hatunge. Þæt nigoðe mægen
þære sawle is þæt man forbuge ælce disignesse and lufie godcundne wisdom.
Þæt teoðe mægen þære sawle ys þæt man aweg aweorpe of ðam mode ealne
þone yflan lust þæs lichaman flæsces. Þæt endlyfte mægen þære sawle ys þæt
man forhycge gytsunge and genime wilsume þearflicnesse. Ðonne ys þæt
twelfte mægen þære sawle þæt man hæbbe Godes soðan lufe and ure
nehstena, and na þæt an þæt we lufien þa þe ure frynd synt for Gode, ac eac
þæt we for Godes lufe and for his ege lufien þa ðe ure fynd syndon for þysse
worulde. Ðys synt þa twelf mægenu. Of ðam beoð ymbscridde eallra
rihtwisra manna sawla on domes dæge, and of þam hie scinað beforan Godes
gesyhðe. Men ða leofestan, þas mægenu we magon begytan gyf we toforan
asettaþ ða heofonlican þing eallum eorðlicum þingum.

Item 91 fol. 170r XCI. Predicatio bona omnibus Christianis.

Quicumque uoluerit placere deo primum requirat quo possit modo
diligere eum, quia primum et maximum mandatum est in lege deum diligere,
170v sicut scriptum est: Diliges dominum deum tuum ex toto corde tuo /170v/ et
ex tota anima tua et ex tota uirtute tua (cf. Mark 12, 30). Est quoque
5 secundum simile huic: Diliges proximum tuum tamquam teipsum (cf. Matthew
22, 39; Mark 12, 31), In his quidem duobus mandatis totius legis consistit
plenitudo. Tota enim dilectio dei in obseruatione mandatorum eius constat,
sicut saluator ait: Ipse est qui diligit me qui mandata mea custodit (cf. John
14, 15; 14, 21). Et iterum: Uos amici mei estis si feceritis que precipio uobis
10 (cf. John 15, 14). Item alibi: In hoc cognoscent omnes quia mei discipuli
estis, si dilectionem habueritis ad inuicem (John 13, 35). Hoc etiam affirmat
Sanctus Iohannes euangelista dicens: Hoc mandatum habemus a deo, ut qui
diligit deum, diligat et fratrem suum (I John 4, 21). Si quis autem interrogare
uoluerit quis est ille proximus quem precepit dominus diligere sciat omnem
15 Christianum posse intelligi qui opera Christi unanimiter excercet cum fide et
spe et caritate.

Tria ergo haec pernecessaria sunt unicuique homini, fides ut credat in
deum omnipotentem, trinum persona et unum substantia; spes, ut certe speret
aeterna premia; caritas, ut sit plenus dilectione dei et proximi quia omnes in
20 baptismo filii dei sanctificamur ut fratres simus spiritaliter in

---

2. B omits; in lege deum. 5. P: tamquam, as Mark 12, 31; B: sicut. 9. B adds:
ego, before: precipio. 18. B adds: patrem after: deum.

3-4. The Scriptural quotation is given exactly as in Item 20, fol. 39r. In Item 20, an
explanation is abstracted from Alcuin, De. Virt. cap. 3 (PL 101, 615).
2-16. Based on Alcuin, De Virt. cap. 3 (PL 101, 615-16). Except for the quotation
similar to John 14, 15; 14, 21 (lines 8-9), the Scriptural texts are as Alcuin, but
not always the same words. Compare also Alcuin's citation of Romans 13, 10:
Plenitudo legis est dilectio, with lines 6-7. For lines 13-16 cf. Alcuin (PL 101,
616).
17-24. Compare Alcuin, De Virt. cap. 4 (PL 101, 616) for initial idea, but
the extension is very close to Item 22 fol. 43r, now ed. Spencer, Medieval Studies
44 (1982), p.283.

caritate perfecta secundum deum. Maneamus ergo in dilectione dei et proximi sicut predictum est ut ipse in nos semper perseueret, sicut Iohannes ait: Karissimi, deus caritas est, et qui manet in caritate, in deo manet, et deus in eo (I John 4, 16).

25   Deinde post haec necesse est et illa respuere quae non diligit deus, sicut psalmista ait: Quicumque diligitis dominum odite malum (Psalm 96, 10), que Salomon dinumerat dicens (items in this list from Proverbs 6, 16-19): Sex sunt que odit dominus et septimum detestatur; oculos sublimes, id est, superbos humilibus nolentes consentire; linguam mendacem, sicut propheta

30 ait: Odisti omnes qui operantur iniquitatem; perdes omnes qui loquuntur

171r mendacium (Psalm 5, 7); manus effunden-/171r/-tes innoxium sanguinem, sicut Isaias ait: Abominabiles sunt oblationes uestrae quoniam manus uestre sanguine plene sunt (cf. Isaiah 1, 13 and 1, 15); cor machinans cogitationes pessimas, sicut propheta ait: Dominus scit cogitationes hominum, quoniam

35 uanae sunt (Psalm 93, 11); sicut alibi scriptum est: Mala cogitatio deducit ad mortem; pedes ueloces ad currendum in malum, sicut propheta ait: Ueloces pedes eorum ad effudendum sanguinem (Psalm 13, 3), et alibi: Veloces sunt ad malum, pigri ad omne bonum; proferentem mendacia testem fallacem, sicut Salomon ait: Falsus testis non erit impunitus (Proverbs 19, 9); et eum

40 qui seminat inter fratres discordias, de cuius persona dictum est: Non uult

---

23. B omits: karissimi. 24. P: eo; B: illo. 34. P: propheta; B: psalmista.
37. B omits: sunt. 39. B omits; eum, before: qui.

27-40. The items in the list are from Proverbs 6, 16-19: oculos sublimes ... inter fratres discordias. For similar citations of Proverbs (without additional Scriptural texts) see Ps.-Bede, Collectanea (PL 94, 545) and Ps.-Isidore, Liber de Numeris VII.16.

filiu[s] dei uocari qui noluerit pacem amplecti, non considerans dictum saluatoris: Beati pacifici quoniam filii dei uoca[bu]ntur (Matthew 5, 9). Certum est ergo quod si dei filii uocantur qui pacem faciunt, procul dubio Satanae sunt filii qui conf[un]dunt; quicumque igitur in his malis

45   perseuerauerint, dificile pre cęteris sanari possunt nisi ueram poenitentiam egerint et ab illo ueniam postulauerint qui dixit: Etiam post mille peccata uenite ad me et ego sanabo uos.

Festinemus ergo, fratres karissimi, per uias domini et ambulemus in illis. Hae sunt enim, recta fides, certa spes, perfecta caritas, perseuerantia

50   in bonis actibus, bonitas, constantia, patientia, lenitas, pax, oboedientia, longanimitas, sollicitudo sancta, studium mentis in sanctis meditationibus, castitas, misericordia, iusticia, studium scientiæ legis dei, timor domini, amor optimarum rerum, contemptus temporalis glorie, affectio caelestis patriae in qua cęlestia possidentur bona quę preparauit deus diligentibus se, id

55   est, uita sine morte, iuuentus sine senectute, lux sine tenebris, gaudium sine

171v   tristitia, pax sine distantia, uoluntas sine iniuria, regnum sine com-/171v/- mutatione. Haec omnia mereamur inuenire in regnum caelorum cum Christo domino qui uiuit et regnat in secula seculorum. Amen.

---

41. P: filium; B: filius. 42. P: uocantur; B: uocabuntur, as Matthew 5, 9. 44. P: confidunt; B: confundunt, as Gregory in Coll. Can. Hib. 21, 7 (ed. p.64). 44. P: in his malis; B: ex uobis in malis. 48. P: et; B: ut. 49. P: hae; B: hec.

42-4. Scriptural text plus comment, Coll. Can. Hib. 21,7 (ed. p.64) citing Gregory, Regulae Pastoralis Liber, Tertia Pars cap. 23 (PL 76, 92). The composer of our Latin collection used both books.

55-57. Seven Joys of Heaven theme; see T. D. Hill in bibliography.

Vercelli XXI Scragg (Szarmach 84, 38-44) cf. Latin 48-54.

Men þa leofestan, uton efestan and uton gan þurh Godes wegas. Þæt synt soðlice Godes wegas: riht geleafa and gewiss hiht and fulfremed soð lufu and þurhwunung on godum dædum and godnes and anrædnes and geþyld and liðnes and sybb and hyrsumnes and langsumnes and halig ymbhidignes and modes bigeng on haligum smeaungum and clænnes and mildheortnes and rihtwisnes and dryhtnes ege and lufu godcundra þinga and forhogung hwilwendys wuldres and gelustfullung þæs heofonlican eðles, on ðam beoð heofonlice god ða God gegearwað þam þe hine her on worulde lufiað and his willan wyrcað oð hira endedæg.

Item 34 fol.79v XXXIII. Item alia de Resurrectione Domini.

Uidete, fratres karissimi, et considerate quam carissimos nos dominus habere dignatus est et quomodo nos amare disposuit, quia pretio tam carissimo nos redemit, non enim angelo, non archangelo, non patriarchis, nec prophetis, non auro, non argento, non alia speciali materia, sed de suo sancto

5 sanguine nos redimere dignatus est. Quapropter, karissimi, pensate quanta propter peccata nostra sustinere debemus si dei filius tanta pro nobis cruciamenta, qui sine peccato est, pertulit, qui peccatum non fecit nec inuentus est dolus in ore eius; qui cum malediceretur non maledicebat; cum pateretur non cominabatur (I Peter 2, 22, 23) sed percutienti se mitissime

10 dicebat: Si male locutus sum, testimonium perhibe de malo. Sin autem bene, quid me cedis? (cf. John, 18, 23). Et iterum: Pater ignosce illis, nesciunt enim quid faciunt (cf. Luke 23, 34). Et tradebat semetipsum iudicanti se iniuste tamquam agnum innocentem et dum haec omnia pro nobis pateretur,

14 ad extremum, in cruce suspensus, lancea perforatus est et exiuit de latere

80r eius sanguis et aqua. Unde Iohannes apostolus dixit /80r/: Tres sunt, qui testimonium dant: sanguis, aqua et spiritus (cf. I John 5, 8). Quid per sanguinem nisi redemptionem nostram? Quid per aquam nisi baptismi sacramentum? Quid per spiritum nisi sanctificationem nostram significat, quia ex his perficimur filii dei? Deinde post haec mortuus et sepultus est pro

20 nobis et dum illud sacr[um] corpus in sepulchro iacuit anima eius descendit ad

---

2-3. J omits: amare ... nos. 4. P, B, R: nec prophetis; J: non prophetis. 4. J omits: de. 10. P, J, R: sin; B: si. John 18, 23: si. 16. J adds: et before: aqua. 19. R omits: pro nobis. 20. P: sacro, corr. to: sacrus; B, J: sacro; R: sacrum.

2-29. Based on Ps.-Caesarius 17 (PL 67, 1080A), with extensions and additional scriptural quotations. The printed text in PL has a large lacuna at sanguine nos redemit (1080A, l.13) which is extant in an early MS. Vatican Palat. lat. 216, fols. 128v-130v, and includes some phrases in Pembroke which are missing from PL.

infernum. Inde eripuit primum hominem Adam qui per quinque milia ducentos

uiginti et octo annos propter suas culpas in infernum detinebatur. Vnde

dominus per Osee prophetam dicit: O mors ero mors tua, morsus tuus ero

inferne (cf. Osee 13, 14). Ideo dominus Iesus Christus morsus inferni fuit

25 quia partem inde abstulit et partem ibi reliquit. Illos iustos detulit et in

suum regnum secum collocauit. Et illos impios et sacrilegos, id est,

Farahonem cum sociis suis Dathan et Habiron, Sodomę et Gomorrae

sceleratores mortuosque in peccatis, hereticos in inferno reliquid. Ita faciet

in die iudicii: separabit [impios] de medio iustorum et mittet eos in

30 supplicium aeternum, iustis autem reddet mercedem laborum suorum in

conspectibus angelorum.

Vnde quidam tractator ait: Certum est, fratres karissimi, quia si assidue

cogitemus quam magna sunt beneficia domini nostri quae nobis, non

precendentibus meritis nostris, ab eo donata sunt, peccata nobis numquam

35 dominari permittemus, et si forte subrepserint, cito per poenitentiam

80v emendari curabimus. Quis enim /80v/mente concicepere potest, non dicam

uerbis possit exponere, quanta sunt circa nos beneficia dei nostri? Fecit enim

nos primum, cum non essemus; reparauit nos postea, cum perissemus. Nasci

enim propter nos, fratres karissimi, per humilitatem in mundo dignatus est

40 dominus Iesus et mortem pro nobis uoluntarię suscepit ac pretioso nos

---

21. J adds: et, before: inde. 22. B adds: et, after: unde. 22. P, B, R: infernum; J: inferno. 24. P, J, R: inferne; B: inferni; Osee 13, 14: inferne. 26. B omits: et. 27. P: Faraonem, with 'h' superscript; B, J, R: Pharaonem. 28. P, B, R: mortuosque; J: mortuos et. 28. P: infernum, corr: to inferno; B, J. R: infernum. 28. P, J, R: faciet; B: faciat. 29. P: minos deleted, iniquos in margin; B, J, R: impios. 30. J omits: in conspectibus angelorum. 34. B omits: nostris. 35. P, B, R: permittemus; P corr. to: permitteremus; J: permittimus. 36. B, J, R, omit: potest. 37. P, J, R: possit; B: posuit. 37. P, J, R: dei; B: domini. 39. B, J, R omit: fratres karissimi. 40. B, J, R omit: dominus Iesus. 40. J omits: nos.

27.   These noted as great sinners in Coll. Can. Hib. 27,10 (ed. pp.88-89).
32-40. Based on Caesarius 57.3 (Morin I, 252).

sanguine liberauit, ad inferna descendit et ab aeternę mortis faucibus nos eripuit et diabolum cum suis satellitibus in infernum deorsum suppressit. Et non solum nos redemit sed etiam caelorum nobis aeterna premia repromisit. Haec ergo omnia, fratres karissimi, pio et benigno animo cogitemus, et

45 quantum possumus cum dei adiutorio beneficiis suis uicem rependere festinemus. Non reddamus mala pro bonis sed in quantum ualeamus uoluntati ipsius obtemperare fideliter studeamus.

Offeramus ergo sancta munera Christo redemptori nostro, primum tenentes in illo fidem rectam, spem certam, caritatem perfectam; et post

50 haec humilitatem, benignitatem, mansuetudinem, continentiam, abstinentiam, patientiam, temperantiam, mentesque humiles et laudabiles mores. Haec sunt dona et munera deo nostro grata et beneplacita quę illi quidem offeruntur sed offerentibus prosunt.

Rogo ergo uos, fratres, et per illum cuius pretioso sanguine redempti

55 estis ammoneo ut, totis uiribus, hęc omnia in animo teneatis et de animę uestrę salute attentius cogitetis. Et nolite obliuisci preceptum Christi per

81r quod nobis caelorum regna promittit dicens: Estote misericordes /81r/ sicut et pater uester misericors est (Luke 6, 36). Et iterum: Beati misericordes quoniam ipsi misericordiam consequentur (Matthew 5, 7). Et iterum: Beati

60 mundo corde quoniam ipsi deum uidebunt (Matthew 5, 8).

---

41. B, J, R omit: ab; as Caesarius. 43. J omits: nobis. 44. J omits: et. 45. P, J, R: uicem; B: inuicem. 45. P, B, R: rependere; J: reprehendere. 51. B omits: patientiam. 52. B, J, R add: enim, after: haec. 52. P, B, R: deo; J: domino. 52. P, B, R: beneplacita; J: multiplicata. 53. P, B, J, R: sed; but a later hand corrects P to: ut. 54. J adds: karissimi after: fratres. 54. P, J, R: et; B: ut. 55. B omits: ut. 59. P, J, R: ipsi; B: ipsis. 59. B omits: et iterum.

41-47. Based on Caesarius 57.3 (Morin I, 252). 48-53. Extended from Ps.-Augustine 136.6 (PL 39, 2015) but with verbal echoes.

Vercelli XXI Scragg (Szarmach 84-85, 67-96) cf. Latin 38 (Nasci enim) - 68 (prestare solet)

Uton eac geþencan georne, men ða leofestan, mid arfæstum and mid wellwillendum mode hu dryhten ælmihtig þurh eaðmodnesse hyne sylfne for ure þearfe to men gehywode on þyssum middangearde þurh ða eadigan fæmnan Marian buta ælces weres gem an an, and hu he deað for us onfeng, and hu he [us] alysde fram deoflum and fram helle witum mid his deorwyrðan blode, and hu he nyðer stah to hellwarum and us alysde of gomum þæs ecan deaðes, and hu he ðone deofol on helle mid his wæggesiðum ofþrihte. And na þæt an þæt he us þanon alysde, men ða leofestan, ac eac swylce he us behet þa ecan meda þæs heofonlican rices. Uton efstan nu þæt we magon him gewrixl agyldan on swa myclum swa he us gefultumian wille ongean ealle þa god þe he us forgifen hæfð. Uton ne agildan yfel ongean his god, ac on swa myclum swa we magon uton hycgan þæt we getreowlice him hyrsumien swa his willa sie. Uton bringan and offrian dryhtne, urum alysende, halige lac, æryst þæt we gehealdon on him rihtne geleafan and gewissne hiht and fulfremede soðe lufe and eaðmodnesse and wellwillendnesse and geþwærnesse and gehealdsumnesse and forhæfdnesse and geþyld and gemetfæstnesse and eaðmode mod and heriendlice þeawas for Gode and for worulde. Ðas gifa and þas lac syndon þancwyrðe and well gecweme urum dryhtne, and witodlice gif hie beoð him brohte fram us, hie us myclum fromiað. Ðig we eow biddað and myndgiað and eac halsiað þurh þone þe us alysde ealle mid his ðam deorwyrðan blode þæt we gehealden ealle ðas foresædan þing on urum mode of eallum urum mihtum. And uton ealle geornlicor be urra sawla hælo [geþencan] þonne we ær þyssum dydon, and na to þæs hwon ne forgiten we Cristes sylfes bebod þurh þæt he us behet heofona ricu, þus cweðende: 'Beoð mildheorte swa swa eower fæder ys mildheort'. And eft he cwæð: 'Eadige beoð þa mildheortan, for ðam þe [hie] begytaþ mildheortnesse'. And eft he cwæð: 'Eadige beoð þa clænheortan, for ðam þe hie geseoð God'.

Witodlice we cumað orsorge on domes dæge toforan Cristes þrymsetle, and beoð rihtwise þonne on ecum gemynde. And we beoð fram him forð gecigede to þam heofonlican gebeorscipe mid þam mærum heahfæderum Abrahame and Isace and Iacobe and eallum haligum werude. He us gegearwað þa heofonlican for ðam eorðlicum and þa ecan þing for þam hwilendlicum þingum þysse worulde , gif we ælmyssan don willað on urum life, and gif we dædbote don willaþ urra misfenga, and gif we þa hingriendan fedaþ and him drinc gesyllað, and gif [we] þa nacodan be urum mihtum scrydað, and gif we þa elðeodigan onfoð þonne hie ure be[ð]urfen.

Si igitur aelymosinas facimus, si poenitentiam agimus, si esurientes pascimus, si sitientes potamus, si nudos secundum uires nostras uestimus, si peregrinos accipimus, et si haec omnia diligenter agimus, securi ante tribunal Christi in die iudicii ueniemus, et tunc in memoria ęterna iusti erimus (cf.

65 Psalm 111, 7), et ad conuiuium caeleste cum Abraham et Isaac et Iacob (cf. Matthew 8, 11) ab illo prouocabimur, qui pro terrenis caelestia, pro temporalibus sempiterna, pro modicis magna, pro mortalitate aeternitatem, nobis semper prestare solet. Placere ergo ei studeamus a quo nobis cuncta bona procedunt, quia nichil a nobis exigit nec petit nisi quod proficit nobis ad

70 salutem animę nostrę ut cum illo regnemus in secula seculorum. Amen.

---

66. P, J, R: illo; B:illa.   67. P, J, R: mortalitate; B: mortalitalitate.   68. B omits: ei.   69. P, J, R: exigit; B: exiguit.   69. P, B, R: petit; J: petiit.

68-69. Ps.-Aug. 136.6.

Extracts.

1. Item 24 fol. 48r XXIIII. Omelia in Dominica iiii in Quadragesima.

   Extract fol. 50r ll.17-21:-

   Tunc miseri peccatores, superbi et auari (B omits this phrase), iudices mali et adulteri, impii et heretici, fornicatores et mendaces, dolosi et inuidi, malum pro malo reddentes, et iniuriam pauperibus facientes.

   Vercelli XXI Scragg (Szarmach 83, 15-19):-

   be ðam earmum synfullum ys on Cristes bocum awriten and be ðam ofermodigum and be ðam gytserum and be ðam yfeldemum and be ðam unrihthæmerum and be ðam arleasum and be ðam gedweolenum and be ðam forligergendrum and be ðam leasfyrhtum and be ðam facenfullum and be ðam andigum and be ðam þe yfel ongean yfel agyldað and be ðam þe þearfum ænige teonan gedoð.

2. Item 39 fol. 90r. Pembroke no title.

   Extract fol. 90v ll.11-12:-

   cum ingenti gemitu, assiduis orationibus et largioribus elimosinis debemus dei clementiam implorare.

   Source:- Caesarius 208.2 (Morin, II 833):-

   cum ingenti rugitu uel gemitu, adsiduis orationibus uel largioribus elemosinis debemus dei misericordiam inplorare.

   Vercelli XXI, Scragg (Szarmach, 84, 33-35):-

   and symle we sceolon biddan Godes mildheortnesse mid ormættre geomrunge and mid syngalum gebedum and mid rumgyfullum ælmessylenum.

3. Item 50 fol. 117v XLXI (sic). Omelia in Passione Sancti Iohannis Baptistę.

   Extract fol. 119v ll.12-14:-

   Ubi est lux lucis et fons luminis, ubi est gaudium sempiternum, ubi claritas angelorum et claritas sanctorum, ubi est honor perfectus et letitia sine fine (J omits: Ubi est lux . . . sanctorum).

Vercelli XXI, Scragg (Szarmach 87, 203-204):-

Þær is leoht ealles leohtes, þær is se eca gefea, þær is seo ece torhtnes eallra engla, þær is seo swete lufu eallra haligra, þæ[r] is wyrðment and ece blis butan ælcum ende.

Oxford, Bodley MS. Junius 85, 86 ed. A. M. L. Fadda, Nuove Omelie Anglosassoni (Firenze, 1977), p.25 11.251-254):-

ðær bið leohtes leoht ond willa ðæs leohtes and þær bið ece gefea ond þer bið ængla breohtenes and haligra lufu ond þer bið seo ece ar . . . ac ðær bið blis butan ænde.

----

4. Item 25 fol. 50v XXV. Omelia in Dominica V^a in Quadragesima.

Extract fol. 52v 11.18-23;-

Ubi est serenitas sine nube, gaudium sine tristitia, lux sine tenebris, uita sine morte, iuuentus sine senectute, decor sine demutatione, splendor mirabilis lucidior splendore solis, aeternitas semper manens et regnum sine fine in quo sunt agmina angelorum et congregatio iustorum ibi semper manentium.

Vercelli XXI Scragg (Szarmach 87, 204-208):-

Þær is smyltnes butan genipe, þær ys gefea butan unrotnesse, þær is leoht butan þysstrum, þær is lif butan deaðe, þær is geoguð butan ylde, and þær is wlite butan awendednesse, and þær ys wundorlic beorhtnes leohtre [þonne þære] sunna[n] beorhtnes and þær ys ecnes symle wuniende and rice butan ende, on þam synt engla weredu and rihtwisra togelaðung þær symle wuniendra.

----

5. Item 48 fol. 111v XLVIII. Item alia de Sapientia.

Extract fol. 113v 11.7-11:-

Ubi cum Christo semper habitant sancti et iusti, inmaculati et recti, boni et mansueti, electi et perfecti, mites et misericordes, patientes et recte iudicantes, deum diligentes et caritate splendentes, benigni et pacifici.

Vercelli XXI Scragg (Szarmach 87, 210-212):-

Þær wunia [þ] þa haligan menn him sylfe and rihtwise and þa unwemman and þa godan and þa geþwearan and þa gecorenan and þa fulfremedan and þa byliwyttan and þa mildheortan and þa geþyldigan and þa rihtwisan deman and þa gesybsuman.

Tristram III

The homiliary in Cambridge, Corpus Christi College MS. 162 is, as Scragg says, (Anglo-Saxon England 8 (1979), p.242) 'an orderly collection' drawing mainly on two earlier collections, Oxford, Bodley MSS. 340, 342, and Cambridge, Corpus Christi College MS. 198, but also containing seven more anonymous items. These last seven include three sermons for Rogationtide (now published from this manuscript in Bazire-Cross as Homilies 1-3) followed by a sermon In die ascensionis domini (Tristram III). The first two Rogationtide sermons are variant texts of Vercelli Homilies XIX and XX respectively; the 'thrust' of the third sermon, also for Rogationtide, 'was towards a visualization' 'of the physical terrors of the Last Days and, especially, of Doomsday' 'and of the sensual delights in the Heavenly City' (Bazire-Cross p.41), a considerable topic within Vercelli XXI, but the fourth sermon in the liturgical sequence (for Ascension Day) is unique in this Corpus Christi manuscript. We recall that the three Vercelli sermons (XIX, XX, XXI) drew variously for material on items within the Pembroke-type collection, which is fused with other material. The same method is found in the fourth sermon (for Ascension Day), which largely uses material from two Pembroke items, 41, 42, (printed below) both for Ascension Day. It is also clear from a comparison with the Latin sources, where relevant, in relation to the corrections made to the base text, that the Ascension Day sermon was copied from an earlier piece already in Old English. Such information collated here may suggest, but not demonstrate, that a sequence of three Rogationtide sermons as Vercelli XIX, XX, XXI, followed by an Ascension Day sermon as in C.C.C.C. 162 could have been a sequence in an earlier vernacular manuscript.

Hildegard Tristram published the Ascension sermon in her doctoral dissertation as no. III of her Vier altenglische Predigten, pp.162-172, but said little about the content of the sermon. I have now been greatly helped by Jane Moores who re-edited the vernacular sermon from manuscript and compared it with the Latin sources as an undergraduate dissertation at Liverpool 1985, under the supervision of Joyce Bazire. They report some misreading of the manuscript or proof-reading error by Tristram and/or some debatable deduction at:

Tristram 1.115: bylihwytlice: MS.: bylitwytlice. Read: byli[h]wytlice.

Tristram 1.115: demdon; MS.: demde, with deletion-point under the final 'e' and superscript 'on'. Read: demd[on].

Tristram 1.129: stigan; MS.: astigan. Read as manuscript.

Tristram 1.131: gegyrelan; MS.: gygyrlan, with deletion-point under the first 'y' but no superscript. Read as manuscript.

Also Tristram 1.51: heofon'es' as MS ('es' superscript). The base text normally presents 'heavens' as plural. Only once it is singular (1.134) without correction, but both base text (ll.15, 237, 255) and corrector elsewhere (1.135) present the accusative as: heofonas. Read: heofon [as] or possibly: heofon.

Both sermons in the Latin collection celebrate the day as a time of joy, triumph and final liberation from the devil's rule, and both describe Christ's physical ascension as in Scripture, but otherwise their emphasis is different. Item 41 (fol. 93v) concentrates mainly on the apostles, the calming of their fears, the answering of questions about the second advent and the command to their preaching mission, with applications to the priestly offices of the present. Item 42 (fol. 95v), a shorter sermon, is directed more pointedly to the ordinary Christian, enumerating virtues to be attained, vices to be avoided, tortures of the sinners' hell and delights of the believers' heaven.

By choosing the second Latin sermon as the basis for his own, the Anglo-Saxon composer indicated his purpose and audience, but he takes from the first a descriptive passage and the Grandis honor ('mycel wurðmynt') sequence which is made applicable to all Christians. To his translated, or adapted, selection he himself adds his own introduction and conclusion, drawing on Scripture and his own liturgical memory.

He begins (ll.1-11) with an exhortation to glory and delight in the Ascension (as with many Ascension Day sermons and our two Pembroke sermons) but with an immediate recall of Christ's birth, which Herod feared, and resurrection, which the Jews feared. With adjectives and descriptive nouns he briefly presents Christ's victorious regality in Ascension (ll.12-15) but then reverts to Scriptural account in

Acts cap. 1, the epistolary reading for Ascension Day, and Mark cap. 16, the Gospel reading for the day, as setting and introduction for the physical ascension. Verses from these Scriptural chapters are the basis for the information in the section, ll.15-34, but the description is freely presented. Pembroke item 41 has a little of this information, but I prefer to think that the Anglo-Saxon has recalled the Scripture chosen for the feast-day.

Yet at ll.35-48, the scene of the ascension, our vernacular composer takes some phrases from the description in Pembroke item 41 ll.105-115, part of which he translates closely towards the end of his own sermon (ll.228-234). We note:

i.   'hine onfeng beorht wolcn fram heora eagum' (ll.36-37), cf. Acts 1, 9: <u>et nubes suscepit eum ab oculis eorum</u>, but item 41 l.105 <u>in nube clara</u> cf. 'on beorhtum genipe' (l.229).

ii.   'twegen weras þa wæron ymbscrydde mid beorhtum reafe' (ll.39-40), cf. Acts 1, 10: <u>duo viri astiterunt . . . in uestibus albis</u>, but item 41 ll.111-112: <u>duo uiri stetere, amicti ueste clara.</u>

iii.   'hwæt wundrige ge þus þas heofonlican heahnysse behealdende? Soðlice þes hælend þe fram eow genumen is and gebroht is on fæder swyðran healfe' (ll.42-45), cf. Acts 1, 11: <u>quid statis aspicientes in coelum? hic Jesus, qui assumptus est a uobis in coelum,</u> but item 41 ll.112-114: <u>Quid admiramini caelorum alta? Iesus enim hic qui assumptus est a uobis ad patris dexteram.</u>

iv.   Also the reference to Christ's return at Judgement (ll.45-48) is an idea from Pembroke item 41 l.115, not from Acts cap. 1, although the Anglo-Saxon develops the idea differently from the composer of the Pembroke-type collection.

Then the Anglo-Saxon inserts an invocation (ll.51-65) to the Creator who made all creation and formed the first man Adam, betrayed by the devil, forced out of Paradise, taken to torment, redeemed (with us, says the preacher) and again led to the joy of paradise from which he had been driven. The intercession (ll.60-65) follows as a direct prayer that the Lord give us eternal rest at Judgement, because of the Ascension. The whole prayer may have a liturgical source, but it forms an introduction to the use of the opening two paragraphs of Pembroke item 42 in ll.66-100 (as illustrated below), which call on us to glory in the Ascension, recall Adam's sin, and state that after the Ascension (not Resurrection, as normally) the souls of the holy may await the resurrection of the body in perpetuam felicitatem l.14 ('on ðære ecan gesælignysse' l.95) while the souls of the sinners may wait for their bodies in hell.

The rather close translation of the Pembroke sermon continues to l.123, with expansion and omission of Latin word or phrase in order to simplify some Latin concepts and to hold the audience firmly to the needs and statements of the faith. Then the Anglo-Saxon omits a Latin section about offering holy gifts, in a list of virtuous attitudes, and concentrates, with the Latin, on the wonders of the day (ll.124-26). This section in the Latin (ll.37-54), with parallel Old English (ll.127-163), is an imaginative elaboration on varied Scriptural hints. The two in white garments of Acts 1, 10 are multiplied to many angels on a ladder as Genesis 28, 12 (Jacob's ladder), ascending and descending (Genesis 28; 12) but applied to the Son of Man in John 1, 51. It is these angels who ask Uiri Gallilei quid admiramini? and command the disciples to remain in Jerusalem. But the heavenly vision also presents Christ standing in heaven (as Stephen saw him in Acts 7, 55) before the high altar (as in the visualization of heaven in the Apocalypse of John 6, 9; 8, 3). They look down on souls in torment, without Scriptural basis, but in a scene obviously influenced by the popular apocryphon, Visio S. Pauli, as indicated by the distinctive tortures of these sinners a little later. Such a vision, full of concrete detail, would be an effective reminder of the alternatives, already presented to the audience and re-iterated within the section.

After the elaborated picture, the Latin composer concludes (ll.55-72) with his exhortation to prepare our hearts so that we may experience the varied (and lengthily-listed) delights of heaven. This section is closely followed by the Anglo-Saxon preacher (ll.164-190). And he continues (ll.193-226), without resistance, to the impressive collocation of Scriptural testimonies of Christ's love and rewards for the faithful in the Grandis honor sequence of Pembroke item 41 ll.82-104. We recall that this Latin sermon was directed towards the apostles, as was Gregory's Homilia 29 in

Evangelia from which some phrases and ideas are taken. But, as Jane Moores has pointed out to me, there are some adaptations in the Old English (underlined) which broaden the specific statements about the apostles to the body of Christian believers, e.g.

i. 'Uton gemunon hu micel wurðmynt hit byð us on ðam toweardan life þæt we þær scinað on godes rice swa sunne gyf we his willan her on worulde wyrcað' (ll.193-196).

Cf. Grandis, inquam, honor est eis ut fulgeant sicut sol in regno patris eorum, et sedeant super duodecim thronos iudicantes duodecim tribus Israel (ll.82-84).

ii. 'Hwæt he us eallum þone wurðmynt geann þe he his apostolum geuðe and him to cwæð: Swa swa min fæder me lufode swa ic lufode eow . . .' (ll.197-199).

Cf. Grandis honor est eis quibus filius dei dicit: Sicut dilexit me pater, et ego dilexi uos (ll.85-86).

The Englishman also inserts 'nu' (now) in some of the other items of the sequence, as a simple means of adaptation to the general audience.

The composer of the Latin sermon (item 41 l.105) has now to refer to the physical event of the Ascension which follows logically from the final Grandis honor quotation, Ascendo ad patrem meum (ll.103-104). Here the Anglo-Saxon follows him closely for a brief passage, which had been echoed sporadically to expand and change Scripture earlier. In the Old English (ll.228-234) it is a repetition of the ascension scene but the vernacular composer omits some Latin phrases of description and runs on to the prayer (ll.235-241), which is an antiphon in the Latin (ll.116-119) as identified in the edition below.

The Latin sermon (item 41) ends immediately with a brief phrase of benediction, but the Englishman believes that he must leave his audience with restated warnings and exhortations in an extended passage (ll.242-264) of his own. He has, however, used the Latin collection, as its composer would have wished, by abstracting effective material and by adapting and fusing it into a composition of his own.

Item 41 fol.93v XL. Omelia in Ascensione Domini.

Uocem iocunditatis ac dulcedinis de resurrectione domini ac uictoria Christi annuntiate, fratres karissimi, in medio catholici [populi] et usque ad extremum terrę dicite, quia liberauit dominus populum suum a peccatis eorum et de captiuitate qua per inuidiam diaboli tenebantur, captiui in

5 tenebris et in umbra mortis, sicut propheta dicit: Eduxit dominus populum suum in exultatione et electos suos in lętitia (Psalm 104, 43, Vulgate). Cantate igitur domino canticum nouum, eodem propheta dicente, quia mirabilia fecit (cf. Psalm 32, 3). Mirabilia quidem Christus fecit quando ab inferis uictor resurrexit; descendere enim prius dignatus fuerat de sede

10 patris qui in cęlo cum patre coaeuus et coaequalis fulgebat. Et tamen homo factus est per misericordiam nostrę salutis causa. Natus enim ex Maria uirgine, pannis inuolutus, in presepio positus, in carne circumcisus, a Iohanne in Iordane baptizatus, a diabolo in deserto temptatus, a Iudeis persecutus, ab ipsis etiam comprehensus, et ad extremum flagellatus atque crucifixus,

15 mortuus et sepultus est, et ad inferna descendit, et postea tertia die de sepulchro uiuus surrexit. Deinde per quadraginta dies suis precepit discipulis quę facere deberent et docere, quibus et prebuit seipsum uiuum post

94r passionem suam, in multis argumentis / 94r / apparens et loquens eis de regno dei (Acts 1,3).   Et conuescens, precepit eis ab Hierosolymis ne

20 discederent, sed expectarent promissionem patris, quam audistis, inquit, per

---

2. P: apostoli; B, J: populi. 10. P, B: fulgebat; J: fuerat. 11. B adds: est, after: natus. 18. J omits: eis; B: apparens eis loquens. 19. P, J: eis; B: illis.

os meum (Acts 1,4). Dicebat enim eis: Vado parare uobis locum (John 14,2); et iterum: Ueniam ad uos, et gaudebit cor uestrum (cf. John 16,22). Nisi enim ego abiero, paraclitus non ueniet ad uos; dum autem assumptus fuero, mittam eum uobis (cf. John 16,7). Cum autem uenerit ille, spiritus ueritatis,

25 docebit uos omnem ueritatem et que uentura sunt annuntiabit uobis (John 16,13 with omissions). Ego enim rogabo patrem pro uobis, et alium paraclitum mittet ad uos, ut maneat uobiscum in aeternum (cf. John 14,16). Apostoli igitur, qui conuenerant in unum, interrogabant eum de his omnibus dicentes: Domine si in tempore hoc restitues regnum Israel? (Acts 1,6), ac si

30 dicerent si in diebus nostris erit consummatio seculi et restitutio regni. Dixit autem eis: Non est uestrum nosse tempora uel momenta que pater posuit in sua potestate (Acts 1,7), quasi diceret, cur queritis tempora uel momenta aduentus domini que signis preuenientibus et prodigiis reuelabuntur in suo tempore quorum tamen diem uel horam nemo scit, neque angeli in celo, neque

35 filius hominis (Mark 13,32, cf. Matthew 24,36), id est, omnes sancti, qui sunt Christi corpus, et angeli celorum diem iudicii nesciunt, sed pate[r] solus. Per id enim patrem et filium et spiritum sanctum intelligimus sicut saluator ait: Ego et pater unum sumus (John 10,30); et iterum: Qui uidet me, uidet et patrem, quia ego in patre et pater in me est (cf.John 12,45; 14,20); et iterum:

40 Nemo nouit filium nisi pater et patrem quis nouit nisi filius, (cf. Luke 10,22);

---

23. B omits: dum ... uobis (line 24). 24. P, B: uobis; J: ad uos; John 16,7: ad uos.
30. B omits: restitutio. 36. P: pate; B, J: pater. 37. J has inverted order of Scriptural quotation after: intelligimus, i.e. 37-39. 40. J: nemo nouit patrem nisi filius et filium quis nouit nisi pater.

8-20. Some phrases, including some quotations from Scripture, taken from Munich 6233, fols. 158v-159v.

nouit igitur filius diem iudicii et horam similiter sicut et pater et spiritus
sanctus sed ideo a corpore suo, id est, ab omnibus sanctis, diem iudicii
abscondit, ut sollicitudinem semper habeant uigilandi, sicut ipse in aeuangelio
dicit: Vigilate et orate et estote parati, quia nescitis qua hora dominus uester
45 ueniet, sero, an media nocte, an galli cantu (cf. Mark 13,35). In his scilicet
94v temporibus noctis dominus noster / 94v / specialiter aduentum suum
significauit, propterea noluit reuelare aduentus sui tempora discipulis sed [ut]
semper uigilarent et orarent, ne seducerentur per fallaciam inimici. Sed
accipietis, inquit, uirtutem superuenientis spiritus sancti in uos, et eritis mihi
50 testes in Hierusalem, et in omni Iudea, et Samaria, et usque ad ultimum terrę
(Acts 1,8), ac si diceret, sicut enim prophete testimonium de meo aduentu
predixerunt in carne, ita uos et successores uestri meae resurrectionis eritis
et ascensionis testes. Et ideo dixit eis: Euntes in mundum uniuersum,
predicate euangelium omni creaturę (Mark 16,15), id est, omni homini, in quo
55 consistunt omnia elimenta ex quibus conditus est mundus. Qui uero non
crediderit condemnabitur (Mark 16,16). Fortasse aliquis apud semetipsum
dicit, ego iam credidi saluus ero; uerum dicit si fidem operibus implet. Sed
ille uerissime credidit qui uerba dei, quę audierit, operibus exercet, et
baptizatus fuerit, id est, qui omnia, quę in baptismo promittit, perseueranter
60 custodit. Qui uero non crediderit condemnabitur (Mark 16,16), id est, qui

---

43. P, J: sicut ipse; B: sicut quod se. 45. B adds: an mane, after: sero. 47. J adds:
ut. 48. B omits: uigilarent. 49. P: eritis, after correction; B, J: eritis. 49. J
omits: mihi. 50. J omits: Iudea et. 52. B adds: et, before: uos. 55. B adds after
mundus: qui crediderit et baptizatus fuerit saluus erit. 56. P, B: apud; J:
ad. 59. B, J omit: qui, before: omnia.

41-47. Some phrases, including the quotation from Scripture, taken from Munich 6233,
fol. 159v.
53-57. Some words, and ideas, taken from Gregory, Hom. 29 in Evang. 1-3 (PL 76,
1214-15).

fidem in deum non habet, nec opera eius exercet, ipse non saluabitur.

Signa autem eos qui crediderint hęc sequentur: in nomine meo daemonia eicient; linguis loquentur nouis; serpentes tollent; et si mortiferum quid biberint, non eis nocebit; super ęgros manus imponent et

65 bene habebunt (Mark 16,17-18). Sunt autem multi qui querunt[ur] et murmurant quia hęc signa modo per sacerdotes facere minime uident, non intelligentes quidem quia sancta aecclesia cotidie spiritaliter facit quod tunc per apostolos dominus corporaliter faciebat. Quid enim aliud sacerdotes faciunt nisi dęmonia eicere quando per exorcismi gratiam manum credentibus

70 imponunt et habitare malignos spiritus in eorum mente contradicunt? Et qui secularia uerba derelinquunt et conditoris sui laudem et potentiam quantum

95r preualent narrant, quid aliud faciunt nisi nouis linguis / 95r / loquuntur? Qui dum bonis suis exortationibus de alienis cordibus malitiam auferunt, quid aliud faciunt nisi serpentes tollunt, id est, odium, inuidiam, detractionem et

75 cętera uitia? Et qui exemplo bonę operationis proximorum uitam roborant qui in propria actione titubant, quid aliud faciunt nisi super aegros manus imponere ut bene habeant et sanentur? Quę nimirum miracula tanto maiora sunt quanto per hęc non corpora suscitantur sed animę uiuificantur.

Grandis ergo honor credentibus in Christum donatur ut sint uidelicet

80 fratres domini Iesu Christi et filii patris altissimi, ut sint heredes dei,

---

65. P: querunt; B, J: queruntur. 70. B omits: qui. 71. P, B: secularia; J: claria. 72. P: loquuntur; B, J: loqui et. 73. B, J omit: dum, before: bonis. 73. J omits: suis. 74. P: tollunt; B, J: tollere. 75. B adds: mala, after uitia. 75. P, B: qui; J: que. 75. P, B: operationis; J: orationis. 75. P, J: uitam; B: uita. 76. P: titubant; B: titubabant; J: tibuant. 80. B, J add: nostri, before: Iesu.

62-78. Many phrases, and ideas, from Gregory, Hom. 29 in Evang. 4 (PL 76, 1215-16).

coheredes autem Christi (cf. Romans 8, 16-17).

Grandis, inquam, honor est eis ut fulgeant sicut sol in regno patris eorum (cf. Matthew 13,43) et sedeant super duodecim thronos iudicantes duodecim tribus Israel (cf. Luke 22,30).

85   Grandis honor est eis quibus filius dei dicit: Sicut dilexit me pater, et ego dilexi uos; manete in dilectione mea (John 15,9); et iterum: Uos amici mei estis, si feceritis quę precipio uobis (John 15,14).

Grandis honor est quibus dicit: Quodcumque petieritis patrem in nomine meo, dabit uobis (cf. John 16,23); item: Ipse [enim]pater amat uos,
90   quia uos me amastis, et credidistis (John 16,27).

Grandis honor est eis pro quibus patrem filius supplicat dicens: Pater sanctę, salua eos in nomine tuo, quos dedisti mihi (cf. John 17,11), et: ut cognoscat mundus quia tu me misisti, et dilexisti eos, sicut et me dilexisti (John 17,23).

95   Grandis honor est credentibus de quibus filius dicit: Pater, quos dedisti mihi, uolo ut ubi ego sum, ibi sint et hi mecum; ut uideant claritatem meam, quam dedisti mihi, et ego dedi eis (cf. John 17,24 and 22); et iterum:

Grandis honor est eis quibus saluator oscula pacifica dedit dicens: Pacem relinquo uobis, pacem meam do uobis (John 14,27), et iterum:

100   Grandis honor est eis quibus saluator ad patrem rediens dicebat: Tempus

---

89. B, J add: enim, before: pater; as John 16,27. 92. P, B: tuo quos; J: meo quod; John 17,11: tuo quos. 93. B omits: et, after: sicut. 99. B adds: Pacem meam do uobis, at beginning, thus presenting the phrase twice.

Tristram III 169-70, 193-222 (with modern punctuation); cf. Latin 82-100.

and uton gemunon hu micel wurðmynt hit byð us on ðam toweardan life þæt we þær scinað on godes rice swa sunne gyf we his willan her on worulde wyrcað.

Hwæt he us eallum þone wurðmynt geann þe he his apostolum geuðe, and him to cwæð: Swa swa min fæder me lufode swa ic lufode eow; wuniað on minre lufe; and: ge beoð mine frynd, gyf ge þa þing doð þe ic eow bebeode.

Eala micel weorðscipe is hit þam nu þe he þa to cwæð: Swa hwæt swa ge on minum naman minne fæder biddað he eow sylþ; and: He lufað eow, for þam ðe ge me lufodon, and on me gelyfdon.

Eala micel wurðmynt is hit þam ðe he his fæder fore halsode þus cwæþende: Eala þu halga fæder, gehæl þa on þinum naman, þe ðu me sealdest; and: þæt middaneard oncnawe þæt þu me sendest; þæt syndon ealle þa ðe on me gelyfað.

Eala micel wurðmynt ys þam gelyfendum þe godes bearn big sæde: Eala fæder, he cwæð, þa ðe þu me sealdest, ic wille þæt hi beon þær þær ic beo; þæt hi geseon mine beorhtnysse, þe ðu me sealdest, and þa ðe ic him sealde.

Micel wurðmynt is nu þam ðe se hælend sealde gesibsume cossas þus cwæðende: Ic læte to eow sibbe, and ic sylle eow mine sibbe.

Micel wurðmynt is nu þam þe se hælend to cwæð, þa he to his fæder for to heofona rices wuldre: Hit is tima þæt ic

est ut reuertar ad eum qui me misit (cf. John 16,5); uos autem benedicite

95v   deum / 95v / et enarrate omnia mirabilia eius (cf. Psalm 104, 2); et iterum:

Grandis honor est eis quibus ipse dixit: Ascendo ad patrem meum, et patrem uestrum, deum meum, et deum uestrum (John 20,17).

105   Et cum hęc dixisset, uidentibus illis, eleuatus est (Acts 1,9) in nube clara et ipse quidem expansis manibus ferebatur in cęlis et benedicebat eis (cf. Luke 24, 50-51) dicens: Pax uobis (Luke 24,36); et nub[e]s suscepit eum ab eorum oculis (cf. Acts 1,9) intuentibus illis aera.   Ecce ubique creatura creatori suo prestat obsequium.   Astra indicant nascentem, patientem

110   obnubunt.   Recipiunt nubes ascendentem et redeuntem ad iudicium comitabuntur.   Cumque intuerentur in cęlum, ecce, duo uiri stetere, amicti ueste clara, iuxta illos (cf. Acts 1,10) dicentes: Quid admiramini caelorum alta?   Iesus enim hic qui assumptus est a uobis (cf. Acts 1,11) ad patris dexteram, ut ascendit, ita ueniet, id est, in eadem forma carnis atque

115   substantia, ueniet iudicaturus in qua uenerat iudicandus.   Illi autem, una uoce, clamabant dicentes: O rex glorię, domine uirtutum, qui triumphat[o]r hodie super omnes cęlos ascendisti, ne derelinquas nos orphanos, sed mitte promissum patris in nos spiritum ueritatis ut semper nobiscum maneat in aeternum, et tecum uitam habeamus aeternam per infinita secula seculorum.

120   Amen.

---

102. P, B: deum; J: eum. 104. B, J add: ad, before: patrem uestrum; P as John, 20,17. 106. P, B: celis; J: celum. 107. P: nubs; B, J: nubes. 110. B omits: nubes. 111. B omits: uiri. 111. P, B: stetere; J: steterunt. 113. B omits: qui. 116. P: triumphatur; B, J: triumphator. 118. B omits: semper . . . aeternum et (119). 120. J omits: Amen.

Tristram III 171, 223-234; cf. Latin 101-108.

gehwyrfe up to þam þe me hider niðer asende; and bletsiað ge god and
gecyðað ealle his wuldru.

Eala micel wurðmynt is nu þam ðe he sylf to cwæð: Ic astige to minum
fæder, and to eowrum fæder, and to minum gode, and to eowrum gode.

And þa ða he þas þing sæde, þa wearð he up ahafen on beorhtum genipe,
him geseondum, and he wæs fered on heofonum aþenedum handum, and he
bletsode hi þus cwæðende: Si sibb mid eow; and þæt genip hine underfeng
fram heora eagum; and hi stodon and beheoldon þa lyfta.

Tristram III 163-64, 38-48; cf. Latin 111-115.

And þa ða hi beheoldon þa lyfte, þa stodon þær twegen weras, þa wæron
ymbscrydde mid beorhtum reafe, and þa stodon wið ða apostolas and þus
cwædon: Eala ge galileiscan weras hwæt wundrige ge þus þas heofonlican
heannysse behealdende? Soðlice þes hælend þe fram eow genumen is and
gebroht is on his fæder swyðran healfe. Mid swa micclum wuldre swa ge nu
gesawon hine upp to heofonum astigan mid eall swa micclum wuldre he eow
eft to cymð on ðam micclan domesdæge.

Tristram III 171,234-241; cf. Latin 115-119.

and hi þa clypedon anre stefne þus cwæþende: Eala wuldres cyning, drihten
mægna, þu ðe nu todæg sigorgend astige ofer ealle heofonas, ne forlæt þu us na
fæderlease, ac asend to us þines fæder behat (þæt is soðfæstnysse gast) þæt he
wunige symle on ecnysse mid us, and þæt we habbon ece lif mid ðe on
heofona rices wuldre.

SOURCES FOR LATIN
108-111. Ecce . . . comitabantur. Bede, Expos. Act. Apost. (ed. Laistner p.8).
116-119. O rex . . . ueritatis. Antiphon. Hesbert, Corpus III, 4079.

Item 42   fol.95v   XLII.   Item alia in eodem die.

Gloriari nos oportet semper, fratres karissimi, et gaudere quia dominus ac redemptor noster, post redemptionem humani generis et diaboli triumphum, hodie cum magna uictoria ad cẹlos ascendisse legimus, et ad patris dexteram in magna lẹtitia cum substantia carnis qua nos redimere

5   dignatus est sedisse.   Credimus etiam inde illum uenire in gloria maiestatis suẹ, cum angelis et archangelis, iudicare omnes homines, iustos et peccatores, et tunc reddet unicuique secundum opera sua (cf. Matt. 16, 27).

Illud quoque scire et intelligere debemus quod, ante passionem domini,

96r   omnes sanctorum animẹ / 96r / in inferno sub debito preuaricationis Ada[e]

10   tenebantur, donec auctoritate domini per indebitam eius mortem de seruili conditione et diaboli capiuitate liberarentur. Post ascensionem uero domini ad cẹlos, omnes sanctorum animẹ cum Christo sunt, et, exeuntes de corpore, ad Christum uadunt, expectantes resurrectionem sui corporis, ut ad integram beatitudinem et perpetuam felicitatem cum ipso pariter immutentur.   Sicut

15   et peccatorum animẹ, in inferno sub timore positẹ, expectant resurrectionem sui corporis, ut cum ipso pariter ad pẹnam conuertantur aeternam.

Caueamus igitur, fideles Christi, ne sine excussatione pro nostris neglegentiis ante tribunal domini trepidi ueniamus quando cẹperit exquirere quid ei reportemus pro omnibus quẹ pro nobis passus est.   Consideremus ergo

20   quod Petrus apostolus dicit: Karissimi, Christus passus est pro nobis, uobis

---

1. P, J: dominus; B: dominum. 2. P, J: redemptor noster; B: redemptorem nostrum. 4. B adds: nostre, before: carnis. 6. J omits: et archangelis, after: angelis. 9. P, B: Adam; J: Ade. 12. P, J: de corpore; B: a corpore. 13. J adds: et, before: resurrectionem.

Tristram III 164-65, 66-78 (with modern punctuation); cf. Latin 1-7.

Men ða leofestan, us gedafenað eac þæt we symble wuldrien and geblissien, for ðam ðe hit is gerædd on halgum bocum, þæt drihten ure alysend, æfter alysednysse mennisces cynnes, and æfter þam mæran sige þe he deoflu ofercom, on þysum dæge mid micelum sige to heofonum astah þær hine heriað on ecnysse ealle heofonlice werodu. Eac swilce we gelyfað þæt he þanon cume on wuldre his mægenþrymmes, mid englum and heahenglum, to demenne eallum mancynne, rihtwisum and synfullum, and þonne he agylt anra gehwylcum æfter his sylfes weorcum.

Tristram III 165-66, 79-100; cf. Latin 8-16.

And þæt we sceolon witan and ongytan þæt, ær drihtnes þrowunge, ealra haligra manna sawla wæron gehæfte on helle for Adames gylte, oð ðone fyrst þe drihten for urum lufon on geþrowode and þone biteran deað onbyrigde and us þa æt deoflum alysde and mid him to heofonum gelædde, ealle þa ðe fram frymðe þisse worulde his willan worhton and his bebodum filigdon. Ealle drihten on þam mæran dæge his upstiges, þe we nu todæg wurðiað, he mid him to heofonum gelædde and nu synt þær wunigende on ecere blisse. And þonne þa godan of þysum life ferað þonne gelæt hi engla werod on þa heofonlican ricu þæt hi þær geanbidion þone ærist heora lichamena þæt hi æfter domesdæge wunien mid lichaman and mid sawle on ecnysse mid drihtne, on þære anwealdan eadignysse and on ðære ecan gesælignysse. Swa þæra synfulra manna sawla on helle beoð under ege asette and geanbidiað ærist heora lichomena þæt hi æfter domesdæge mid lichaman and mid sawle beon gecyrrede to ecum witum mid deoflum wunigende.

Tristram III 166, 101-109; cf. Latin 18-20.

Men ða leofestan uton us nu warnian þæt we þonne ne cumon forhte toforan drihtnes domsetle for urum gyltum þonne he ongynð us acsian and smeagian hwæt we him ongean broht hæbben for eallum þam þingum þe he for us geþrowode. Uton besceawian hwæt se mæra godes þegen sæde Petrus: Eala ge leofestan menn, he cwæð, uton ongitan þæt Crist for us þrowode,

---

SOURCES FOR LATIN

No direct sources for the Latin words, apart from Scriptural echoes and quotations, have been identified. Echoes of a theme and of apocryphal texts noted below.

relinquens exemplum ut sequamini uestigia eius; qui peccatum non fecit nec inuentus est dolus in ore eius; qui cum malediceretur, non maledicebat; cum pateretur, non comminabatur; sed tradebat se mitissime iudicanti se iniuste (cf. I Peter 2, 21-23). Considerate ergo quod sequitur ut sequamini uestigia

25 eius. Exemplum enim tribulationum reliquit nobis non diliciarum, contumeliarum non pomparum, flagellorum, dolorum, opprobriorum et spinarum crucis, uulnerumque mortis.

Pensemus ergo, karissimi, quanta propter peccata nostra sustinere debemus, si dei filius, qui sine peccato est, tanta pro nobis cruciamenta

30 pertulit. Non reddamus ergo ei mala pro [bonis] sed in quantum possumus uoluntati ipsius semper obtemperare studeamus. Offeramus ei cotidie sancta munera, fidem rectam, humilitatem, benignitatem, mentes humiles et lauda-

96v / 96v / -biles mores, supra haec autem caritatem perfectam. His igitur muneribus cum ipso ascendere hodie studeamus in gloria quia hęc solemnitas

35 ascensionis domini hodie per totum mundum manifeste cęlebratur, in qua multa mirabilia facta sunt.

Apostoli enim, aspicientes Iesum euntem in cęlum, longissimam scalam uiderunt inter cęlum et terram et angelos super eam ascendentes et descendentes (cf. John 1,51; Genesis 28,12) in uestibus albis atque dicentes:

40 Uiri Galilei quid admiramini? hic Iesus qui assumptus est a uobis in cęlum,

---

28. B adds: fratres, before karissimi. 30. P: nobis; B, J: bonis. 31. J adds: ergo, before: ei. 37. B adds: illum, after: Iesum.

Tristram III 166-67, 110-123; cf. Latin 21-27.

and he us lærde þa bysne þæt we sceoldon filigan his bebodum and larum and weorcum; se þe næfre nan facn næs on his muðe gemet ne ut gangende; ne nanne mann ne wyrgde he þa ða man hine wirigde; ac he sealde hyne sylfne swiðe byli[h]wytlice þam ðe hine on unriht demd[on]. He cwæð eftsona, Petrus se gecorena drihtnes þegen and ealdor ealra þæra leorningcnihta þe drihtne sylfum filigdon on þysum life: Uton witan, he cwæð, þæt drihten us forlæt þa bysna manigra geswinca, næs nanra ræsta, and teonena næs nanra glencga, swingla and sara, and hospas and manega oðre yfelu þing he þrowude for urum lufon.

Tristram III 167, 124-126; cf. Latin 35-36.

Men ða leofestan us is micclum þes dæg to mærsigenne and to wuldrigenne for ðam þe manega wundru gewurdon on þysum dæge.

Tristram III 167, 127-134; cf. Latin 37-40.

Þæs hælendes leorningcnihtas gesawon on þysum dæge ane lange hlædre betweonan heofonum and eorðan. Þa hi hine gesawon to heofonum astigan and hi gesawon englas ægðer ge up ge nyðer on ðære hlæddre faran on hwitum gygyrlan and þus cwæþende: Eala, ge Galileiscan weras, hwæt wundrige ge? Þes hælend þe fram eow genumen is on heofon,

ita ueniet ut uidistis eum euntem in cęlum (cf. Acts 1,11). Sed ite ad
Hierusalem et ibi manete donec ueniat uobis spiritus paraclitus ab
omnipotenti deo qui uos docebit omnia quę uobis promissa sunt a domino Iesu
Christo. Et iterum: Uiderunt filium dei ante sublime altare in alta cęlorum
45   stantem et patrem suum laudantem ac alleluia dulcissime canentem et
multitudinem angelorum canenti respondentem: Amen. (cf. Acts 7,55; on
altar cf. Apocalypse of John 6,9; 8,3).   Et iterum: Viderunt animas
peccatorum in poenis miserabiliter a daemonibus alligatas. Hęc autem
om[n]ia ideo illis ostensa sunt ad nos premonendum ut semper desideremus
50   caelestia et caueamus hęc loca infernalia ne intremus in illa; in quibus est
cotidie dolor sempiternus, tristitia sine lętitia, abundantia lacrimarum sine
consolatione, in quibus cotidie cruciantur peccatores.   Alii enim pendunt ibi
ex pedibus, alii ex manibus, alii ex uerticibus, alius ad genua, alius ad
umbilicum, aliusque ad labia, alii usque ad capillos capitum eorum.

55   Nos igitur cogitemus quę recta sunt quibus placatur deus et eadem
faciamus; preparemus corda nostra, uacuemur uitiis, repleamur uirtutibus;
cum omni alacritate semper desideremus caeleste appetere regnum ubi
summus rex ac summi milites semper habitant, ubi premium perpetuum, ubi
97r   manna cęleste, uita sine morte, iuuentus / 97r / sine senectute, lux sine
60   tenebris, gaudium sine tristitia, pax sine discordia, securitas semper uiuendi

---

43. P, J: que; B: quicumque. 49. P: omia; B, J: omnia. 52. B adds: cotidie (a
second), after: cruciantur. 52. J omits: ibi. 54. P, B, after labia: alii;   J:
aliique. 54. J omits: ad, after: usque. 55. P, B: nos; J: nosque. 55. P, B, after
deus: et; J: ut. 59. B adds: ubi, before: uita.

Tristram III 167, 134-142; cf. Latin 41-45.

swa he cymð eft swa swa ge gesawon hine nu faran on heofonas. Ac gað to Hierusalem and wuniað þær oð ðæt eow cume se frefrigenda gast fram ælmihtigum gode se eow lærð ealle þing þe eow behatene synt fram drihtne hælendum Criste. And eft hi gesawon godes sunu standan ætforan þam healican weofde on heora heannyssum and hi hyne gehyrdon his fæder herian.

Tristram III 167-68, 142-163; cf. Latin 47-54.

And eft hi gesawon synfulra manna sawla on witum earmlice fram deoflum gewriðene. Ealle þas þing, men ða leofestan, him wæron ætywede to ðam þæt hi sceoldon us forewarnian, and þam bið wa geborenum þe þylcum larum hyran nellað þe hi on bocum for ure þearfe awriton; and uton na forgytan þæt we symle sceolon gewilnian þa heofonlican, and uton us warnian wið ða hellican stowa þæt we ne gan on ða. On þam is dæghwamlice ece sargung, and unrotnys buton blisse, and teara genihtsumnyss buton frofre, þær beoð cwylmede dæghwamlice þa synfullan. Sume þær hangiað be þam fotum, þæs þe us halige gewritu onwrigen habbað, and sume þær hangiað be þam handum, and sume þær hangiað be þam sweorum, and sum þær beoð besenced oð ða cneow on þam hatan pice, and on ðam fyre, and sum þær bið besenced oð ðæne nafelan, and sum þær bið besenced oð ðone muð, and sume þær hangiað be heora feaxe on þam þuruhhatan fyre.

Tristram III 168-69, 164-174; cf. Latin 55-60.

Men ða leofestan uton geþencan þa þing þe rihte synt on ðam bið gegladod god, and uton don þæt sylfe and uton gegearwian ure heortan mid godum weorcum, and uton beon geæmtigode fram leahtrum, and uton beon gefyllede of mægenum, and uton gewilnian symle þæt we gegyrnon mid ealre hrædnysse þæt heofonlice rice, þær se healica cyning and þa healican cempan symle eardiað; þær is ece med, and þær is heofonlic mete, þær is ece myrhþ, and rice buton awendednysse.

SOURCES FOR LATIN

42-54 The specified tortures of sinners are reminiscent of those presented in the Visio S. Pauli (or Apocalypse of Paul). For another example of such a list in Old English see Bazire-Cross, p.63, and discussion, p.58.

59-60 uita...discordia and l.64: regnum sine ammutatione, see discussion in Bazire-Cross pp.11-12 of this theme, named by T. D. Hill as 'The Seven Joys of Heaven' in Notes and Queries 214 N.S.16 (1969), pp.165-66.

sine timore mortis; ubi pascuntur sancti propter eorum labores quibus placuerunt deo; ubi est beatitudo angelica et felicitas perpetua; ubi nec ira, nec indignatio, neque tenebr҄, nec ulla mala sunt, sed lux lucida et securitas sempiterna et regnum sine ammutatione.

65   Oportet nos ergo, fratres karissimi, istum contemnere mundum ut possimus sequi Christum saluatorem nostrum. Caueamus ne perdamus uitam perpetuam propter uanam huius mundi gloriam sed semper laudemus dominum, super cheru[b]in [et seraphin] sedentem, c҄lum et terram regentem; quem laudant angeli et archangeli, quem uenerantur prophet҄ et

70 apostol[i], quem semper desiderant turb҄ uirginum uidere, qu[oni]am ipse est plenitudo et perfectio omnium sanctorum de cuius aspectu semper l҄tantur in c҄lo; cum quibus ad supernam c҄lestem patriam nos perducere dignetur saluator mundi, qui cum patre et spiritu sancto uiuit et regnat in secula seculorum. Amen.

---

64. P, J: ammutatione; B: mutatione. 68. P: cheruphin; J: cherubin; B: cherubyn et seraphin; cf. Old English. 70. P: apostolici; B, J: apostoli. 70. P: quam; J: quoniam; B: quia.

Tristram III 169, 175-190; cf. Latin 66-72.

Men ða leofestan, us gedafenað þæt we forhicgen þisne middaneard þæt we magon filigan Criste urum alysende fram hellewitum. And uton warnian þæt we ne forspillon þæt ece lif for þyses middaneardes idelan wuldre, ac uton symle herian urne ecan drihten þone þe sitt and ofersyhþ þa eadigan engla werodu on heofonum, þe genamode synt cherubin and seraphim. Se is reccend heofones and eorðan and ealra gesceafta, þone heriað englas and heahenglas, þone arwurðiað witegan and þa apostolas þe drihtnes leorningcnihtas wæron her on worulde, þone symle gegyrnað haligra fæmnena mænigo to geseonne, for ðam ðe he is gefyllednys and fulfremednys ealra haligra, and hi symle blissiað on heofonum ætforan his gesihþe.

Assmann XI

The sermon edited by Bruno Assmann (<u>Angelsächsische Homilien</u> pp.138-143), as his no. XI, is extant in three manuscripts, Cambridge, Corpus Christi College 198 art. 20, 419 art. 14 and Oxford, Bodley 340 art. 20 (Ker, <u>Catalogue</u> pp.78, 116, 362 respectively). Assmann edited his text from the last two manuscripts only, but his edition is sufficient for source-study, especially since C.C.C. 198 arts. 1-43 (including our sermon) had as exemplar 'a set of homilies of the Bodley type', as Peter Clemoes recorded in the reprint of Assmann's edition (Darmstadt, 1964), p.XXXI.

Two scholars have found sources for the vernacular sermon, Karl Jost (<u>Anglia</u> 56 (1932) pp.306-307), noting contacts with Theodulf's <u>Capitula</u>, and Joseph B. Trahern Jr. (<u>Anglo-Saxon England</u> 5 (1976) pp.111-113), recording abstracted translations from Caesarius of Arles, <u>Sermo</u> 199, and a 'recollection', which needs a little discussion, from <u>Sermo</u> 197.4. Now, of course, we shall demonstrate that Pembroke items 20, 21, both entitled as for the first Sunday in Lent, were used as direct sources for Assmann XI. These two Latin sermons were copied from the Pembroke-type collection in 'Le sermonnaire carolingien de Beaune' (Paris BN lat. 3794) and their sources were detailed by Raymond Étaix (<u>Revue Aug.</u> pp.109-110), independently confirming the use of the Theodulfian extracts for items 20 and 21, and Caesarius, <u>Sermo</u> 199 for item 21, but adding Caesarius, <u>Sermo</u> 183, and <u>Sermo</u> 64 <u>ad fratres in eremo</u> for item 20, and Caesarius, <u>Sermo</u> 188 for item 21. I have merely added a recollection of Alcuin <u>De Virt.</u> for item 20.

The two Pembroke items for a Sunday in Lent now support the title in two manuscripts (Bodley 340, C.C.C. 198) of the vernacular sermon as for the third Sunday in Lent, and also the comment within Assmann's base text (C.C.C. 419): 'Nu is eac to witanne ... þæt we scylon þas lenctentide mid swiðe micelre begymene healdan' (p.140 ll.49-50), which contradicts the general title 'Larspell' in this manuscript. The Old English sermon should be regarded as one for Lent not as a general sermon.

The priestly audience for Pembroke item 20 is particularly clear since the composer has drawn almost entirely on two sermons and a tract, all directed to priests (see also above on the 'Collection and its background'). But he interweaves his selected passages to emphasize the major observances of Lent, fasting and almsgiving, as is well exemplified in both selections and omissions from Theodulf's Capitula, and insertion from one of the sermons. Having opened with Scriptural warnings to silent priests, as presented in the two sermons, the composer then draws on Theodulf cap. 28 to iterate that no excuse will be allowed for not teaching as best one can. Avoiding detail in Theodulf caps. 29-33 on the necessity of teaching other Christian acts, named as prayer, confession, works of mercy, and obedience to parents, he sees Theodulf Cap. 34 on the prime commandments, love of God and neighbour, but takes his actual phraseology mainly from Sermo 64 ad fratres and Alcuin De Virt. on this love, with one sentence from Theodore cap. 34. Theodulf caps, 35, 36, admonish businessmen and tradesmen and give detail of Lenten observances, so our composer leaves these aside and chooses caps. 37-39 on fasting and almsgiving, omitting, however, specific moderations or prohibitions on food and drink in cap. 40. He concludes with Theodulf caps 41 and 44 on the necessity of communion and the purity of those receiving it, omitting commands to abstain from lawsuits, and also from wives, in caps. 42, 43. The selections form a coherent presentation.

Pembroke item 21, the second sermon for the day, again concentrates on the main acts for Lent, fasting with almsgiving and repentance, abstracting and adapting mainly from two sermons of Caesarius of Arles. The first of these, Sermo 199, discourses on fasting with almsgiving, using the text: Frange esurienti panem tuum (Isaias 58, 7); the second, Sermo 188, in fact a sermon for Advent and preparation for Christ's Nativity, includes paragraphs on almsgiving and repentance, which deeds Caesarius himself (188.3) regarded as applicable for all periods of special observances. These were used by the Pembroke composer. To this information our Latin writer added more reminders, probably from his own recollection of other admonitions in Theodulf's tract, as a conclusion to his sermon: on bringing to church materials for lighting it, on confession, on oblations, on abstaining from intercourse with wives before the sacrifice, on being true Christians, on holding good family relationships, on loving God and on holding His precepts. The two Latin items provide good instruction for the observances of Lent.

The Old English writer treats his two main sources with some freedom, although closely following the Latin for some of his selections and thus defining the sources. But he omits sections from the Latin, rearranges the Latin order, accepts some ideas but substitutes his own words, and, on occasion, extends the Latin, in order to produce an effective sermon of his own. The second Latin sermon (Pembroke 21) considers the same main subject as the first, so some sections are omitted from this whose topics have already been covered, notably from Pembroke 21 (ll.1-21) which discusses the special fasting in Lent (from Caesarius _Sermo_ 199. 1 and 2), a subject already presented in the Old English (ll.49-62) from Theodulf _Capitula_ cap. 37, via Pembroke 20 (ll.53-63), and also from Pembroke 21 (ll.41-48), citing Scripture (Luke 6, 31 etc., from Caesarius _Sermo_ 199.8) which had already been quoted in Old English (ll.39-43) from Pembroke 20 (ll.39-41). Pembroke 20 itself probably took this quotation from Caesarius _Sermo_ 199.8, although immediately turning to Theodulf _Capitula_ cap. 34 for the sequential words. The Anglo-Saxon's omissions from the first Latin sermon, Pembroke 20, are partly for abbreviation of the rather full sequence in Latin of orders and prohibitions, but one of these excisions certainly changes the emphasis of the Old English sermon, where the writer omits Pembroke 20 ll.25-33, from Theodulf _Capitula_ cap. 28, addressed directly to priests on the necessity and manner of teaching. Other omissions from this Latin sermon are ll.46-51, on the heavenly rewards for observing the commandments of true love (_caritas_), and ll.63-67 from Theodulf _Capitula_ cap. 38.

The Anglo-Saxon substitutes on occasion and, at other times, accepts an idea but offers his own extension. At Assmann XI ll.34-39 he substitutes his own explanation of the two prime commandments, which in the Latin (Pembroke 20 ll.37-38) is taken from Alcuin's tract _De Virtutibus_, by defining 'a neighbour' as everyone, in stating that we are all 'brothers' in God, probably recalling Matthew 12,

50 which is quoted in Pembroke 21 ll.35-36. At ll.67-79 the Englishman inserts a command to go to confession (67-72), before developing the Latin statements (71-73) with his own words (72-79) and adding a near-citation of Luke 21, 34 against excessive drinking.

At l.79 the Anglo-Saxon is ready to abstract from the second Pembroke sermon and reverses the Latin order by looking first to the example of the cup of cold water as minimal almsgiving for a poor man, as in Pembroke 21 ll.36-40. Although Trahern (op. cit. p.112) noted an echo from Caesarius Sermo 197.4 for the phrase in Assmann XI ll.79-81, it is an adaptation of Pembroke 21 ll.36-37, as illustrated below. Even in this passage the Englishman elaborates on the Latin, adding his own Latin quotation on keeping almsgiving secret: Abscondite etc. (ll.88-90). This phrase is not in the Vulgate Scripture, although it is similar to a quotation (?) of Ecclesiasticus 29, 15 as presented in Pseudo-Augustine Sermo 312.1 (PL 39, 2343): Claude ... eleemosynam in sinu pauperis et ipsa pro te orabit.

Our vernacular writer now returns to a full quotation and explication of Isaias 58, 7, Frange esurienti panem etc. (ll.91-97) which had been broken up by explanation in Pembroke 21 (ll.22-23, 26), and then he follows Pembroke 21, ll.51-65 very closely for the series of questions on why we should share with the poor (ll.97-107), and for the exhortation to adorn ourselves with virtues and to reject vices like poison from our hearts (ll.107-115, see the extract below). In the following passage, detailing acts and prohibitions, the brief Latin warning, et hoc etiam cauendum est ne cantica luxuriosa uel diabolica dicatis (ll.72-73), is echoed in the Old English ll.119-121, but to the devilish songs of the Latin, diabolical practices are added, ll.121-126. Such practices are also listed within Ælfric's sermon on Auguries in Ælfric's Lives of Saints ed. W. W. Skeat, vol. I, E.E.T.S. OS. 76, 82 (1881, 1885, repr. 1966), p.372 ll.130-131 and p.374 ll.148-50. The composer sums up by reiterating admonitions in his conclusion.

The Anglo-Saxon preacher certainly uses the Latin material as he wished, and produced a progressive sermon on the particular observances for Lent.

Item 20 fol. 38r XX. Omelia in Quadragesima Dominica i.

Audite, filioli mei, et intelligite quomodo sacra scriptura uos ammonet et ad regna caelorum inuitat et uiam ostendit, quomodo mala mundi istius euadere possitis et ad uitam aeternam, Christo adiuuante, peruenire. Clamat enim dominus per prophetam ad sacerdotes qui presunt populo, ut uos debeant
5 ammonere et annuntiare uobis uiam ueritatis. Dicit enim: Clama, ne cesses; quasi tuba exalta uocem tuam, et annuntia populo meo peccata eorum et domui Iacob scelera eorum (cf. Isaias 58,1.). Quod si non annuntiaueris
38v iniquo iniquitatem suam, sanguinem / 38v / eius de manu tua requiram (cf. Ezekiel 3,18; 33,8). Uidetis ergo, fratres karissimi, si diligenter adtenditis
10 quod omnes sacerdotes domini, non solum episcopi, sed etiam presbiteri et ministri ecclesiarum, in grandi sunt periculo si dei sermones uobis non annuntiauerint. Unde dominus per prophetam dicit: Audiens ex ore meo sermonem, annuntiabis eis ex me (Ezekiel 33,7), ex me non ex te. Uerba mea loqueris non est quod ex eis tamquam de tuis i[mp]leris. Considerate ergo,
15 fratres, si pro semetipso unusquisque uix poterit in die iudicii reddere rationem quid de sacerdotibus futurum est a quibus omnium animę requirentur. In his siquidem omnibus necesse est sacerdotibus ut uobis uiam dei annuntient et semitam ostendant uobis per quam uitam possitis habere aeternam. Sed tamen cauendum est uobis, fratres karissimi, quia si nobis
20 periculosum est non annuntiare multo magis uobis perniciosius erit si

---

13. J omits: ex me; (the second). 14. P: quod; B, J: quo. 14. P: infleris; B, J impleris. 17. P, B: siquidem; J: quidem. 18. P, B: et; J: ut.

Assmann XI, 138, 1-14 ; cf. Latin 1-12.

Gehyraổ nu, men þa leofestan, hu þas halgan bec eow myngiaổ and eow þone weg ætywiaổ and eac in gelædaổ to heofena rice, and hu ge magon þa yfelu þisses middaneardes forbugan and gode gefylstendum to ổam ecan life becuman. Clypaổ ure drihten þurh his witegan swiổe stiổlice to ổam preostum, þe godes folce wisian scylan, þæt heo eow myngian and cyổan eow soổfæstnesse weg, and þus cweổ: Clama, ne cesses; quasi tuba exalta vocem tuam, et adnuntia populo meo peccata eorum. Ðæt is on urum geþeode: Clypa, ne ablin ổu, ac ahefe up þine stefne swa beme and cyổ minum folce heora synna. Gif þu þonne nelt þam unrihtwisan his synna cyổan, þu bist his sawle scyldig. Her ge magon gehyran, broổru ổa leofestan, þæt ealle godes mæssepreostas and biscopas and oổre godcunde lareowas synd on mycelre frecednysse, gif heo eow godes bebodu ne cyổaổ.

Assman XI, 138-39, 14-25; cf. Latin 12-20.

Be ổam cweổ drihten þurh þone witegan: Audiens ex ore meo sermonem meum, adnuntiabis eis ex me, non ex te. Ðæt is on urum geþeode: Of minum muổe gehlystendum þu bodast hym mine spræce of me, næs of þe. Nu ge magon ongitan, hwylcne ege þa mæssepreostas habbaổ toweardne, þonne god wile girnan to hym ealra þara sawla, þe hym her on life betæhte synd. Þonne we witan, þæt anra manna gehwylc mæg earfoổlice be his agenre sawle gescead agyldan on domes dæg. Forþam us is micel þearf, þæt we eow þone weg cyổen and þæt siổfæt ætywen, þe ge þurh magon to ổam ecan life becuman. And eac eow is to warnienne, forổan gif hit us is frecenlic, þæt we hit eow ne cyổen, hit is eow micele mare frecednes,

---

SOURCES FOR LATIN

1-8.   Sermo 64 ad Fratres in Eremo, PL 40, 1347, with a little addition at Isaias 58,1; cf. Caesarius 183.1 for Scripture.

9-17.   Caesarius of Arles Sermo 183.1 (Morin, II 744) with some verbal echo and much addition.

17-19. Cf. ideas in Sermo 64 ad Fratres, PL 40, 1347.

nolueritis implere quę annuntiauerimus uobis; dicente domino per prophetam:
Si autem annuntiante te ad impium ut a uiis suis conuertatur, ipse conuersus
non erit in inquitatibus suis, morietur, et tu animam tuam de uindicta eius
liberasti (cf. Ezekiel 33,9). Vnde quidam sapiens ammonet sacerdotes dicens:

25 Hortamur uos paratos esse ad docendas plebes. Qui scit scripturas, prǽdicet
scripturas; qui uero nescit, saltim hoc, quod notissimum est, plebibus dicat:
Ut declinent a malo et faciant bonum, inquirant pacem et sequa[n]tur eam
(cf. Psalm 33,15). Quia oculi domini super iustos, et aures eius ad preces

39r eorum. Vultus autem domini super facientes mala ut perdat / 39r / de terra

30 memoriam eorum (Psalm 33,16,17). Nullus ergo se excusare poterit, quod
non habeat linguam, unde possit aliquem aedificare. Mox enim, ut quemlibet
errare uiderit, prout ualeat, aut arguendo, aut obsecrando, aut increpando, ab
errore retrahat, et ad peragendum opus bonum sepius hortetur. In primis
igitur homo Christianus hoc debet scire, et in corde firmiter tenere, quod

35 primum et maximum mandatum est, domino dicente: Diliges dominum deum
tuum ex toto corde tuo et ex tota anima tua et tota uirtute tua (cf. Mark 12,
30). Hoc quidem nobis demonstrat ut toto intellectu, tota uoluntate, et ex
omni memoria deum semper diligamus. Addidit quoque: secundum simile est
huic: Diliges proximum tuum, sicut teipsum (Matthew 22,39). Hoc est

40 siquidem quod in aeuangelio scriptum est: Omnia quecumque uultis ut

24. J omits: sapiens. 24. P, B: sacerdotes; J: sacerdos. 25. J omits: esse. 26. J
adds: scripturas; after: nescit. 26. P, J, Th: quod notissimum est; B: qui
nouit. 27. P, J, Th: faciant; B: facient. 27. B, Th: sequantur; P: sequatur; J:
persequantur. 28. P, Th: ad; B, J: in; Ps. 33,16: in. 29-30. B omits: Vultus ...
eorum. 36. P, J: ex tota anima; B: in. 36. B adds: in, before: tota uirtute. 37. P,
J: nobis; B: uobis. 38. J omits: est.

Assmann XI, 139, 25-29; cf. Latin, 21-24.

þæt ge nellen gefyllan, þæt we eow to eowre sawle þearfe cyðað. Þonne þurh þone witegan is gecweden: Gif þu bytst þam synfullum, þæt he of his unrihtan wegum gecyrre and he gecyrran nelle of his unrihtwisnessum, he swelt and þu hæfst alysed þine sawle fram his witum.

Assmann XI, 139, 29-40; cf. Latin, 33-40.

Ealra ærest sceal ælc cristen man witan and on his heortan trumlice healdan þæt æreste bebod and þæt mæste, þæt is, þæt he lufige his drihten mid ealre heortan and mid eallum mode and mid eallum mægne. And oðer bebod is þysum fulgelic, þæt is, þæt ælc man lufige his nextan swa hine sylfne. Nu wenð manig man, þæt þis sy gecweden be his freondum, þe him gesibbeste synt and þurh mægrædenne nehste. Ac hit nis be ðam gesibban na swiðor gecweden, þonne be ðam fremdan. Ac ure ælc is oðres nehsta þurh þone rihtan geleafan, þe we to urum drihtne habbað, and we synd gebroðru gecigede, forðy þe god is ure fæder on heofonum. Þy cweð se hælend on his godspelle: Omnia quaecumque vultis, ut

SOURCES FOR LATIN

21-24.	No source, except Scripture.
25-27.	Theodulf of Orleans, Capit. cap.28, PL 105,200, almost verbatim.
28-30.	Theodulf, cap. 28, PL 105, 200 omits: Vultus . . . eorum, but the new edition in Mon. Germ. Hist., includes it as Theodulf.
20-33.	Theodulf, cap.28, almost verbatim.
33-36.	Sermo 64 ad Fratres, PL 40, 1347,
37-39.	Cf. Alcuin, De Virt. cap.3, PL 101, 615.

faciant uobis homines, ita et uos facite eis (cf. Luke 6,31).   Hęc est ergo

uera caritas quę deum diligit plusquam se [et proximum tamquam se] et qui

nichil uult ali[i] facere nisi quod sibi uult fieri. Si hęc uero amore, fratres, in

animo posueritis, et ista prima precepta, cum summa reuerentia et cum

45   gaudio, uolueritis suscipere, tunc ad alia bona, deo adiuuante, poteritis

peruenire. Promisit enim his qui diligunt eum resurrectionem post mortem et

uitam perpetuam et dilicias paradysi et gaudia cum angelis.   Unde ibi post

haec [nec senectus separat, nec mors occumbit uel occurrit, sed

est] stabilitas et securitas iuuentutis et pax perpetua diligentibus deum et

50   amantibus illum. Haec autem per assiduitatem et perseuerantiam boni operis

et per continentiam de malo et facientibus bona promissa sunt.

39v   Scire ergo / 39v / debetis, fratres karissimi, quod haec quadragesima

sicut quidam [sapiens] ait: Cum summa obseruatione custodiri debet, ut

ieiunium in ea preter dies dominicos, qui de abstinentia subtracti sunt,

55   nullatenus soluatur, quia ipsi dies decimę sunt anni nostri, quos cum omni

religione sanctitatis transigere debemus.   Nulla in his occasio sit ad

soluendum ieiunium, quia alio tempore solet ieiunium caritatis causa disolui,

isto uero nullatenus debet;   quia in alio tempore ieiunare in uoluntate et

arbitrio cuiuslibet positum est; in hoc uero non ieiunare pręceptum domini

60   transcendere est.   Et in alio tempore ieiunare, premium abstinentię

---

41. J omits: ergo.   42. P, B, Th: caritas; J: fraternitas.   42. P, B, Th: que, quae;
J: qui.   42. B, J, Th: et proximum tamquam se; P omits.   43. P, B, Th: nichil,
nihil; J: nil.   43. B, J, Th: alii; P: alio;   43. J omits: amore.   47. P, J: gaudia;
B: gaudium.   48-49. J: nec senectus...sed est; so B except: occumbit uel; P omits.
53. B, J: sapiens; P erasure.   56. P, B, Th: transigere; J: transire.   59. P, J, Th:
arbitrio; B: in arbitrio.

Assmann XI, 139-40, 41-48; cf. Latin 41-46.

faciant vobis homines, ita et vos facite illis. Ðæt is on urum geðcode: Don ge
oðrum mannum ælc ðara þinga, þe ge willan, þæt hy eow don. Se man hæfð rihte
lufe and soðe, þe god lufað ma, þonne hine sylfne, and his nyhstan swa swa hine
sylfne, and nanum oðrum men ne deð, butan swa swa he wile, þæt man him do. Gif
ge þonne þas ðreo forman bebodu on eower mod asettað and mid healicre
arwurðnesse and mid micelum gefean onfon willað, þonne magon ge mid godes
fultume becuman to oðrum godum dædum.

Assmann XI, 140, 49-58; cf. Latin 52-60.

Nu is eac to witanne, broðru þa leofestan, þæt we scylon þas lenctentide mid
swiðe micelre begymene healdan, þæt we þurh nan þing nænne dæg þis fæsten ne
abrecon, ne on æte, ne on drence, butan sunnandagum.   On ðam nis nan fæsten
geboden.   On oðre tide men gewuniað, þæt hy þurh oðra manna lufe hwilum fæsten
forlætað; on þisse tide hit ne mæg nateshwon beon forlæten.   On oðre tide is on
æghwylces mannes willan and on his scriftes dome gesett, hu he for his synnum
fæste.   On ðisse tide gif man ne ful fæst, man forgymð godes agen bebod.   On
oðerre tide se ðe wel fæst, gestrynð him mede æt gode.

SOURCES FOR LATIN

41-43.   Theodulf, Capit. cap.34 (PL 101, 202).
43-51.   Sermo 64 ad Fratres, PL 40, 1347, with variation of word and addition.
53-60.   Theodulf cap.37, almost verbatim.

adquirere est. In hoc uero preter infirmos aut paruulos quisquis non ieiunat, poenam sibi adquirit, quia in eosdem dies dominus, et per Moysen et per Heliam et per semetipsum sacro ieiunio consecrauit. In diebus quoque ieiunii huius temporis, fratres karissimi, aelemosina frequentius facienda est; et

65 cybum de quo quisque uti debuerat, si non ieiunaret, pauperibus erogare debet, quia ieiunare et cybos prandii ad cẹnam reseruare non mercedis, sed cyborum est incrementum.

Cauendum est quoque quod multis in usu est; solent enim plures, qui se ieiunare putant, mox ut signum audierint ad horam nonam, manducare, qui

70 nullatenus ieiunare credendi sunt, si ante manducauerint, quam uespertinum cẹlebretur officium.   Concurrendum est enim ad missas, et postea

40r auditis / 40r / missarum solemnitatibus, siue uespertinis officiis, largitis prius ẹlemosinis, ad cybum accedendum est.   Si uero aliquis necessitate constrictus fuerit, ut ad missam conuenire non ualeat, aestimata uespertina

75 hora, et completa oratione sua ieiunium [ab]soluere debet.

Sciendum est quoque quod in singulis diebus dominicis in quadragesima, preter hos, qui excommunicati sunt, sacramenta corporis et sanguinis Christi ab omnibus fidelibus sumenda sunt, et in Cẹna Domini, et in uigilia Pasche, et in die resurrectionis domini penitus omnibus communicandum est Christianis,

80 et ipsi dies Paschalis ebdomadẹ omnes aequali religione colendi sunt.

---

62. B, J, Th omit: in, before: eosdem. 62. P, J, Th: dies; B omits. 65. J omits: de, before: quo, but erasure. 68. P, J: usu; B: usum. 75. J, Th: absoluere; P: soluere; B: abscondere. 77-78. B omits: sacramenta ... sunt.

Assmann XI 140, 58-62; cf. Latin 61-63.

On þisse tide se ðe rihtlice ne fæst, he gestrynð him helle wite, butan hit for untrumnesse oððe for geogoðe sy, forðam þe ure drihten gehalgode þas ilcan dagas þurh Moysen and Heliam and þurh hine sylfne, þæt heora ælc gefæste feowertig daga and feowertig nihta.

Assmann XI, 140, 62-67; cf. Latin 68-71.

Earnostlice is to warnienne wið þæt, þe manega men on gewunan habbað, þæt synd þa ðe wenað, þæt hy fæstende synd rihtlice, gif hy etað, sona swa hy þæt belltacen gehyrað þære nigoðan tide, þæt is seo nontid. Ac hit nis na to gelyfanne, þæt hy fæstende synd rihtlice, butan hy æfter hyra mæssan þæs æfenes tid wurðunga gebiden.

Assmann XI, 141, 72-79 is greatly extended from the Latin 71-73. See introduction.

Þonne beoð hy Cristene, gif he þis eall gelæstað, and hy scylon embe þa nigoðan tide heora mæssan gestandan and æfter þam heora æfenþenunga, syððan don heora ælmessan swa forð, swa him fyrmest gehagie, and þonne mid miclum godes ege gangan to heora mete and þær don, swa se hælend on þam godspelle beot and þus cweð: Cavete, ne graventur corda vestra in crapula et ebrietate (Luke 21, 34). Dæt is on Englisc: Warniað, þæt eowre heortan ne beon gehefegode on oferfylle and on druncennesse.

SOURCES FOR LATIN

61-63.	Theodulf Capit. cap.37, almost verbatim.
63-67.	Theodulf cap.38, closely.
68-75.	Theodulf cap.39. Initial phrase added.
76-80.	Theodulf cap.41, closely.

Ammonendus est igitur populus ut ad sacrosanctum sacramentum corporis et sanguinis domini nequaquam indiferenter accedat, nec ab hoc nimium abstineat, sed cum omni diligentia atque prudentia eligat tempus, quando aliquandiu ab opere coniugali abstineat, et uitiis se purget et uirtutibus

85 exornet, aelemosinis et orationibus insistat, et sic ad tantum sacramentum accedat; quia sicut periculosum est inpurum quemque ad tantum sacramentum accedere, ita etiam periculosum est ab hoc prolixo tempore abstinere, nisi qui excommunicati sunt. Caeteris uero temporibus communicandum est religiosis quibusque sanctę uiuentibus qui pene omni die

90 id faciunt. Haec precepta implendi uirtutem nobis prestare dignetur saluator mundi qui cum patre et spiritu sancto uiuit et regnat in secula seculorum. Amen.

---

82. B, Th: indifferenter; P: indiferenter; J: differenter.   83. P, B, Th: diligentia; J: indulgentia.   89. P, B, Th: uiuentibus; J: ecclesie.

81-90.   Theodulf _Capit_. cap. 44, with some adaptation of word.

Item 21 fol.40r XXI. Item alia in Die Initii.

Rogo et ammoneo uos,   fratres karissimi, ut in isto legitimo ac sacratissimo tempore quod de suo sancto ieiunio dominus consecrauit, exceptis dominicis diebus nullus ex uobis prandere presumat, nisi forte ille quem ieiunare i[n]firmitas non permittit; quia in aliis diebus ieiunare aut remedium aut premium est, in quadragesim[a] autem non ieiunare peccatum est. Alio enim tempore qui ieiunat, accipiet indulgentiam peccatorum; in quadragesima uero, qui potest ieiunare et non facit, patietur poenas.   Unde etiam ipse caueat qui ieiunare non preualet ut secretius sibi soli, aut si est alius infirmus, cum illo in domo sua preparet quod ei necessarium sit, et illos qui ieiunare preualent ad prandium non inuitet, quia non ei oportet ut aliquem tunc sanum roget ad comedendum secum, ne sibi augeat etiam de alterius gula peccatum. Quia, si hoc fecerit, non solum scit deus sed etiam et homines sobrii possunt intelligere, illum non pro i[n]firmitate ieiunare non posse, sed pro gula non uelle.   Cum gemitu ergo et suspirio et animi dolore manducet, pro eo quod aliis ieiunantibus ille abstinere non potest, et pro eo quod ieiunare non potest, precuret amplius aelemosinas pauperibus erogare, ut peccata quę non potest ieiunando curare, possit aelemosinas dando redimere.

Bonum est ergo, fratres, ieiunare sed melius est ęlemosinam dare si possibilitas non fuerit ieiunandi.   Si autem quis utrumque potest, duo sunt bona; sed elemosina sola sufficit sine ieiunio, ieiunium uero sine ęlemosina

---

2. B omits: sancto. 4. P: imfirmitas; B, J: infirmitas. 5. P: quadragesimo; B, J: quadragesima. 9. J adds: infirmo, after: illo. 13. J omits: pro, before: infirmitate. 13. P: imfirmitate; B, J: infirmitate. 14. P, J: manducet; B: manducat. 18. P, B: fratres; J: fratres karissimi.

1-17. Caesarius 199.1 (Morin, II 803-04).
18-21.   Caesarius 199.2.

41r   non sufficit / 41r / . Unde dominus per prophetam hortatur et ammonet aelemosinam fieri dicens: Hoc est ieiunium quod elegi,   frange esurienti panem tuum (Isaias 58,7).   Considerate, fratres, quia non dixit ut integrum daret, sed 'frange' inquit, hoc est dicere, ut etiam si tanta tibi paupertas

25   fuerit ut non habeas nisi unum panem, ex ipso frangas et pauperibus tribuas et aegenos uagosque, inquit, induc in domum tuam (cf. Isaias 58,7). Hoc uero significat ut si aliquis ita pauper est, ut non habeat unde tribuat cybum, etiam in uno angulo domus suę peregrinis et aegenis uagisque saltim pręparet lectulum.   Quid nos ad haec dicturi sumus, fratres, uel quam excusationem

30   ante tribunal aeterni iudicis habebimus, qui amplas et spatiosas domus habemus, et uix aliquando dignamur excipere peregrinum, non considerantes quod in omnibus peregrinis Christus suscipitur, sicut ipse dixit: Hospes fui, et suscepistis me (cf. Matthew 25,35) et: quandiu fecistis uni ex his fratribus meis minimis, mihi fecistis?   (Matthew 25,40), qui sunt autem fratres alio

35   loco demonstrat dicens: Quicumque fecerit uoluntatem patris mei, qui in cęlis est ipse meus frater et soror et mater est (Matthew 12,50).   Ille autem qui non habet unde faciat aelemosinam, non pertimescat; sufficit ei uoluntas bona. Sed quis poterit se excusare, cum etiam pro calice aquę frigidę mercedem nobis dominus reddere promiserit?   Et ideo 'frigide' dixit, ne forte posset

40   aliquis dicere se uasculum ubi aquam calefaceret non habere.

---

21. J adds: dicens, after: hortatur. 22. J omits: dicens. 23. B adds after tuum: et egenos uagosque induc in domum tuam (Isaias, 58,7). 23. B adds after integrum: panem. 25. J adds: tantum, before: unum. 30. P,J: domus; B: domos; Caesarius: domos. 32. P, J: suscipitur; B: suscipiatur. 33. J adds: non, before: suscepistis. 34. B, J add: eius, after: fratres. 36. J omits: et, before: soror. 37. J omits: aelemosinam. 37. J omits: ei.

Assmann XI, 141-42, 91-97; cf. Latin 21-29.

And ure drihten cweð eft on oðre stowe þurh his witegan: <u>Frange esurienti</u>
<u>panem tuum et egenos vagosque induc in domum tuam.</u>   He cweð: Brec
þinne hlaf þam hingriendan and þa wædlan and þa ælþeodigan gelæd in to þinum
huse. Midþam þe he cweð: Brec þinne hlaf, he getacnað, þæt þu scealt of
þam þone þearfan aretan, and þeah þu mare næbbe, þonne ænne hlaf.

Assmann XI, 141, 79-91; cf. Latin 36-40.

And se man, þe næbbe, of hwan he mæge rumlice ælmessan syllan, ne
onðracige he forðam, þeh he lytel hæbbe.   Þonne drihten us mede behet, gif
we þam þearfan, þe ðæs neod bið, geræcað cuppan fulle coles wæteres, and for
ðy he cwæð be ðam colan wætere, þæt nan man ne ðorfte hine beladian, þæt
he fæt næfde, on hwy he hit wyrman mihte.   Do gehwa georne on godes est,
beþam þe hine fyrmest onhagie. And þæt is to witanne, þeah ðe seo ælmesse
on ælcne sæl god beo gedon, huru þinga man sceal on þissum dagum hy dælan
swa forð, swa mannes mihta fyrmeste beoð. Þonne hit be ðam awriten is:
<u>Abscondite eleemosynam in sinu pauperis et ipsa orat pro vobis ad dominum.</u>
Ðæt is on Englisc: Behydað þa ælmessan on þæs þearfan greadan and heo gebit
for eow to gode.

SOURCES FOR LATIN

21-34. Caesarius 199.3, omission, addition, but verbal echoes.
36-37. Caesarius 199.2; cf. 197.4.
38-40. Caesarius 199.3 at beginning, adaptation but ideas and some verbal
        echoes.

Omnia ergo compleuit qui quod potuit fecit, quia uoluntas perfecta faciendi reputabitur pro opere facti. Sed tamen unusquisque consideret

41v / 41v / ut sic pauperi tribuat, quomodo, si ipse in tali necessitate esset, sibi fieri uellet. Hec uero qui fecerit, noui et ueteris testamenti praecepta

45 compleuit, implens illud euangelicum: Omnia quęcumque uultis ut faciant uobis homines bona, ita et uos facite illis similiter. Haec est enim lex et prophetę (cf. Matthew 7,12 and Luke 6,31).

Ammonemus uos iterum, fratres karissimi, ut in his sanctis diebus non solum a concubinis sed etiam a propriis uxoribus abstineatis. Et hoc etiam

50 sciendum est quia licet omni tempore proficit aelimosinas facere, praecipue tamen in his diebus secundum uires nostras amplius erogare debemus. Non enim est iustum in populo Christiano ad unum deum pertinente alios inaebriari et alios famis periculo puniri, dum nos et omnis populus unius domini serui sumus et uno pretio redempti sumus, et si bene agimus, ad unam

55 beatitudinem pariter ueniemus. Cur ergo pauper tecum non accipit cybum qui tecum accept[ur]us pariter regnum? Quare [pauper] non accipit ueterem tunicam tuam qui tecum accepturus est in cęlo immortalitatis stolam? Quare pauper non meretur accipere panem tuum qui tecum similiter meruit accipere baptismi sacramentum? Cur indignus est accipere reliquias cyborum tuorum

60 qui tecum uenturus est ad conuiuia angelorum?

---

41. P, J: qui quod; B: quicquid. 44. P, B: ueteris; J: ueteri. 46. J adds: bona, before: similiter. 48. J omits: in, after: ut. 52. P, J: pertinente; B: pertinentes. 54. B adds: in hac uita, after: agimus. 55. B adds: omnes, before: ueniemus. 55. P, J: ergo; B: autem. 56. P: acceptus; B, J: accepturus. 56. B, J add: pauper, after: quare; Caesarius: pauper. 56. P, J: accipit; B: accipiat.

Assmann XI, 142, 97-107; cf. Latin 51-60.

Men ða leofestan, hit nis na riht on Cristenum folce, þæt sume scylon mid oferæte and mid oferdrence beon oferlede and sume hungre cwylmede. Þonne we ealle synt anes drihtnes ðeowas and mid anum wyrðe gebohte, þæt is mid his agenum blode, þe he for eall mancyn ageat, and gif we wel doð, þonne mote we ealle to anre eadignesse becuman. For hwi ne mot se ðearfa onfon þines metes, þe mid ðe is to onfonne heofona rice? Hwi ne mot se ðearfa onfon þine ealdan gewæda, þe mid ðe is to onfonne þæs undeadlican gegyrlan on neorxna wange? Hwi nis se wyrðe, þæt he onfo þinra metelafe, þe mid þe is to cumenne to engla gebeorscipe?

SOURCES FOR LATIN

41-47. Caesarius 199.8.
48-49. Caesarius 188.3 (Morin, II 768).
50-60. Caesarius 188.4 with much verbal echo.

Haec ergo cogitantes, fratres karissimi, hoc ammonemus ut ad istos dies castitate nitidi, caritate splendidi, aelimosinis emundati, et bonis operibus adornati, per Christi adiutorium, nos preparemus. Et iracundiam et inuidiam

42r et odium / 42r / omnemque malitiam uelut uenenum de cordibus nostris

65 respuamus, ut postea cum fide recta et bona uoluntate ad aecclesiam ueniamus ad supplicandum deum pro peccatis nostris, et unusquisque homo studeat ut sciat symbolum et orationem dominicam et qui amplius non potest saltim duabus uicibus in die oret, mane uidelicet et uespere dicens symbolum primum, deinde dominicam orationem. Et omnibus dominicis diebus

70 et cunctis festiuitatibus praeclaris tam uespertinis uigiliis et matutinis quam et ad missas caelebrandas frequenter ueniatis et ibi dei uerba sollicite audiatis orantes humiliter cum puro corde et mundo corpore. Et hoc etiam cauendum est ne cantica luxuriosa uel diabolica dicatis neque quando ad aecclesiam conueniatis neque in domibus uestris, nec ullam diabolicam

75 culturam facere presumatis, sed quando ad aecclesiam conueniatis, cum timore et silentio et summa reuerentia, intrate in domum dei et ibi stantes nichil aliud faciatis nisi orare tantum pro peccatis uestris et laudare nomen domini. Uerba otiosa aut secularia nolite ipsi ex ore uestro proferre, et eos qui qui proferre uoluerint castigate. Pacem cum omnibus custodite, et quos discordes

80 agnoscitis, ad concordiam reuocate. Et quando ad aecclesiam conuenitis

---

61. P, B: hoc; J: hec. 65. J omits: cum. 67. P: qui; B: qui iam; J: si; Theodulf: qui. 68. P, J: duabus; B: duobus. 71. B, J omit: et, before: ad missas. 71. P, J: dei uerba; B: uerbum dei. 74. P: conueniatis; B, J: conuenietis. 75. P: conueniatis; B, J: conuenietis. 76. P, J: intrate; B: intrare. 77. P, J: faciatis; B: facietis. 80. P, J: agnoscitis; B: agnoscatis. 80. P, B: conuenitis; J: conuenietis.

Assmann XI, 142-43, 107-128; cf. Latin 61-80 (echoes of word and idea but adaptation and extension).

Broðru þa leofostan, utan us gegearwian on þyssum dagum, þæt we synd on ðam mæran æriste ures drihtnes þurh clænnesse wlitige and fægere and þurh soðe lufan scinende and mid ælmesdædum aclænsode and mid eallum godum weorcum gefrætewode.   And ælce yrsunge and andan and hatunge and ealle yfelnesse utan aworpan fram urum heortum eal swa atter and gelomlice mid rihtum geleafan and mid godum willan to cyrcan cuman and þær mid micelre geornfulnesse æt gode biddan forgifennesse ealra þara gylta, þe we dæghwamlice wyrcað.   And wite ælc man swiðe georne, þæt he cunne his Credan, on ðam he sceal geandettan his rihtan geleafan, and his Pater Noster, on ðam he sceal him æt gode are biddan ge þisses lifes, ge þæs toweardan. And ælcum men is swiðe to warnienne wið idele spræce and þæt man idele leoð ne singe on ðysum dagum, þe ymbe hæðenscipe and ymbe galscipe geworhte syndon.   And næfre nan man ne geþristlæce ænigne deofles bigencg to donne, ne on wiglunge, ne on wiccedome, ne on ænegum idelum anginne.   And þæt nan man ne sece to nanre wellan, ne to nanum stane, ne to nanum treowe, ne nan man his cild þurh þa eorðan ne teo, forðam se ðe þæt deð, he betæcð þæt cild eallum deoflum and seo moder forð mid.   Ne nan man nane neode ne sece, butan to gode sylfum and to his halgum.

SOURCES FOR LATIN

61-65.   Caesarius 188.6, some ideas and words, much addition.
67-69.   Theodulf, Capit. cap.23, PL 105,193.
76-80.   Caesarius 188.6, some ideas and words.

incensum cereolos et oleum et omnia quę necessaria sunt ad inluminandum in
aecclesia ibidem date quia dominus ait: Non apparebis in conspectu
42v   meo / 42v / uacuus (Exodus 23,15, et alia).   Confessiones uestras sacerdotibus
confidite et eos rogate ut pro peccatis uestris rogent deum ut indulgeat uobis.
85   Oblationes per dies dominicos et pro uobis et pro uestra familia deo offerte et
de ipsis postea secundum consilium sacerdotis communicate, ante plures tamen
dies a propriis uxoribus abstinentes ut puro corde et casto corpore secundum
sacrificium accipere possitis quia hoc dignum et acceptabile est apud deum.

Sciendum est ergo, fratres karissimi, quia sicut Christiani fideles abluunt
90   peccata sua quę neglegenter agunt per sacras oblationes et per aelimosinas et
per puram orationem, per ieiunium et abstinentia[m] et per bona opera, ita et
uos [t]aliter debetis agere in omnibus, semper meditantes pro quid nati estis in
mundo - quid aliter nisi ut semper benefaciatis? et si aliquid per ignorantiam
uel stultitiam contra deum egistis, per bona opera hoc frequentius emendetis, et
95   hoc uobis sollicite sit ad memoriam reducendo (sic) ut in domibus uestris cum
coniugibus propriis sic uiuatis quomodo Christiano decet, parentibus honores
impendatis et uos inuicem diligatis, legem dei filiis uestris per fidem
catholicam cum summa disciplina doceatis, ut ipsi sciant et intelligant deum
diligere et timere et eius precepta seruare et parentes honorare quia hoc bene
100   placitum est deo.   Haec mandata in nobis implere saluator mundi dignetur, qui
cum patre et spiritu sancto uiuit et regnat in secula seculorum. Amen.

---

87. P: appropriis; B, J: a propriis. 91. P: abstinentia; B, J: abstinentiam. 92. P:
aliter; B, J: taliter. 94. B omits: uel stultitiam. 100. P, J: nobis; B: uobis.

Assmann XI, 143, 128-134; cf. Latin 81-84.

Ac þonne ge to cyrican cumen, þonne bringe ge eowre ælmessan to godes weofode, swa eow fyrmest gehagie, forðam drihten cweð: <u>Non apparebis in conspectu meo vacuus.</u> Ðæt is on Englisc: Ne ætyw þu þe on minre gesihðe idelhende. And doð gelomlice eowre andetnesse eowrum scrifte and hine biddað, þæt he eow to gode þingie, þæt ge motan eowra synna forgyfnesse geearnian.

Assmann XI, 143, 134-140; cf. Latin 92-99.

Men ða leofestan, to hwy synd we elles on ðisne middaneard acenned, butan þæt we scylan mid micelre eadmodnesse urum drihtne hyran and swa hwæt swa we þurh ungewis oððe þurh hwylce dysignesse gedon habban, þæt eadmodlice mid micelre hreowsunga and mid godum dædan betan þa hwile, þe us god þæs fyrstes geunne. Healdan we nu georne godes æ and his bebodu and þam þærto wisien, þe us underþeodde synt,

Assmann XI, 143, 140-144. Extra.

forðam þe ure drihten behet þam þe hine lufiað and his bebodu healdað, þæt hy motan æfter þam æriste habban ece lif and neorxna wanges gefean mid fæder and mid suna and mid halgum gaste a worulda woruld a butan ende. Amen.

SOURCES FOR LATIN

No source identified.

Extract.

Item 21 fol. 40r XXI. Item alia in Die Initii.

Extract fol. 41v l.25-42r l.2:-

> hoc ammonemus ut ad istos dies castitate nitidi, caritate splendidi, aelimosinis emundati, et bonis operibus adornati, per Christi adiutorium, nos preparemus. Et iracundiam et inuidiam et odium omnemque malitiam uelut uenenum de cordibus nostris respuamus.

Assmann XI , 142, 107-113:-

> utan us gearwian on þyssum dagum ... þurh clænnesse wlitige and fægere and þurh soðe lufan scinende and mid ælmesdædum aclænsode and mid eallum godum weorcum gefrætewode. And ælce yrsunge and andan and hatunge and ealle yfelnesse utan aworpan fram urum heortum eal swa atter.

For the Latin

cf. Item 2 fol. 5v II. Omelia in iii Dominica ante Natale Domini.

Extract fol. 7r ll.17-24:-

> preparemus nosmetipsos fortiter, per Christi adiutorium, ab omni luxuria carnis abstinentes et (B adds: de) bonis operibus fulgentes ut simus castitate nitidi, caritate splendidi, elimosinis mundati, simplicitatis gemmis et sobrietatis floribus adornati, ad solemnitatem regis aeterni. Ut haec autem omnia implere ualeatis, fratres karissimi, iracundiam, odium, et inuidiam cum omni malitia de cordibus uestris tamquam uenenum respuere debetis.

Source for Latin - Caesarius 188.6 (Morin, II 769):-

> Hoc enim ammonuimus, fratres, ut quia natalis domini inminet, tamquam ad nuptiale et caeleste convivium, ab omni luxuria nitidi et bonis operibus adornati per Christi adiutorium, nos praeparemus, elemosynas pauperibus erogemus, iracundiam vel odium velut venenum diaboli de cordibus nostris respuamus.

Note that the Pembroke composer extends Caesarius's words in both passages, items 2 and 21, but the Assmann XI closely follows the extract from item 21.

Bruno Assmann used the only two manuscript-texts for his edition (Angelsächsische Homilien pp.144-50) of his sermon XII, extant in the manuscripts, Cambridge, Corpus Christi College 198 art. 22 and Oxford, Bodley 340 art. 22 (Ker, Catologue pp.78 and 363 respectively), and his text is reprinted for the Old English text below. Both manuscripts entitle the sermon as for the fifth Sunday in Lent, and its opening sentence indicates that the address was intended for a period of special observance:

'Men ða leofestan, us is on ælcne sæl geornlice to smeagenne and to hycgenne, hu we ... ures drihtnes willan mid godum dædum and mid halgum mægenum gefyllan magon and huru on ðisse halgan tide, þe eallum mannum to hreowsunge and to dædbote geset is.'

We note the contrast between 'on ælcne sæl' (on every occasion) and 'on ðisse halgan tide' (in this holy time) in this initial statement.

The contents of the sermon, together with the new direct source, Pembroke item 23, reinforce the hint that 'this holy time' was Lent. The main topic of the first part of the sermon is the excess in drunkenness - as the preacher says: 'nothing is worse for a Christian than drunkenness' (ll.17-18) - obviously an effective theme in a period of rigorous fast, and the second part draws directly on Pembroke no. 23, which was designated for the third Sunday in Lent, for a presentation of other vices and Christian needs.

The English composer used three main sources for his sermon, but added other comments and treated his known Latin reading with some freedom. His introductory statements (Assmann ll.1-18) record common admonitions, that this 'holy time' is set 'for repentance and penitence' (ll.4-5), and, although a man may not go to church every day, he should attend on Sundays and other festival-days, for matins, mass and vespers, confess his sins, hear the holy service and then go to his meal with alms and enjoy it with temperance and moderation, without excess in food or drink 'because nothing is worse than drunkenness' (ll.17-18). Within this section there is a slight echo of Pembroke item 23, but even this echo emphasises the Anglo-Saxon's control of his material.

Compare: Oportet nos, fratres karissimi, omni die dominico ad ecclesias dei cum humilitate et silentio et sobrietate conuenire (ll.1-2, below),

with: 'Us is ðonne swiðe gedafenlic, þæt we gelomlice ure circan secan and ðær mid micelre eadmodnysse and stilnysse us to urum drihtne gebiddan ...' (ll.5-7).

The most notable omission from the Latin is sobrietas which, in one of its applications, is the opposite of ebrietas, a theme retained for main emphasis later.

Drunkenness is castigated at length (Assmann ll.18-81), the English author weaving together statements from selected paragraphs within two forceful sermons of Caesarius of Arles, as Karl Jost demonstrated (Anglia 56 (1932) pp.307-309). The order of the selections again indicates conscious choice of material (viz Caesarius Sermo 46.8, 46.4, 46.6, 46.8, Sermo 47.4, 47.5, 47.7), and some adaptation, e.g. where Caesarius 46.8 addresses clerics the Anglo-Saxon generalises to 'every man' (l.21). Where he names or refers to his source as Sanctus Augustinus (l.40) and 'he bytt eft on oðer stowe' (l.51) and 'he cwyð eft' (l.66), the selections follow the Latin more closely, although even in these passages the ideas are presented differently in word on occasions.

Neither of these two sermons of Caesarius is used within the items of the Pembroke-type collection. Indeed, if a preacher wished to warn his congregation about drunkenness, the Latin sermonary would be lacking, for no elaboration on that vice is found within any of its items. But on other necessary Christian acts and other dangers for Christians, including some with power and substance, Pembroke item 23 had relevant information from Theodulf's Capitula and Alcuin's moral florilegium De Virtutibus. Here the Anglo-Saxon accepts the Latin composer's selections and arrangements since he follows Pembroke item 23 in the same order, but he abbreviates by omission of sentences and phrases (as illustrated in the facing texts below). This general confirmation of the direct source for Assmann XII is indicated by detailed comparison of the Old English source, for which one example is sufficient here:-

Assmann 11.81-85: 'Men þa leofestan, we mynegiað eac ælcne getreowfulne man, þæt he gelomlice lufige cumliðnysse and nanum cuman ne forbeode, þæt he ne mote on his huse gerestan, forðan ðe manega gode gelicodon þurh þæt, þæt hi cuman onfengon and him arwurðlice þenodon'.

Pembroke item 23, 11.22-24: Ammonendi sunt quoque fideles ut hospitalitatem frequenter diligant, et nulli hospitium prohibeant, quia multi per hospitalitatis officium deo placuerunt.

Theodulf, Capitula cap. 25: Admonendi sunt ut hospitalitatem diligant, et nulli hospitium praebere detrectent ... Dicendumque illis qualiter multi per hospitalitatis officium Deo placuerunt ...

We note that Assmann XII 'ælcne getreowfulne man' reflects Pembroke fideles, and 'gelomlice' frequenter, which are not in Theodulf, although the Anglo-Saxon re-explains some Latin phrases.

One passage in Pembroke item 23 (11.73-76) is this Latin composer's own extension of his sources and this is used in Assmann XII 11.135-139, as illustrated below.

Pembroke item 23 thus provides information, including Scriptural testimonies and phrases, for Assmann XII on hospitality, perjury, bearing false witness and even on concealing the truth, on the four ways in which judgement is perverted, on the penalty for vices, in Pembroke at this point (1.66) on perjury, but in Assmann XII (11.124-125) extended to homicides, fornicators, drunkards and perjurers, some kinds of sinner from Pembroke (11.34-36); finally, on the end of a man's life being more important than the beginning. 'He who perseveres unto the end, he shall be saved' (Assmann XII 11.150-151) and shall receive the eternal reward.

Item 23 fol.46r   XXIII.   Omelia in Dominica iii in Quadragesima.

Oportet nos, fratres karissimi, omni die dominico ad ęcclesias dei cum humilitate et silentio et sobrietate conuenire.   Si enim infelices Iudei tanta deuotione caelebrant sabbatum, ut in eo nulla opera terrena exerceant, quantomagis Christiani in die dominico soli deo uacare, et pro animarum
5   suarum salute certatim debent ad aecclesias eius concurrere.

Tanta ergo in eo debet esse obseruantia, sicut quidam sapiens ait, ut preter orationes, et missarum solemnia, et ea quę ad uescendum in illo die pertinent nihil aliud in eo fiat.

Ueneranda est itaque dominica dies quia in ea lucem deus in principio
10   condidit, in ea manna de cęlo in heremo pluit, in ea redemptor humani generis sponte sua pro nostra salute a mortuis resurrexit, in ea spiritum sanctum super apostolos infudit, et multa alia quę enarrari perlongum est.

Scire etiam debet quod conueniendum est cuilibet Christiano die sabbati cum luminaribus ad aecclesiam, concurrendum est quoque ad uigilias
15   uespertinales uel ad matutinum officium.   Concurrendum est etiam cum oblationibus pro se suisque omnibus ad missarum solemnia, et hoc quoque sciendum est quod dum ad aecclesiam conuenitur nulla causa dici debet uel audiri, nulla iurgia sunt habenda, sed tantummodo deo uacandum est, in
19   caelebratione uidelicet sacrorum officiorum et in exhibitione aelimosinarum.
46v   Et postea cum dei laudibus apud / 46v / amicos et proximos et peregrinos

---

1. P, B: dominico;   J: dominica. 4. P, B: dominico;   J: dominica. 5. J omits: debent. 8. P, B: nihil, J: nil. 13. B, J, Theodulf: conueniendum; P corr. to: conueniens, from:conueniem.um by later hand. 20. B omits: dei.

Assmann XII, 144, 5-7; cf. Latin 1-2.

Us is ðonne swiðe gedafenlic, þæt we gelomlice ure circan secan and ðær mid micelre eadmodnysse and stilnysse us to urum drihtne gebiddan and godes word gehyran.

SOURCES FOR LATIN

1-5. cf. Caesarius of Arles, Sermo 13.3, (Morin, I 66).

6-21. Theodulf, Capitula, cap.24, PL 105 cols.198-99, with difference of individual word on occasions, additions, and not in the order of cap.24.

12. multa alia ... perlongum est. The composer knows longer 'Sunday lists'. One, from Pseudo-Augustine Sermo 167.2, PL 39,3070, is used in the sermon in die Sancto Pasche at fol.79r.

spiritaliter epulandum est.

Ammonendi sunt quoque fideles ut hospitalitatem frequenter diligant, et nulli hospitium prohibeant, quia multi per hospitalitatis officium deo placuerunt, dicente apostolo: Per hanc enim placuerunt quidam deo, angelis
25 in hospitio susceptis (cf. Hebrews 13,2). Et iterum: Hospitales inuicem sine murmuratione (I Peter 4,9).   Et ipse dominus ad iudicium ueniens dicturus est: Hospes eram et suscepistis me (cf. Matthew, 25,35), ac si dixisset: Ideo uenite et habitate in aeterna tabernacula (cf. Luke 16,9 for idea).   Sciant ergo quicumque amant hospitalitatem, quod Christum uere in hospitibus
30 recipiunt. Predicandum est etiam ut periurium fideles caueant et ab hoc sum[m]opere se abstineant, scientes hoc grande scelus esse, et in lege et in prophetis, uel etiam in aeuangelio prohibitum (cf. Matthew 5,33). Audiuimus autem quosdam parui pendere hoc scelus, et leuem quodammodo periuriis poenitentię modum imponere.   Qui uero nosse debent talem de periurio
35 poenitentiam imponere debere, qualem de adulterio et de fornicatione, de homicidio et de ceteris criminalibus uitiis imponere debent.   Et siquis post perpetratum periurium, aut quodlibet criminale peccatum, timens poenitentię duritiam, ad confessionem uenire noluerit, ab aecclesia poenitus repellendus est, et ab omni communione et consortio fidelium, ut nullus cum eo comedat,
40 neque bibat, neque oret, neque in sua eum domo recipiat.

---

21. J omits: est; so Theodulf, cap.24. 25. B omits: in, before: hospitio. 31. P, B: sumopere; J: summopere. 31. B adds: quod, after: hoc. 31. P, J: esse, B: est. 32. B omits: uel, after: prophetis. 33. B adds: non, after: quosdam. 35. B omits: de, after: et. 37. P, J: perpetratum; B: pertratum. 37. J omits: timens.

Assmann XII, 147, 81-95; cf. Latin 22-36.

Men ða leofestan, we mynegiað eac ælcne getreowfulne man, þæt he gelomlice lufige cumliðnysse and nanum cuman ne forbeode, þæt he ne mote on his huse gerestan, forðan ðe manega gode gelicodon þurh þæt, þæt hi cuman onfengon and him arwurðlice þenodon.   And ure drihten is to cweðenne, þonne he to ðam dome cymð: Hospes eram et suscepistis me. Þæt is on urum geðeode: Ic wæs cuma and ge onfengon me.   Witon ðonne ða ðe cumliðnysse geornlice for godes lufan begað, þæt hi Crist sylfne on ðam cuman onfoð.   Ælcum geleaffullum men is eac swiðe to warnigenne wið manaða, forðan ðe hi synt swiðe forbodene ægðer ge on ðære ealdan æ, ge on ðam godspelle.   Manega men tellað to lytlum gylte, þæt hi oðre men mid manaðum beswicen, ac witun hi, þæt hi beoð eal swa miceles wites scyldige, swa ða manslagan and ða unrihthæmeras and ða oferdrinceras.

SOURCES FOR LATIN

22-30. Theodulf, Capitula, cap.25, PL 105 col.199 with omission, change and small addition.

30-40. Theodulf, Capitula, cap.26, with changes of word.

47r   Dicendum est eis iterum ut a falso etiam testimonio se abstineant, / 47r /

scientes et hoc grauissimum scelus esse, et ab ipso domino in monte Sinai

prohibitum, dicente eodem domino: Non falsum testimonium dices (cf.

Exodus 20,16, Deuteronomy 5,20).   Salomon dicit: Falsus testis non erit

45   impunitus (Proverbs 19,9).   Quicumque ergo falsum testimonium profert

contra proximum suum, extinguetur lucerna eius in die ultimo, quia qui metu

cuiuslibet potestatis ueritatem occultat, iracundiam dei super se prouocat,

tunc enim magis timet hominem quam deum.   Falsidicus testis tribus est

personis obnoxius; primum deo, cuius presentiam contemnit; deinde iudici,

50   quem mentiendo fallit; [postremo innocenti, quem falso testimonio ledit]. Si

falsi testes separantur, mox mendaces inueniuntur. Uterque autem reus est,

et qui ueritatem occultat, et qui mendacium dicit; quia et ille prodesse non

uult, et iste nocere desiderat.   E contrario autem beatus est cuius

testimonium in conspectu domini probabile inuenitur.

55   Quattuor siquidem modis iustitia in iudiciis subuertitur: timore,

cupiditate, odio, amore.   Timore, dum metu potestatis alicuius ueritatem

dicere uel iudicare quislibet pauescit; cupiditate, dum premio muneris alicuius

corrumpitur iudex; odio, dum cuiuslibet inimicitię causa nocere alteri

desiderat; amore, dum amicos uel propinquos contra iustitiam defendit

60   potentior. His quattuor modis saepe aequitas iudicii subuertitur, et

---

41. J omits: etiam. 44. J adds: uero, after: Salomon. 46. P, B and Alcuin: qui; J: quicumque. 48. P, B and Alcuin: falsidicus testis; J: falsi testis decus. 50. P, J: mentiendo; B: interiendo. 50. P omits: postremo innocenti, quem falso testimonio ledit, as in B, J and Alcuin. 52. J omits: et, before: ille; P, B and Alcuin: et ille. 52. B omits: prodesse. 54. P, B: inuenitur; J: inueniatur; Alcuin: inuenietur. 58. P, B and Alcuin: corrumpitur; J: corrumpit.

Assmann XII, 147-48, 95-103; cf. Latin 41-47.

Eac is manna gehwilcum þearf, þæt he hine forhæbbe fram leasum cyðnyssum, forðam hit is swiðe hefig gylt and fram urum drihtne sylfum forboden, ða he wið Moysen spræc on ðære dune, þe man hæt Sinai, and ðus cwæð: Non falsum testimonium dices. Þæt is: Ne sæge ðu na lease cyðnysse. And Salomon cwæð, þæt leasa gewita ne sceolde beon ungewitnod, and swa hwilc man swa sægð leasunga on his nehstan, his leohtfet bið acwænced on ðam ytemestan dæge. And se ðe þæt soð wat and hit for æniges woruldlices mannes ege forsugað, he gecigð godes yrre ofer hine.

Assmann XII, 148, 104-06; cf. Latin 51-53.

Ægðer is ðonne scyldig wið god ge se ðe þæt soð bediglað, ge se ðe ða leasunga sægð, forðan ðe se ðe ða leasunga sægð, wile derian, and se ðe þæt soð wat, nele fremian.

Assmann XII, 148, 106-118 ; cf. Latin 55-60.

On feower wisan bið rihtwisnys on dome forhwyrfed: for ege and for gytsunge and for hatunga and for lufe. Ðonne bið seo rihtwisnys ðurh ege forhwyrfed, þonne se dema forhtað for æniges anwealdes þingum, þæt he na dear soð asecgan and riht gedeman. Hio bið forhwyrfed for gytsunge, þonne þæs deman heorte bið mid sumere mede ablend and eac forðan þe he wile ðæne unscyldigan a woh bereafian. Heo bið eac forhwyrfed for hatunge, ðonne se dema gewilnað, þæt he wile ðam unscyldigan for sumum oðrum þinge derigan. Eac bið seo rihtwisnys þurh lufe forhwyrfed, þonne se dema bewereð his freond and his magas ongean riht and ða fremdan mid unrihte bereafað. Mid þisum feower ðingum bið rihtwisnys oftust on dome forhwyrfed and

---

SOURCES FOR LATIN

41-43. Theodulf, Capitula cap.27, with changes of word.
44-64. Alcuin, De Virtutibus et Vitiis Liber, cap.21, PL 101, col.629, with variation of word.

N.B. Both Theodulf and Alcuin cite Proverbs 19,9, Alcuin alone ascribing it to Salomon.

innocentia leditur.   Magis autem dolendi sunt qui opprimunt pauperes quam qui

47v   patiuntur iniuriam.   Illi enim qui opprimuntur, temporalem / 47v / miseriam

cito finiunt;   illi uero qui opprimunt eos per iniustitiam, aeternis flammis

deputantur.

65   Sciant ergo quicumque hoc scelus perpetrauerint quod, aut tali poenitentia

necesse est purgari, ut superius dictum est de periurio, aut tali damnatione et

excommunicatione damnari, sicut superius scriptum est, id est, aut septem

annis in arta erumna sint, aut ab aecclesia repulsi, et ab omnium fidelium

communione deiecti, dicente domino: Quid prodest homini si totum mundum

70   lucretur, animę uero suę detrimentum patiatur (cf. Matthew 16,26, Mark

8,36).   Quippe cum aliis uideatur pius existere, sibimet autem crudelis

existat.

Festinare ergo debemus, fratres karissimi, et emendare uitam nostram:

quod antea male fecimus defleamus, et ulterius peccare cessemus, quia non

75   requiret deus quales abantea fuimus, sed quales circa finem nostrum

asstiterimus.   Cum aliquid in uos boni esse uideritis [non ad uestram laudem

sed ad dei putetis et malum cum uideritis] neglegentiae uestrae uel culpae

deputetis.   Hoc igitur sciendum est quod non initium boni operis quaeritur in

Christiano, sed finis, quia de fine suo unusquisque iudicabitur. Sunt enim qui

80   bene incipiunt et male finiunt conuersationem suam sicut Iudas, primo

---

63. P, B and Alcuin: iniustitiam; J: iustitiam. 65. P, B and Theodulf: poenitentia; J: penitentie. 66. P, B: purgari;   J: pugnari. 66-67. P, J: damnatione   et excommunicatione; B: dampnatione excommunicationis. 75. P, J: abantea; B: antea. 76. J omits: esse, after: boni. 76-77. J: non ad uestram laudem sed ad dei putetis et malum cum uideritis; B: non uestram laudem queratis sed ad dei reputetis et malum cum uideritis; P omits. 78-79. B omits: non initium . . . quia.

Assmann XII, 148, 118-122; cf. Latin 61-64.

unscyldige men gederede. And miccle swiður synt to bemænenne þa ðe þa earman ofðricceað mid unrihte, þonne þa ðe þæne teonan þoliað, forðan ðe þa ðe þæne teonan þoliað, geendiað hredlice þa hwilwendlican yrmðe, ac ða þe hi mid unrihte bereafiað, beoð betæhte ecum ligeum.

Assmann XII, 148-49, 122-135; cf. Latin 65-72

Witun ðonne þa ðe ðyllicne gylt þurhteoð, þæt hi synt mid þære ilcan dædbote to clænsigenne, þe ða manslagan and þa unrihthæmeras and ða oferdrinceras and þa manswaran, þæt is þæt hi sceolon seofon gear mid micelre angsumnysse hreowsian oððe hi man sceal ut of godes circan anydan and fram ealra getrywfulra manna gemanan awurpan. Be ðisum þinge cwæð se hælend on ðam godspelle: Quid prodest homini, si universum mundum lucretur, animae vero suae detrimentum patiatur? Þæt is on urum geðeode: Hwæt fremað þam men, þeah ðe he ealne middaneard gestryne, and his sawul þolige ece forwyrd? Witodlice þa men, þe ðyllice gyltas doð, þeah hi fram oðrum mannum syn geðuhte arfæste, hi synt him sylfum swiðe wælhreowe, þonne hi nellað heora earman sawle gehelpan, þe sceal on ðam ungeændudan witum ealle þas unrihtan dæda þolian.

Assmann XII, 149, 135-144; cf. Latin 73-80

Men, us is swiðe þearle to efstanne, þæt we ure lif and ure þeawas gebeterian and þæt we bewepan, þæt we ær to yfele gedydon, and ofer þis ðære syngunge geswican, forðan ðe god ne besceawað na, hwilce we ær wæron, ac he besceawað, hwilce we beon, þonne we dælan sceolon sawle and lichaman. Þæt is to witanne, þæt god ne secð na þæs godan weorces angin, ac he secð þæne ænde, forðan ðe ælc man sceal beon demed be ðam geearnungum, þe he hæfð, þonne he of ðisum life hwyrfan sceal. Sume men onginnað god to donne, ac hi hit endiað yfele, swa Iudas dyde. He wæs ærest

SOURCES FOR LATIN

65-72. Theodulf, Capitula cap.27, with variation of word.

78-80. Alcuin, De Virtutibus, cap.26, PL 101 col.632.

apostolus et postea proditor domini et facti sui conscius, laqueo se suspendit
(cf. Matthew 27,5).   Paulus male coepit et bene finiuit, primo persecutor,
postea predicator.   Uirtus igitur boni operis est perseuer[a]ntia, domino
84 dicente: Qui perseuerauerit usque in finem hic saluus erit (Matthew 10,22;
48r 24,13).   Non igitur qui coeperit bonum / 48r / sed qui perseuerauerit in bono,
hic saluus erit.   Tunc enim placet deo nostra conuersatio quando bonum quod
inchoamus perseueranti fine complebimus.   Bonum ergo non coepisse, sed
perfecisse, uirtus est.   Non inchoantibus enim premium promittitur sed
perseuerantibus datur.   Ideo unusquisque instantissime bona que̜ coepit
90 perficere contendat ut perpetuam a domino mereatur mercedem accipere in
caelestibus.

Prestante domino nostro Iesu Christo qui cum patre et spiritu sancto uiuit
et regnat in secula seculorum.   Amen.

---

81. B omits: et, after: apostolus.   83. P: perseuerentia;   B, J: perseuerantia.   89. P,
J: coepit, cepit;   B: fecit.   92. J omits: nostro.

Assmann XII, 149-50, 144-158; cf. Latin 81-93.

apostol and syððan he sealde urne drihten to cwale and on ænde hine sylfne on grine aheng. And sume men onginnað yfel to donne, ac hi hit geendiað wel, swa Paulus dyde. He wæs ærest godes circena ehtere and syððan he wæs bodigend and acoren lareow. Þæt is ðæs godan weorces mægen, þæt man þæron ðurhwunige æt his ende, swa ure drihten on ðam godspelle cwyð: <u>Qui perseveraverit usque in finem, hic salvus erit</u>. He cwæð, þæt se beo hal on ðam toweardan life, þe her ðurhwunað on godum dædum. Gif we god beginnað and we on ðam þurhwuniað æt urum ende, þonne licað gode ure drohtnung. Efste þonne ælc man, þæt he anrædlice gefulfremige þa god, þe he beginne, þæt he þurh þæt geearnige, þæt he onfo þære ecan mede on heofonan rice. Þa us gegearwige se drihten, þe mid fæder and mid sunu and mid þam halgum gaste leofað and rixað on ecnysse a buton ende. Amen.

SOURCES FOR LATIN

81-90. Alcuin, <u>De Virtutibus</u>, cap.26, PL 101 col.632, with omissions.

Karl Jost (Wulfstanstudien pp. 178-182) has argued that one author composed Assmann XI and XII together with a sermon, entitled Alia in dedicatione aeccelesie, in one of its manuscripts, edited by Rudolf Brotanek (Texte und Untersuchungen pp.15-27) as his Sermon II. Jost also stated, without argument (Anglia 56 (1932) p.306 note 2) that this author also composed the sermon printed by A. O. Belfour (Twelfth-Century Homilies pp.50-58) as his Sermon VI. The argument for the common authorship of the first three sermons was based on a similar attitude by the writer to the then known sources, but, more importantly, also on certain stylistic distinctions, including distinctive choice of vocabulary, which were common to one and another of the three. It was a scholarly and progressive study of its time and its conclusions have been accepted by Peter Clemoes in the Introduction (p.XXXI) to the reprint (1964) of Assmann's edition. Now, however, we should be cautious of firm conclusions on common authorship based on stylistic analyses of limited anonymous material, especially since Helmut Gneuss (Anglo-Saxon England 1 (1972) pp.63-83) has discussed distinctive linguistic practices within a 'school', and M.R. Godden, with selected examples but in a convincing brief study (English Studies 61 (1980), pp.206-223), has demonstrated changing individual choice of vocabulary over a period in 'Ælfric's changing vocabulary'. The caveat, however, is offered at this stage not to throw doubt on Jost's conclusions, but to ask that a fuller comparative study be undertaken now of the four sermons against other anonymous pieces, particularly those in the same manuscripts or of the same period.

But on the assumption that such a study will be completed, we may comment on the choice of sources in the four sermons, and methods of use, re-emphasising however that these comments can only be ancillary to full linguistic analysis as evidence of common authorship. Assmann XI, XII (as indicated above) and Belfour VI certainly used sermons from the Pembroke-type collection. Joan Turville-Petre (Traditio 19 (1963) pp.55-56) briefly discussed Belfour VI in relation to those vernacular texts which were either variants of Vercelli Homily III (such as Belfour V) or, as she argued, had a relationship to a then undiscovered Latin source, now defined as Pembroke item 22, for the second Sunday in Lent (see list of sources). She noted (p.56), and illustrated (p.67 seq.) that the Old English vocabulary of Belfour VI was different from that in Vercelli III (Belfour V), and thus that Belfour VI was not dependent on the other vernacular version, but that the two drew separately on the same Latin source. She also recorded differences of attitude to the common source (pp.55-56) which have relevance here: 'Many passages present in V3 (Vercelli Homily III) are lacking, and there are three additional passages, of a simple and crude kind. The first (Belfour 52.23-54.14) is an excursus on the punishments of hell, concluding Penance. The second (54.17-24) is at the head of the section Vigils, and it treats of wrongful vigils, given to drunkenness and revelry. The third concludes the section Prayer (56.12-23), with reflections of the devices of avaricious men; this seems more appropriate to Almsgiving and may be connected with the displacement of Prayer'. Now, in relation to the known direct source, Pembroke item 22, some minor additions may be noted: p.50 ll.4-7, an elaboration on the Trinity; p.52 ll.5-8, an echo of 2 Peter 2, 22, Proverbs 26, 11, on the dog returning to his vomit as illustration of a sinner repeating his sin. We may also note that the addition noted by Turville-Petre (Belfour p.54) includes a Scriptural citation in Latin, Circuet querens quem deuoret, a part-quotation of I Peter 5, 8 on the continual alertness of the devil. Obviously, Belfour VI treats its Latin source with the same freedom as do Assmann XI and XII, adding passages and re-arranging Latin material, and, like Assmann XI, using extra Scriptural quotations.

These three sermons are for Lent, but the fourth, Brotanek II, is for the Dedication of a Church, and does not use the Pembroke-type collection for its main Latin source. For this festival Pembroke item 77 chose Caesarius, Sermo 227, which was a choice in the influential homiliaries of Paul the Deacon and in the recension of the Roman homiliary by Alanus of Farfa (see list of sources). Brotanek II chose Caesarius Sermo 229, and speculations why he rejected Sermo 227, if he did, may vary, but remain speculations. We recall, however, that the composer of Assmann XII chose Caesarius Sermones 46 and 47 for his lengthy description of drunkenness, possibly because the Pembroke-type collection had no extensive elaboration on that vice. So Caesarius (as might be expected in this period) was known to the putative author, as Augustine, of course. The author of Brotanek II treated his main source with the freedom exemplified in the other sermons, omitting the whole of Caesarius Sermo 229, paragraph 3, placing some ideas in a different order from those in his source, extending some ideas in his own words, inserting two passages (fol. 167a ll.3-8, fol. 169b ll.15-20) on the delights of heaven, and also including a quotation in Latin, Non solum qui faciunt sed etiam qui consentiunt facientibus digni sunt morte perpetua (fol. 169b ll.2-4), an adaptation of Romans 1, 32.

The second of the two inserted passages on heaven, which concludes the sermon, is reminiscent of some endings of sermons in the Pembroke-type collection, mingling positive delights with the formulaic 'delight without' distress or opposite.

Brotanek II fol. 169b ll.15-20: 'þær is ece med and þær is lif butan deaðe and þær is gefea butan unrotnysse and þær is leoht butan þystrum and þær is wlite butan awendednysse and þær is ece bliss and ece gefea mid þam ecean fæder'.

The Latin phrase for 'ece med' is found in Caesarius 229.6, although, when translating the phrase from Caesarius earlier, the author has substituted 'to þære ecean blisse' for ad aeterna praemia, and one may see some of the 'crudity' of extension noted by Turville-Petre for Belfour VI in the repetition of 'gefea'. But the 'x without y' sequence is exactly as Pembroke item 25, fol. 52v ll.18-20:

Ubi est ... gaudium sine tristitia, lux sine tenebris, vita sine morte ... decor sine demutatione.

Obviously, in the Pembroke text, the sequence is yet another variation on the common theme called 'The seven joys of heaven' which persists particularly in 'insular' texts, but it includes one rare phrase decor sine demutatione. In no other Latin example in print or in manuscript, seen as yet, does the phrase occur, and the only other examples of the corresponding Old English phrase 'wlite butan awendednysse' are in Vercelli Homilies XX and XXI (as illustrated above) which, in XXI, clearly translates the Pembroke sequence in item 25 fol. 52v.

If the hint is valid, we could have four sermons in Old English, having access to the Pembroke-type collection, which exhibit the same kind of attitude to their sources. Such information is too indistinctive to begin to speak of common authorship. Many Old English pieces adapt their Latin sources and the authors of some Vercelli sermons do this with items from the Pembroke-type collection. Firmer speculation on this point is dependent on a full linguistic analysis.

INITIA SERMONUM

Ad inluminandum humanum genus, quod per inuidiam diaboli perierat, scire et intelligere debemus... Item 44.

Ad sancti ac beatissimi istius patris nostri cubŧ, cuius hodie festa cẹlebramus... Item 75.

Angeli grece vocantur, aebraice malaoth, latine uero nuntii interpretantur... Item 54.

Audite, filioli mei, et intelligite, quomodo sacra scriptura uos ammonet... Item 20.

Audite me, filioli mei, et liberate uos; currite pro uobis in bonis operibus... Item 46.

Benedictus Deus et Pater Domini nostri I. C., cui quidem soli ab hominibus reddenda est benedictio... Items 68-72.

Conueniendum est in unum nobis, fr. k., ad huius diei sollempnitatem, quia hodie Christus... Item 15.

De eo quod a cantoribus placide ac suaue canendum sit: Studendum summopere cantoribus... Item 96.

De sancto Petro apostolo, primo et principe apostolorum, hodie nos oportet loqui... Item 45.

Doctorum est omnes cum modestia ammonere quẹcumque debeant agere... Item 90.

Dominus ad prophetam Iezechiel, cum mitteret eum ad predicandum filiis Israel, dicit: Mitto... Item 28.

Dominus per prophetam prẹdicatoribus loquitur dicens: Aperi os tuum, et ego adimplebo illud ... Item 26.

Ecce adest dies honorabilis Sancti Andreẹ apostoli; uiriliter agite, fr. k., sectando precepta saluatoris... Item 67.

Ecce dies confessionis et humillimae supplicationis adsunt, fr. k., et ideo ammoneo uos... Item 52.

Ecce, fr. k., dies sancti ac spiritales et animẹ nostrẹ medicinales adsunt... Item 38.

Factum est autem cum impleta essent omnia que de aduentu Domini in carne temporibus praedicta per prophetas... Item 2.

Factum est autem postquam emundasset Iesus templum suum ab omnibus scandalis, accesserunt ad eum caeci... Item 27.

Factum est, fr. k., cum implesset Iohannes haec et multa his similia, et cum annorum esset nonaginta .vii... Item 10.

Factum est, fr. k., cum impleta essent omnia quę de aduentu Domini in carne predixerant prophete... Item 43.

Gloriari nos oportet semper, fr. k., et gaudere, quia Dominus ac Redemptor noster... Item 42.

Glorificare oportet et honorare hanc solemnitatem beatorum ac felicium infantium... Item 11.

Haec sunt mirabilia, fr. k., quę in die solemnitatis sui baptismatis Dominus noster... Item 14.

Hoc denuntiare uobis oportet, fr. k., et uos diligentius considerare debetis, ut per terrenorum... Item 18.

Hoc primum omnium inquirendum est humano generi, qualiter mundus a principio creatus... Item 30.

Hodie, dilectissimi, omnium sanctorum sub una solemnitatis lętitia caelebramus festiuitatem... Item 64.

Illud scire et in corde frequenter meditari, et animo uoluntarie recordari debemus... Item 3.

In illo tempore, exiit edictum a Cęsare agusto... Item 6.

Inquirendum est, fr. k., et explanandum per ordinem de origine generis Mariae, et natiuitatis eius solemnitate... Item 51.

Inquirendum est, fr. k., et subtiliter discutiendo inuestigandum quid mysterii continetur in officiis... Item 16.

Intelligendum est, fr. k., et exponendum omnibus noui Testamenti fidelibus... Item 12.

Iudęi ergo quoniam Parasceue erat ut non remanerent in cruce corpora Sabbato... Item 32a.

Iuxta qualitatem audientium formari debet sermo doctorum ut ad sua singulis congruat... Item 89.

Legimus in aecclęsiasticis historiis, fr. k., quod Sanctus Bonifatius, qui quartus... Items 56-63.

Legimus in prophetis cum Niniue ciuitati subuersio immineret... Item 37.

Memorari et recitare decet memoriam Sancti Michaelis, fr. k., cunctis gentibus, toto orbe terrarum dispersis... Item 55.

Officium quidem missę magna ex parte ad solum pertinet sacerdotem... Items 78-88.

Oportet hoc scire et intelligere, fr. k., quod hęc dies, id est quinta feria, in qua caena Domini... Item 29.

Oportet nos disputare, fr. k., de sancto Stephano primo apostolorum diacono. Septem enim ab ipsis... Item 8.

Oportet nos, fr. dil., annuntiare uobis, quod modo dies sanctificati ac uenerabiles sunt, in quibus a uitiis... Item 40.

Oportet nos, fr. k., ad primum sanctę religionis fundamentum catholicam fidem tenere, in qua salus animarum... Item 53.

Oportet nos, fr. k., gaudere hodie et exultare et in unum conuenire, ad laudandum... Item 5.

Oportet nos, fr. k., in sanctitate et iustitia semper seruire et placere Deo... Item 95.

Oportet nos, fr. k., omni die dominico ad ęcclesias Dei cum humilitate et silentio... Item 23.

Oportet nos, fr. k., ut tota mentis intentione inquirere et intelligere studeamus quare Christiani sumus... Item 92.

Oportet nos omnes unanimiter gaudere, fr. k., et pręclarum diem obitus Sancti Martini fideliter uenerari... Item 66.

Parasceven, id est sexta dies sabbati, que preparatio interpretatur... Item 31.

Paulisper de ministratoribus persecutionis Christi, quid actum sit uideamus, fr. k., primus... Item 35.

Postquam Dominus noster I. C. triumphator ad alta caelorum ascendit et in maiestate paterna consedit... Item 65.

Pręcauendum est omnibus bona opera exercentibus, fr. k., quod Dominus dicit... Item 19.

Precauere nos oportet semper, fr. k., octo uitia principalia quę assidue animas hominum iugulant... Item 93.

Predicanda sunt et recolenda miracula, fr. k., et uirtutes, quę huius solemnitate dies... Item 13.

Primum in prędicatione christianus debet populus silentium tenere; deinde, qui habet aures audiendi audiat... Item 17.

Primum omnium inquirendum est omni homini Deum scire uolenti, fr. k., quę sit uera scientia ueraque sapientia... Item 48.

Primum omnium oportet nos memorari, fr. k., et recitare de Deo... Item 1.

Primum omnium tria quaedam unicuique homini pernecessaria sunt: fides, spes, caritas... Item 22.

Quicumque uoluerit placere Deo primum requirat quo possit modo diligere eum, quia primum... Item 91.

Quicumque uult saluus esse, ante omnia opus est ut teneat catholicam fidem... Item 24.

Qvotiescumque, fr. k., altaris uel templi festiuitatem colimus, si fideliter... Item 77.

Qvotiescumque, fr. k., sanctorum martyrum solemnia uoluntarie caelebramus... Item 73.

Rogo et ammoneo uos, fr. k., ut in isto legitimo ac sacratissimo tempore quod de suo sancto ieiunio... Item 21.

Sabbati paschalis ueneratio ideo caelebratur et colitur, quia in eadem die Dominus in sepulchro quieuit... Item 32.

Saepe uos ammoneo, fr. k., praua opera fugere huius mundi... Item 76.

Sanctam et gloriosam solemnitatem natiuitatis Domini nostri I. C., saluatoris cosmi... Item 4.

Sanctum Iohannem adoptiuum Domini filium uenerari oportet, fr. k., cui supra pectus ... Item 9.

Sciendum est, fr. k., et omnibus exponendum fidelibus, quod post ascensionem Domini... Item 49.

Sciendum est, fr. k., quod primum credulitatis fundamentum est fides... Item 94.

Scire et intelligere debemus, fr. k., quod dies conpunctionis et poenitentię modo celebramus... Item 39.

Scitis, fr. k., quod istos quattuor dies cum summa diligentia custodire debetis, in grandi humilitate... Item 36.

Scriptum est, fr. k., in evangelica lectione quod homo quidam peregre proficiscens uocauit seruos suos... Item 74.

Spiritus sanctus per Isaiam prophetam hortatur nos et ammonet dicens: Querite... Item 25.

Spiritus sanctus per prophetam populo christiano diem solemnem constituere hortatur... Item 33.

Ualde honorandus est nobis, fr. k., sanctus Iohannes Baptista, cuius hodie solemnitatem... Item 50.

Uenerari nos oportet, fr. k., hanc solemnitatem Machabeorum, quę hodie celebratur et colitur... Item 47.

Uidete, fr. k., et considerate quam carissimos nos Dominus habere dignatus est... Item 34.

Uocem iocunditatis ac dulcedinis de resurrectione Domini ac uictoria Christi annuntiate... Item 41.

Venerandus est hic dies, fr. k., ab omnibus fidelibus, in quo natiuitas Domini... Item 7.

1.   Additional manuscript

Lincoln, Cathedral Chapter Library MS. 199 (C.3.3) fols. 213r-345r (saec. XII med.-3/4).

R. M. Thomson, who is completing a full descriptive catalogue of the manuscripts to replace R. M. Woolley, Catalogue of the manuscripts of Lincoln Cathedral Chapter Library (Oxford, 1927), has just informed me of a collection of sermons in the named manuscript, some individual items of which correspond to a number in the Pembroke-type sermonary. These corresponding items, within fols. 213r-345r, offer variant texts and indicate further popularity of our sermonary. The Lincoln compiler or scribe omitted some Pembroke-type items and substituted others on occasions for certain festivals, but Professor Thomson's typescript analysis (generously provided) allows the following comparison against the itemization in the list presented above under 'The Latin collection. Sources': Lincoln 2-6, Cross 1-5; Lincoln 7-27, Cross 7-27; Lincoln 28-29, Cross 29-30; Lincoln 31-33, Cross 31-33; Lincoln 35-49, Cross 34-48; Lincoln 53, Cross 50; Lincoln 56-60, Cross 52-55 and 56-63 (now as one sermon); Lincoln 61-62, Cross 65-66; Lincoln 64, Cross 67. We note that the Lincoln selections end at Cross 67, Omelia in natale Sancti Andreae Apostoli, and thus, that the collection does not include any of the general sermons at the end of the Pembroke manuscript.

The Lincoln manuscripts are at present deposited in Nottingham University Library during renovations at the Cathedral, and I have now consulted the manuscript by permission of the Lincoln and Nottingham University Librarians.

A collation of the relevant Lincoln items against those printed whole or in extract above indicates (i) that the Lincoln MS agrees variously with one or another of the manuscripts used in the editions above and has no special filation with any one of these manuscripts; (ii) that the vast majority of the Lincoln variants from the base manuscript Pembroke 25 are also found in one or other of the variant texts recorded in the textual notes to the relevant editions above; (iii) that none of the individual Lincoln variant readings are of consequence for the derivative Old English sections. As a result I have decided not to delay the production of this volume by entering the Lincoln manuscript variants at appropriate places, although future editors of the Old English texts should also consult the Lincoln MS. 199.

2. Additional sources

(a) Item 1 . . . in quarta Dominica ante natale Domini.

The theme of the gifts of the Holy Spirit is discussed at Pembroke 25 fol. 4r l.20–4v l.26. I can now demonstrate that the Pembroke description is enclosed within a fuller abstraction from another text on the subject as represented in the unpublished text in Munich, Bayerisches Staatsbibliothek MS. Clm. 14311 (saec. X, Germany; information from Bernhard Bischoff) fols. 221r-222r entitled: <u>De VII Donis Spiritus Sancti, Agustinus ait</u>. The Pembroke 25 abstract (now fol. 4r l.10-4v l.27) varies slightly in word, has omissions and insertions, but it can be clearly seen from the Munich text printed below where correspondences of word between the two texts are underlined, and correspondences of idea are underdotted, that the Pembroke composer used this passage, although not necessarily from this Munich manuscript. The Munich text reads:

> <u>Egredietur uirga de radice Iesse, et flos de radice eius ascendet.</u> <u>Et requiescet super eum spiritus domini, spiritus sapientie et intellectus, spiritus consilii et fortitudinis, spiritus scientie et pietatis, et repleuit eum spiritus timoris domini</u> (Isaias 11, 1-3). <u>Flos de uirga ascendens Christus est, de</u> integritate <u>sancte Marie</u> homo natus, <u>super quem septiformis spiritus domini in omni plenitudine diuinitatis eternaliter requiescit,</u> non sicut in aliis sanctis

temporaliter secundum uisitationem a deo directam aduenit sed perpetua habitatione permansit; sicut Iohannes Baptista testimonium perhibuit de ipso dicens: Uidi spiritum sanctum quasi columbam de celo uenientem et mansit super eum (cf. John 1, 32) et ego uidi et testimonium perhibui quia hic est filius dei (John 1, 34).

Iste septiformis graciẹ spiritus, qui in patriarchis diuisus est, adunatus in Christo permansit. Igitur in Adam spiritus sapientie fuit, qui omnium creaturarum quẹ cẹli ac terrẹ ambitu concluduntur naturas et rationes cognouit et ideo singulis secundum proprias naturas nomina inposuit (cf. Genesis 2, 19-20). Spiritus intellectus fuit in Noe, qui intellexit, cum sua familia solus, omnium bonum esse, deo credere et obedire, ac ideo, mundo pereunte, arcam meruit in salutem domus suẹ fabricare (cf. Genesis 6, 8; 6, 14). Spiritus consilii fuit in Abraham, qui consilio domini creatoris sui obtemperans, exiuit de terra sua et de cognatione sua et de domo patris sui et peregrinari uenit in terram (cf. Genesis 12, 1) quam filii sui erant in hereditatem accepturi (cf. Genesis 12, 7; 13, 15) qui ob fidei meritum 'amicus dei' appellabatur (cf. Judith 8, 22) et promissionem de Christo in semine suo primus accepit patriarcharum. Spiritus /221v/fortitudinis fuit in Isaac, qui forte animo persecutiones alienigenarum uincebat (cf. Genesis 26) et ideo uiuam meruit inuenire aquam (cf. Genesis 26, 19) et centuplos sui seminis accipere fructus (cf. Genesis 26, 12).

Spiritus scienciẹ fuit in Iacob, qui sciens bonum esse primogenita a suo fratre comparare et paternam accipere benedictionem (cf. Genesis 27, 23) et fraternum declinare odium (cf. Genesis 27, 41) et iniurioso socero fidelem esse qua propter cum turma filiorum et familia multa et grege inumeroso qui tantum in baculo suo fugit, diues et honoratus reuersus est ad patrem (cf. Genesis 30). Spiritus pietatis fuit in Moysen qui, pro populo peccante etiam et se lapidante, orauit ad dominum dicens: Domine, dimitte huic populo peccatum suum, sin autem dele me de libro uitę quem scipsisti (sic) (cf. Exodus 32, 31-2) qua pietate et populo ueniam inpetrauit et sibi apud deum plus aliis sanctis maiorem familiaritatem promeruit ita et conloquio dei (cf. Exodus 33, 11) et legis acceptionem dignus habebatur (cf. Exodus 34).

Spiritus timoris domini fuit in Dauid, qui, persequenti se regi Saul et in suas uenienti manus pepercit, dicens: Absit a me ut manus meas mittam in Christum domini (cf. I Kings 24, 7) idcirco inimico eius allofilorum gladio pereunte regnum accepit a deo sibi donatum et promissionem ut pater uenturi Christi esset.

Hec omnia karimata (sic) septiformis spiritus in Christo Iesu permanserunt. Spiritus sapientię quia est dei sapientia et dei uirtus . . . . .

Munich 14311 contains various texts but notably Pseudo-Alcuin, Commentary on Matthew (printed in PL 100) at fols. 9r-148v, a text which has contacts with Irish commentaries.

(b) Item 1 . . . in quarta Dominica ante natale Domini.

On re-reading this item and considering it in closer detail, I realise that I was misled by the Latin writer's method of presentation into assuming that all the seeming references to Scripture were so. Some are, but some are antiphons and/or responses. The Corpus Antiphonalium Officii (see bibliography) is not accessible at present but references are made to the Pseudo-Gregory, Liber Responsalis (PL 78).

Add:

P 4v l.27-P 5r l.15: De quo propheta dicit: Ueni domine uisitare nos in pace . . . tribus et lingue seruient ei. Antiphons and/or Responses for the Advent season as in PL 78 cols. 725-729.

Also:

P 3r ll.23-25: . . . sicut alibi scriptum est: O clauis Dauid . . . nemo aperit.

Advent 'O' antiphon as in PL 78 col. 732.

P 3r l.25: Ipse est rex regum et dominus dominantium. Cf. PL 78 col. 728.

There may well be more such echoes if it is deemed necessary to consider the item with closer scrutiny.

(c) Item 13 . . . in die Theophaniae.

P 23v ll.11-13: Magi ergo obseruabant sidera in kalendis Ianuariis in capite circuli redeunt[e]s (P, B, J: redeuntis) si stella[m](B, J: stellam) prophet[ic]am (B, J: propheticam) uiderent.

Cf. Vienna Nb 940 fol. 26r: sed sciendum est si per omne tempus sidera obseruabant caeli; non per omne tempus sed in octauo kalendis tantum Ianuarii in quibus in capite circuli redeuntes per annos sidera commutant cursum et in hoc articulo anni semper magi obseruabant caelum si stellam prophetatam (with 'ta' superscript) uiderent.

P 24r ll.7-9: . . . adorauerunt eum dicentes: Adoramus te; glorificamus te; magnificamus te.

Cf. Vienna Nb 940 fol. 28r: . . . adorauerunt eum (Matthew 2, 11) ac si dixissent: Adoramus te; glorificamus te; magnificamus te.

These echoes of the commentary as in Vienna Nb 940 do not appear in other commentaries on Matthew which are used elsewhere in the sermonary.

(d) Item 20 . . . in Quadragesima, Dominica I.

Sermo 64 ad fratres in Eremo (PL 40, 1347) has been recorded as a source for Pembroke item 20 (printed above to illustrate Assmann XI) ll.1-8, 33-36 and 43-51. A text of this sermon is extant in the Vatican Library, Palatine lat. MS 220 fols. 33r seq., items from which manuscripts were printed and discussed by

R. E. McNally, 'In nomine Dei summi: seven Hiberno-Latin sermons', Traditio 35 (1979), 121-143. McNally (121) regarded the manuscript as in 'Anglo-Saxon script', 'from the middle or upper Rhineland', from 'the early ninth century'. He noted (122) that distinctive abbreviations suggested that the manuscript was 'ultimately rooted in an Irish exemplar', and for the texts which he printed 'variant readings in the biblical citations . . . reveal traces . . . of the presence of the Irish element'. He did not scrutinize our sermon, but it may be suggestive to note that it was copied in a centre which had access to insular compositions. But more importantly here Vat. Pal. lat. 220 records a variant text to the one printed in PL 40, of early date, and generally much closer in word to the text of Pembroke 25.

(i)   Item 20 ll.1-8 (and PL 40, 1347).

Cf. Vat. Pal. Lat. 220 fol. 33r:

Audite, filioli mei, et intelligite quomodo sacra scriptura uos admonet et regna celorum inuitat et uiam ostendit, quomodo mala mundi istas (sic)euadere possetis et ad bonam eternam, Christo adiuuante, peruenire. Clamat enim dominus per prophetam ad sacerdotes qui presunt populo, ut uos debeant admonere et adnuntiare uiam ueritatis. Dicit enim: Clama, ne cesses, exalta quasi tuba uocem tuam, et adnuntia populo meo scelera eorum (cf. Isaias 58, 1). Quod si tu non nuntiaueris ('nun' superscript) iniquo iniquitatem suam, sanguinem eius de manu tua requiratur (cf. Ezekiel 3, 18; 33, 8).

(ii)   Item 20 ll.33-36 (and PL 40, 1347).

Cf. Vat. Pal. lat. 220 fol. 33r/33v:

. . . in primis enim hoc Christianus/33v/debet scire, et in corde suo firmiter tenere, quod primum mandatum est, domino dicente: Diligis dominum deum tuum ex toto corde tuo et ex tota anima tua et ex tota uirtute tua et ex tota mente tua (cf. Mark 12, 30).

(iii) Item 20 ll.43-52 (and PL 40, 1347).

Cf. Vat. Pal. lat. 220 fol. 33v/34r:

Si ista uero amore et timore in animo posueritis, et ista prima precepta, cum summa reuerentia et cum gaudio, uoleritis suscipere, tunc ad aliam bonitatem, deo adiuuante, potestis peruenire. Promisit enim his qui diligunt eum resurrectionem post morte (sic) et uitam perpetuam et dilicias paradisi et consortio angelorum. Unde tibi post hec nec senectus separat nec mors non occurrit, sed est stabilitas et securitas inuentutis et pax perpetua diligentibus deum et amantibus illum. Hoc enim per patientiam/34r/boni operis et per continentiam de malo et facientis bonum promissa sunt.

A comparison of the three texts now indicates that the composer of Pembroke, probably abstracted his sections from yet another variant text, which however was closer to that in the Vatican manuscript than to the one printed in PL 40.

(e) Item 40 Item alia (in iiii feria in Letania Maiore).

Pembroke item 40 (printed above pp.111-118, as illustration to Vercelli Homily XIX) now is associated with another sermon extant in Châlons-sur-Marne BM MS. 31(33) fols. 1r-2v (beginning lost) (saec. XI, Saint-Pierre-aux-Monts; see Analecta Bollandiana 89 (1971), pp.71-73 on the manuscript) and in London BL Cotton Vespasian Dii fols. 17v-18v (complete) (saec. XI/XII; see Catalogue of the manuscripts in the Cottonian Library (London, 1802), p.474).

The kind and comparative lack of variation between these two texts (C, V), where they correspond, indicate a close connection between the two and also with their archetype. Pembroke item 40 may well be a rewriting of a variant text, with amplification, omission and adaptation, but there is considerable verbal correspondence and consistent similarity of idea. The only passage in Pembroke item 40 which has no correspondence with C, V, is at pp.117-118 above, ll.81-108.

Cotton Vespasian Dii [V] with variants from Châlons 31(33) [C].

fol. 17v In Letania Maiore.

Dies sanctificati ac uenerabiles occurrunt nobis in hoc tempore, dilectissimi fratres, quo a uiciis purgari, a peccatis mundari, possumus, si cum bono animo et sincera uoluntate ieiunia impleuerimus.

/18r/ Legimus in propheta quia populus Niniuitarum, impius et sacrilegus, ieiunando cum afflictione cordis et corporis, iram dei potuit mitigare. Sic enim scriptum est quia statim ut audiuit populus denunciationem Ionę prophete, quia ciuitas subuertenda erat. Predicauerat ieiunium et inducti sunt saccis, a maiore usque ad minorem, et peruenit uerbum ad regem Niniuę, et surrexit de solio suo et scindit uestimenta sua et indutus est sacco et sedit in cinere et clamauit et dixit: Homines et iumenta et boues et peccora non gustent quicque neque pascantur et aquam non bibant, qui scit si conuertatur et ignoscat deus et reuertatur a furore ire sue et non peribimus. Et uidit deus opera eorum quia conuersi sunt di(sic) uia sua mala et misertus est populo suo. Si enim tam impius populus, et idolis seruiens, placare potuit iram dei, quantomagis uos, fideles Christi, et sanguine eius redempti, poteritis placationem dei impetrare, si cum bono animo et deuoto hoc triduum (C begins; adds: ieiunium) impleueritis.

Certissime namque et uerissime cognoscere potestis quia quociens nobis euenerit aut fames, aut mortalitas hominum, siue peccorum, siue siccitas, aut nimia inundatio aquarum, aut tempestas (C: tempestates), aut qualibet tribulatio non aliunde (C: aliena) nobis eueniunt (C: ueniunt), nisi propter peccata nostra ideo (C omits) quod (C: quia) nos contempnimus dei preceptum. Ideo mittit in nobis (C: nos) flagellum suum (C: omits), non ut pereamus, sed ut emendemur. Isti enim dies sanctificationis (C: sanctificati) sunt in (C omits) ieiunium triduanum ante ascensionem domini sicut illi quadragesimales ante Christi passionem; sed illi dies tristitiam passionis signant, · isti uero leticiam resurrectionis et gloriose ascensionis Christi in celum demonstrant.

Queritur enim a plurimis unde istud triduanum ieiunium in hoc tempore constitutum sit, cum neque eum (C omits) auctoritas antiqua, tradidit (C: tradit), nec Romana consuetudo, tocius ordinis caput, insinuauerit (C: insinuat).

Legimus enim quod a sancto Mamerto, Uienniensium (C: Uiennensium) urbis antistite, hec consuetudo exorta est; eius namque temporibus clades magna percussit populum et in (C omits) ualitudo grauissima ita ut si quidem (C:quem) mortuum ferrent homines ad tumulum, pauci ex ipsis portitoribus reuertebantur in domum, sed, aut super tumulum, aut in uia, cadebant mortui, qua de re (C: causa) prefatus pontifex, congregatis omnibus episcopis Gallie (C: Gallia) qui pro sanctitatis reuerentia ab omnibus honorabilior uidebatur, uoce lacrimabili, episcopis et plebi locutus est; Si deus, inquit, omnipotens pepercit populo Niniuitarum et auertit iram (C adds: suam) ab eis propter ieiunii afflictionem quantomagis nos poterimus placationem domini impetrare, si toto cordis et mentis affectu humiliauerimus animas nostras in ieiunio et fletu. Et iccirco (C: idcirco) hoc ieiunium unanimiter adimplentes, cessauit ira dei a populo, et recuperata est sanitas. /18v/ Hac de causa prefati sancti patres constituerunt hoc tempus ieiunii in omnibus ecclesiis quod numquam potuit ullo tempore dimitti in posteris generationibus.

Ideo rogo et amoneo (C: admoneo) uos, fratres mei, ut in his diebus ieiunium exibeatis et in uiliori habitu et cibo humilietis uos coram deo saluatore nostro qui humiles respicit (C: respexit) et dat eis gloriam (C: gratiam), superbos despicit et reprobat. Multi uero in nobis (C: uobis) sunt, tam uiri quam femine, qui hos dies, non pro humilitate seu deuota supplicatione suscipiunt, sed pro extollentia et uana gloria, preciosioribus uestimentis se induunt et deliciosa sibi conuiuia preparant, et inebriando nimiam uoracitatem sectantes, non pro dei timore, sed pro sua misera exaltatione, conueniunt. Et dum plus debuerant sua minuere peccata, orando et ieiunando et ad ecclesiam ueniendo, magis ea augent suas miseras et delicias et iocunditates sequendo. (C: sua misera iocunditate et delicias sequendo). Tale enim ieiunium reprobat dominus per prophetam dicens:

Ecce in die ieiunii uestri (V omits) inuenitur uoluntas uestra, et omnes debitores uestros repetitis (Isaias 58, 3). Sed hoc est magis ieiunium quod elegi (cf. Isaias 58, 6). Frange esurienti panem tuum et egenos uagosque induc in domum tuam; si uideris nudum, uesti (C: operi) eum et ne despicias (C: despexeris) carnem tuam (cf. Isaias 58, 7). Tunc inuocabis et dominus exaudiet, clamabis et dicet: Ecce, adsum (Isaias 58, 9); quoniam misericors est dominus deus tuus (cf. Deuteronomy 4, 31).

Hoc, ergo, ammoneo (C: admoneo) uos (C omits), fratres mei, ut in his diebus ad ẹcclesiam ueniatis et (C omits) cum summa deuotione ieiunantes et orantes ut misericors deus pacem tribuat, famem repellat, morbos et egrotaciones auferat, pluuiam temporalem tribuat, serenitatem celi largiri dignetur, peccata indulgeat, crimina dimittat, reos absoluat, iniquitates deponat, deuocionem augeat, fidem rectam confirmet, iusticiam amplificet, castitatem concedat, omniumque bonorum operum uirtutem infundat. Nullus in (V omits) his diebus ante horam (C adds: non , for : nonam?) prandere presumat. Lites et contentiones, uel uerba turpia, siue iocunda aut luxuriosa cantica, aut lusus tabularum, exercere presumat, sed magis orationibus (C: orationes) insistat, lectiones et predicationes (V: oraciones) humiliter audiat, discordantes ad concordiam reuocet, pauperes et peregrinos unusquisque ad conuiuiola sua suscipiat, opus seruile nullus facere presumat, et si hec omnia, cum dei adiutorio et cum bona uoluntate, impleueritis, indulgentiam peccatorum et corporis sanitatem et abundantiam temporalem, deo donante, impetrare poteritis; ipso adiuuante qui in trinitate perfecta uiuit (C adds: et regnat deus per omnia secula seculorum. Amen).

(f)   Items 78-88 De officio misae . . .

The opening section can now be more closely identified.

P   159r l.23 (beginning)-l.25, Officium . . . consecrare. Hrabanus, De. Cler. Inst. 2, 1 (PL 107, 325).

P 159v ll.4-12, et oblationes . . . punientur. Based on Theodulf, Capit. cap. v (PL 105, 193), with amplification but with interspersed verbal echoes. But the whole passage, Officium . . . punientur, is a variant text of the first part of a text, entitled De Officio Misse, found in manuscripts of Archbishop Wulfstan's 'Commonplace Book'. This section in the 'Commonplace Book' is no. 40 in Hans Sauer's analysis, Deutsches Archiv fur Erforschung des Mittelalters 36 (1980); see p.355 on Oxford, Bodley Barlow 37, and pp.382-83 on other manuscripts. It may be that a common intermediary source existed for the insertion in the Pembroke-type sermonary and for the section in the 'Commonplace Book'.

(g) Item 96 De eo quod a cantoribus . . .

This whole item (Studendum summopere . . . tenendus est) is a variant text of Amalarius (Pseudo?), Forma Institutionis Canonicorum et Sanctimonialium lib. I cap. cxxxvii (PL 105, 929). The whole collection of Amalarius is as the Council of Aachen 816 A.D. edited A. Werminghoff, Monumenta Germaniae Historica, Legio, Sectio III, Concilia Aevi Karolini I tom. II pars I, (Hanover and Leipzig, 1906), pp. 307 seq. For cap. cxxxvii see p. 414.

(h) Tristram Homily III

Jane Moores has now discovered a third major source for the Old English sermon. The section at Tristram III ll. 12-65 takes all ideas in the same order, with significant verbal echoes on occasions, from a sequence for Ascension Day: Rex omnipotens die hodierna . . ., edited from a number of manuscripts in Analecta Hymnica Medii Aevi vol. 7, ed. G. M. Dreves (Leipzig, 1889), pp. 83-85, and in vol. 53 ed. C. Blume (Frankfurt, 1911), pp. 111-114, but found also in Latin manuscripts from Anglo-Saxon England. The immediate source for the vernacular section is clear, but I have left my now superseded remarks (pp. 175-176 above), partly because the discovery should be highlighted since this is the first occasion that a liturgical sequence has been identified as a source for a vernacular prose sermon, partly because my earlier comments present the context for the 'narrative' sequence and suggest an impetus for the vernacular composer's recall and use. Where I have noted verbal differences from Vulgate Scripture in Pembroke item 41 (p. 176 above), the Pembroke Latin words echo those of the sequence. The vernacular composer has obviously recognised the echoes and turned to the full sequence. Mrs. Moores will discuss the relationships in detail in a forthcoming paper in Anglia.